Contents

THE UNIVERSITY OF WINCHESTER

Martial Rose Library
Tel: 01962 827306

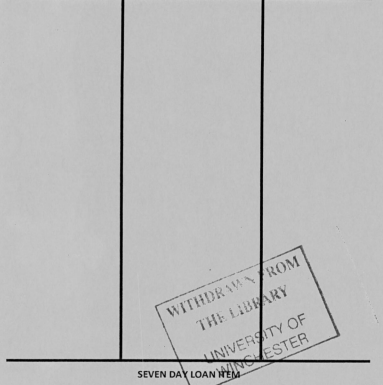

Shaping the Future of Business Education

Shaping the Future of Business Education

Relevance, Rigor, and Life Preparation

Edited by

Gordon M. Hardy and Daniel L. Everett
Bentley University, USA

First published 2013 by
PALGRAVE MACMILLAN

Palgrave Macmillan in the UK is an imprint of Macmillan Publishers Limited, registered in England, company number 785998, of Houndmills, Basingstoke, Hampshire RG21 6XS.

Palgrave Macmillan in the US is a division of St Martin's Press LLC, 175 Fifth Avenue, New York, NY 10010.

Palgrave Macmillan is the global academic imprint of the above companies and has companies and representatives throughout the world.

Palgrave® and Macmillan® are registered trademarks in the United States, the United Kingdom, Europe and other countries

ISBN: 978–1–137–03337–6

This book is printed on paper suitable for recycling and made from fully managed and sustained forest sources. Logging, pulping and manufacturing processes are expected to conform to the environmental regulations of the country of origin.

A catalogue record for this book is available from the British Library.

A catalog record for this book is available from the Library of Congress.

10 9 8 7 6 5 4 3 2 1
22 21 20 19 18 17 16 15 14 13

Printed and bound in Great Britain by
CPI Antony Rowe, Chippenham and Eastbourne

List of Figures

Foreword

Shaping the future of business education is a big and serious issue. I am delighted to have been invited to contribute a short foreword to this important and illuminating book. Shaping such a future is, of course, what EFMD (European Foundation for Management Development) is all about.

No one can deny that that the future is uncertain, and how to reshape it is as yet unclear. The world is still enveloped in a major financial and economic crisis that shows little sign of abating. In this environment, preparing for the world of business is itself fraught with uncertainty. Fortunately, the contributions to this book help define a new path appropriate to the challenge.

The very fact that we face long-term economic challenges means that we need business education – the right kind – more than ever. We need people with the talent and skills to respond to difficult times. Leading this process must be factories of future knowledge – the world's top business schools and the liberal arts universities that in many cases encompass them.

The EFMD has consistently maintained that the primary objective of these leading higher-education institutions must be to deliver (and enhance) excellence in teaching and learning. As the following chapters make clear, they must do this by leavening the professional qualifications required for doing business in a tough global economy with the type of liberal education that produces well-rounded graduates.

How can we reshape business education and business education providers to achieve this?

In the future, successful business schools must equip themselves with adequate resources to accomplish their objectives, including excellent facilities and highly qualified faculty. In tough economic times this may well be easier said than done.

Second, they must provide adequately funded doctoral research programs and other incentives for academics. A lack of qualified faculty may well be one of the factors limiting future progress.

That faculty must also be attuned to the challenges and implications of globalization (as, indeed, must also be the student body and business education curricula).

Finally, and most importantly, they must teach and place into the market students who are capable of acting as globally responsible leaders.

What does that mean? For a start, it means leaders who take sustainability in its widest sense seriously and do their utmost to act in partnership with a wide range of stakeholders, not just the shareholders in an organization.

As I have written elsewhere, I believe that we must encourage more human (and humane) values in management, especially forgiveness and health at work. Leadership training, which may well be the center-piece of a reshaped business education, should aim at developing a style of management that promotes these values.

But if we want the next generation of globally responsible leaders to show the competencies, capacities, and attitudes they will need, then we have to realize that inculcating them is about more than just the simple transfer and acquisition of knowledge. We need to think about ways to prioritize new and more practical ways of learning in business education curricula.

Shaping the future of business education will involve educating students in how they can respond to the challenges of an increasingly complex world. This will mean the use of new and demanding approaches to management education that will introduce substantial changes to the way we prepare the next generation of leaders.

This will, I believe, put globally responsible leadership and corporate responsibility at the heart of the business education curriculum, something that will present providers of business education with an opportunity to expand and enrich their academic offering and to employ new pedagogical approaches.

Corporate global responsibility as a subject in the business education curriculum will allow further integrated multidisciplinary approaches to learning and for co-operation between traditional business school subject areas. As a topic, corporate global responsibility requires both the knowledge and application of a wide set of business fields. As such, it provides a way for business schools to move beyond functional boundaries to a more integrated approach.

This is not just some current management fad. EFMD, through its EQUIS (European Quality Improvement System) accreditation system, is committed to enhancing the quality of management education and to developing and communicating best practices that educate students to think critically and exercise their judgment in responding to new situations and problems.

This book goes a long way to helping in this endeavor. I heartily recommend it to you.

Eric Cornuel
CEO and Director General, European Foundation
for Management Development

Acknowledgments

The editors would like to thank the people who made this work possible: first, the chapter contributors, whose intellectual efforts and devotion to teaching make a difference in students' lives every day; to Virginia Thorp and Keri Dickens, our collaborators at Palgrave Macmillan; to our support team at Bentley University, including Provost Michael Page, Dean of Business Roy ('Chip') Wiggins III, Executive Director of Marketing Communication Katherine Blake, Chief Marketing Officer David Perry, and President Gloria Larson and her cabinet; to those who granted us permission to use their words and images; and of course, to our family and friends, who helped us throughout the process with companionship and good humor.

Notes on Contributors

Anders Aspling is Secretary-General of the Globally Responsible Leadership Initiative (GRLI) – a United Nations Global Compact and European Foundation for Management Development (EFMD) joint venture, a professor at the School of Economics and Management, Tongji University, Shanghai, and an affiliated professor at CENTRUM Católica, Pontificia Universidad Católica del Perú. He earned a master's degree in economics and business administration and a doctorate in business administration from the Stockholm School of Economics (SSE). He has served as the president and dean of the Swedish Institute of Management at the SSE and Dean of the Vlerick Leuven Gent Management School in Belgium. He has been a senior vice president and a member of the group executive board of Siab (now NCC – one of Europe's largest construction companies) and has been chairman, board member, and senior adviser at numerous NGOs in Sweden and internationally. He also serves on boards of universities, corporations, and academic centers around the world as an official member or in an advisory capacity. He is a member of the Dean's External Advisory Board of the Beedie School of Business at Simon Fraser University, Vancouver, and the Advisory Board of the Centre for Business in Society at the University of Stellenbosch, South Africa.

Joan L. Atlas is an adjunct assistant professor in the English and Media Studies Department at Bentley University in Waltham, Massachusetts. She received a BA in English from the University of Rochester and a JD from Suffolk University Law School. After practicing law with Martin, Magnuson, McCarthy & Kenney in Boston, Massachusetts, from 1981 to 2000, she turned to teaching writing, literature, and effective speaking. She has twice received the Community Service Faculty Award from Bentley for her strong involvement in the Waltham community and has also received the Curricular Service-Learning Faculty Award for developing a course in grant writing.

Andrew B. Aylesworth is Associate Professor of Marketing at Bentley University. He has been teaching at Bentley since 1994. He earned an MBA and PhD in Marketing from Indiana University. Prior to that, he was an account executive at Saffer Advertising in Chicago. His primary teaching interests are creativity, advertising, marketing communication and promotion, and marketing fundamentals. His current research interests include enhancing creativity in business and the classroom and improving marketing and business pedagogy. He has trained in the techniques of improvisational comedy and performed in several Boston area shows, and strives to use these techniques to improve the business skills of his students. He has been published in the *Journal of Marketing Education, Journal of Advertising, Journal of Business Research,* and *Advances in Consumer Research.*

Nicole Belmonte is an assistant actuary at Liberty Mutual Insurance Group in Boston. She received her BS in Mathematical Sciences from Bentley College with an International Studies minor, and since then has held various actuarial roles within property and casualty insurance. She is an associate of the Casualty Actuarial Society.

Chris Beneke is Associate Professor of History at Bentley University. He received his BA in Independent Studies (American Civilization) from Cornell University and his PhD from Northwestern University. He is a former director of the Valente Center for Arts and Sciences at Bentley. He is the author of *Beyond Toleration: The Religious Origins of American Pluralism* and co-editor of *The First Prejudice: Religious Tolerance and Intolerance in Early America* (with Christopher S. Grenda). His forthcoming book is titled *Free Exercise: The First Amendment and America's Moderate Religious Revolution.*

Elizabeth A. Brown teaches Business Law at Bentley University. She received her undergraduate degree from Harvard College and her JD from Harvard Law School. She is also the Executive Director in Boston of Golden Seeds, one of the largest angel investor networks in the United States. Prior to coming to Bentley, she was a partner in a leading international law firm, specializing in intellectual property. She practiced law in London, San Francisco, and Boston, advising senior executives at Fortune 500 companies on legal strategies and managing multi-million dollar cases from inception to successful resolution. As President of the Harvard Law School (HLS) Association of Northern California, she developed an innovative series of programs for members and created a new women's network for HLS alumnae in the Bay Area. She is a frequent speaker and writer on the subject of alternative law careers.

Richard J. Cleary is Professor of Mathematical Sciences at Bentley University. He earned a BS in Mathematics from Oneonta State College, MA in Mathematics from the University of Massachusetts, Amherst, and PhD in Statistics from Cornell University. He taught at St. Michael's College in Vermont. He returned to Cornell and served on the faculty and as an associate dean in the College of Engineering until joining the Bentley faculty in 2001. He has won several teaching awards, including the Merrill Scholar Prize at Cornell, the Adamian Award at Bentley, and the Howard Eves Award of the Northeastern Section of the Mathematical Association of America. He enjoys collaboration and has co-authored papers in such wide-ranging areas as auditing, biomedical engineering, vertebrate taxonomy, and baseball.

Mark M. Davis is Professor of Operations Management at Bentley University. He received a BSEE from Tufts University, and an MBA and DBA from Boston University. He worked as a manufacturing engineer for the General Electric Company and was also a programs manager for the U.S. Army Natick Research Laboratories, where he focused on the design of military food-service systems. He is a past president of the Decision Sciences Institute (DSI), served as Program Chair for the 2003 DSI Annual Meeting, as Secretary, as a member of the DSI Board of Directors, and is a past president of the Northeast Decision Sciences Institute. He received Bentley College's Scholar of the Year Award in 1998 and was appointed to the 1996 Board of Examiners for the Malcolm Baldrige National Quality Award. He currently serves on the editorial review board of the *Journal of Service Management* and on the Board of Overseers for Mass Excellence. He is the co-author of two textbooks: *Operations Management: Integrating Manufacturing and Services* (5th edition, with Janelle Heineke) and *Managing Services: Using Technology to Create Value* (with Janelle Heineke).

Samir Dayal is Associate Professor of English and Media Studies at Bentley University. He received his PhD in English from the University of Wisconsin-Madison. He is the Cultural Studies Series Editor for Other Press in New York. He is the author of *Resisting Modernity: Counternarratives of Nation and Masculinity*, and co-editor of *Global Babel: Interdisciplinarity, Transnationalism and the Discourses of Globalization* (with Margueritte Murphy). He is completing a book about Indian cinema as well as another book on global cinema. He is the editor, with an introduction, of Julia Kristeva's *Crisis of the European Subject*, François Rachline's *Don Juan's Wager*, Lucien Gubbay's *Jews under Islam*, Patricia Gherovici's *The Puerto Rican Syndrome* (winner of the Gradiva Award in Historical, Cultural and Literary Analysis and the Boyer Prize for Contributions to Psychoanalytic Anthropology), Robert Rushing's *Resisting Arrest: Desire and Enjoyment in Detective Fiction*, Sanjay

Subrahmanyam et al.'s *Textures of Time*, and Barbara Christian's *Belief in Dialogue*, among other books.

Gregory L. Farber is Interim Director of the Writing Center at Bentley University. He received his BA in English from Bentley College and his MFA in playwriting from Arizona State University. He is a working playwright and theater practitioner who has produced numerous theater festivals and staged readings and also served as Director of Development for Theatre on Fire from 2007 to 2010. His plays have been performed in Arizona, Massachusetts, North Carolina, and most recently in Maryland where 'Weathertician' won UMBC's (University of Maryland, Baltimore County) IN10 competition and was produced as part of their Grrl Parts festival.

Robert E. Frederick is Professor of Philosophy and Chair of the Philosophy Department at Bentley University. He is also a research scholar at the Center for Business Ethics at Bentley, and editor of the quarterly journal *Business and Society Review*. He received a BA degree in Economics from Rice University and an MA and PhD in Philosophy from Brown University. He has published a number of articles in philosophy, business ethics, and environmental ethics, and has edited or co-edited ten books on various topics in applied ethics and philosophy. He has served as a consultant on business ethics for corporations and academic institutions, and has delivered addresses on business and environmental ethics to a variety of professional organizations. Prior to joining Bentley, he worked for nine years for a large financial institution in Atlanta, Georgia, where he was Vice President for Administrative Services.

Gregory J. Hall is Associate Professor of Psychology at Bentley University. He received his PhD from the University of Massachusetts, Amherst. He has served in a variety of capacities at Bentley, including Associate Undergraduate Dean, Behavioral and Political Sciences Department Chair, Director of the Undergraduate Honors Program, and Wilder Professor for Teaching and Learning Initiatives. He has received the Gregory H. Adamian Award for Excellence in Teaching and has been selected three times as the Student Government Association Faculty Member of the Year. His teaching has been recognized with the Innovation in Teaching Award and the Curricular Service Learning Faculty Award. His teaching interests include cyber psychology, financial psychology, personality theory, social and developmental psychology. His recent research and publications focus on facilitating moral reasoning in undergraduate business students.

Dominique Haughton is Professor of Mathematical Sciences and Graduate Coordinator for Business Analytics at Bentley University in Waltham, Massachusetts, and an affiliated researcher at the Université Toulouse 1, France. She received her PhD from the Massachusetts Institute of Technology. Her areas of interest are applied statistics, statistics and marketing, the analysis of living standards surveys, data mining, and model selection. She is Editor-in-Chief of *Case Studies in Business, Industry and Government Statistics* and has published more than 60 articles in journals such as *The American Statistician, Computational Statistics and Data Analysis, Economic Development and Cultural Change, Studies in Family Planning, Journal of Population Economics, Journal of Biosocial Science, Annals of Statistics, Sankhya, Journal of Statistical Computation and Simulation, Communications in Statistics,* and *Statistica Sinica*. She is a Fellow of the American Statistical Association.

Diane M. Kellogg is Associate Professor of Management at Bentley University She received her BS from Brigham Young University and an EdM and EdD from Harvard University. A management consultant to the largest of multi-national corporations, she offers the same expertise gratis to the smallest of NGOs in Ghana. In 2005, she initiated the Ghana Project at Bentley and began engaging others at the university to work on economic development work in the country. Her leadership has led to Bentley faculty and students assisting an NGO to become a fully self-funding business that uses its profits to benefit vulnerable children. In her programs Bentley students learn how to apply business skills in not-for-profit contexts at home and abroad.

Nick A. Komissarov is an associate actuary for Variable Annuities Planning & Forecasting at John Hancock in Boston. He joined John Hancock in the Long-Term Care business. He received his BA in Managerial Economics from Bentley University. He is a Fellow of the Society of Actuaries.

Daniel R. LeClair is Executive Vice President and CEO of Association to Advance Collegiate Schools of Business (AACSB) – the International Association for Management Education. He earned a PhD in economics from the University of Florida. He was the principal architect of AACSB's thought leadership initiatives and Knowledge Services area, which assists business school leaders worldwide to plan and make decisions using comparable data and information about trends and effective practices. He leads the research teams of AACSB and the Global Foundation for Management Education (GFME), a think-tank joint venture of AACSB and the EFMD, and currently serves on the steering committee of the Principles for Responsible Management Education. He has served on numerous industry-wide committees and task forces (for organizations such as the Graduate Management Admission Council (GMAC®), Executive MBA Council, and Aspen Institute Business & Society Program) and is an internationally recognized expert, author, and frequent presenter on business education topics. Prior to joining AACSB, he was an associate professor in the University of Tampa's business school, where he also served as an associate dean.

Fred D. Ledley is Professor in the Department of Natural & Applied Sciences and Department of Management, and Director of the Center for Integration of Science and Industry at Bentley University. He has a BS from the University of Maryland, an MD from Georgetown University, trained in Pediatrics and Genetics at Boston Children's Hospital/Harvard Medical School, and was a post-doctoral fellow with Nobel laureate David Baltimore in the Center for Cancer Research at MIT. He has extensive experience as a scientist, educator, entrepreneur, executive, and author. He has authored more than 170 academic papers in fields ranging from molecular and human genetics to education, bioethics, biopharmaceutical development, and biotechnology, and has served on the faculties of the Baylor College of Medicine and the Howard Hughes Medical Institute. He is Founder and vice president of GeneMedicine, President and CEO of Variagenics, Inc., and a consultant to industry, academia, and government. At Bentley, he spearheaded strategic initiatives to reorganize and reorient the school's science programs and better prepare business students for leadership roles in technology-driven enterprise. His research focuses on strategies for accelerating the translation of scientific discoveries for public benefit.

Eric A. Oches is Associate Professor of Geology and Environmental Sciences, and Chair of the Department of Natural & Applied Sciences at Bentley University. He received a BS in Geology from Purdue University, and an MS and PhD from the University of Massachusetts, Amherst. Prior to his current position, he was a faculty member in the Geology Department and Chair of the Environmental Science and Policy Department at the University of South Florida, Tampa. While his disciplinary research has focused on the reconstruction of Pleistocene and recent climate and environmental changes, he is increasingly engaged in the development of novel interdisciplinary curricula to enhance science literacy in non-science-majors.

Michael J. Page is the Provost and Vice President for Academic Affairs at Bentley University, having joined the university some four years ago as the Dean of Business and the McCallum Graduate School. A native of South Africa, he holds a BS in Civil Engineering from Natal University in South Africa. He served in the South African Navy, and worked as a construction and design engineer before earning an MBA and PhD from the University of Cape Town. Before joining Bentley he served as the Dean of Post-Experience Programs of RSM Erasmus University and as the Executive Director of the Rotterdam School of Management (RSM) B.V., The Netherlands. Previously he was the Dean of Rotterdam School of Management, Erasmus Graduate School of Business, and also served a term as its Dean of Academic Affairs. He joined Erasmus after 16 years as Professor of Finance at the University of Cape Town, South Africa. He is a board member of the AACSB and is Chair of the Initial Accreditation Committee (IAC). Additionally, he is a member of the Accreditation Coordination Committee (ACC), the International Blue Ribbon Committee on Accreditation Quality (BRC), and the Committee on Issues in Management Education (CIME). He is also actively engaged with the international management education industry, including serving on the board of the EFMD and working with its EQUIS accreditation program. He also supports development activities offered by the Central and Eastern European Management Development Association (CEEMAN).

Patricia J. Peknik is a lecturer in the English and Media Studies Department at Bentley University. She received a BS in Journalism from Ohio University, and two master's degrees, one in English and one in History, from Boston University, where she is a PhD candidate in American Intellectual History. Before joining the faculty at Bentley, she worked in Public Relations in Washington, DC and Paris and taught classes in law, history, and English at Boston University.

Emily Roth is an associate professor in the Mathematical Sciences Department and the Actuarial Program Coordinator at Bentley University. She earned a BS in Mathematics and a PhD in Operations Research from the Massachusetts Institute of Technology. Prior to joining the Bentley faculty, she was Senior Member of Technical Staff at GTE Laboratories, Inc. and Assistant Professor of Operations Research and Public Policy at the Carnegie-Mellon University School of Urban and Public Affairs. She is the author or co-author of articles on heuristics for evaluating the behavior of queuing models as well as the application of stochastic processes to business problems.

William T. Schiano is Professor of Computer Information Systems at Bentley University and a former director of Bentley's Master of Science in Information Technology program. He received a BA in Economics from Williams College and PhD in Information Systems from Harvard Business School. He has taught in graduate and executive programs at Aalto University School of Economics, TiasNimbas, Norwegian Business School, the Arthur D. Little School of Management (now Hult International Business School), and the Asian Institute of Management, and facilitates Harvard Business School Publishing's workshops on participant-centered learning. He served as the president of Thoughtbubble Productions, a New York-based new media company, and was a research affiliate at CSC Index Research and Advisory Services.

Jay C. Thibodeau is Professor of Accountancy at Bentley University. He received a BS and PhD from the University of Connecticut. His scholarship is focused on auditor judgment and decision making and audit education. He is co-author of *Auditing and Accounting Cases: Investigating Issues of Fraud and Professional Ethics* (4th edition, with Deborah Freier) and *Auditing and Assurance Services* (5th edition, with Timothy J. Louwers, Robert J. Ramsay, David H. Sinason, and Jerry R. Strawser). In addition, he has published more than 40 articles and book chapters in a variety of academic and practitioner outlets. He received national recognition for his doctoral dissertation, winning the 1996 Outstanding Doctoral Dissertation Award presented by the American Accounting Association's ABO section, and for curriculum innovation, winning the 2001 Joint AICPA/AAA Collaboration Award and the 2003 Innovation in Assurance Education Award.

Heikki Topi is Professor of Computer Information Systems at Bentley University. He earned a PhD in MIS at Indiana University Graduate School of Business. Before joining Bentley in 2000, he held academic and administrative positions at Helsinki School of Economics and Indiana University Kelley School of Business. His research has been published in journals such as *European Journal of Information Systems, Journal of American Society of Information Science and Technology, Information Processing & Management, International Journal of Human-Computer Studies,*

Journal of Database Management, Small Group Research, and others. He is the co-author of *Modern Database Management* (with Jeffrey A. Hoffer and Ramesh Venkataraman) and co-editor of *IS Management Handbook* (with Carol V. Brown). He has been actively involved in national computing curriculum development and evaluation efforts. He serves on the education board of the Association for Computing Machinery (ACM) and on the Computing Sciences Accreditation Board (CSAB).

Catherine A. Usoff is Dean of the Graduate School of Management at Clark University in Worcester, Massachusetts. She was formerly a professor and department chair at Bentley University. She earned a BS in Accounting from Boston College and an MBA and PhD from the Ohio State University. She has published academic articles in accounting and information systems journals and has extensive experience in curriculum development and project-based learning.

Edward Zlotkowski is Professor of English and Media Studies at Bentley University. In 1990 he founded the Bentley Service-Learning Center (BSLC). He received a BA in English and a PhD in Comparative Literature from Yale University. He has written and spoken extensively on a wide range of service-learning and engagement-related topics, and served as general editor of the American Association for Higher Education's (AAHE) 21-volume series on service-learning in the academic disciplines. He is co-author of *Higher Education and Democracy: Essays on Service-Learning and Civic Engagement* (with John Saltmarsh), and is a senior associate at the New England Resource Center for Higher Education.

The Crucial Educational Fusion: Relevance, Rigor, and Life Preparation in a Changing World

Daniel L. Everett and Michael J. Page

Books are the carriers of civilization. Without books, history is silent, literature dumb, science crippled, thought and speculation at a standstill. I think that there is nothing, not even crime, more opposed to poetry, to philosophy, ay, to life itself than this incessant business.

Henry David Thoreau

By propagating ideological inspired amoral theories, business schools have actively freed their students from any sense of moral responsibility.

Sumantra Ghoshal (2005, pp. 75–78)

Introduction

In his classical work, *The Tacit Dimension*, scientist and philosopher Michael Polanyi makes the case that everything we know has a beginning in the unsaid and assumed background information of our culture. Everett (2012) makes a similar case in his book, *Language: The Cultural Tool*, referring to tacit knowledge as the 'dark matter of the mind.' This background, unspoken information is socio-cultural. Tacit knowledge implies that knowing, goal-setting, value, values, and valuation are constructs of the societies in which we live.

So it is with higher education. Because of this role of society in all endeavors of its members, faculty, administrators, staff, and students who have dedicated portions of their lives to the enterprise of higher education should understand the larger context from which their endeavors, as well as the purpose and conception of education, emerges and receives its sustenance. Education as we practice it is not the shadow

1

of a pure idea in a platonic heaven. Its form and content are shaped by our societies. Given the contemporary force of society's concerns, the social conception of higher education cannot be bound by the past. We are under no obligation to continue the model of education for the leisured class of the Greeks seen in Plato's Academy and Aristotle's Lyceum. Nor are we bound to continue the Oxbridge model in which higher education was established in order to prepare young men for the Anglican ministry. One of the most exciting and invigorating challenges of higher education is its fluidity. Like the human mind, higher education thrives through flexibility. It must be ever attentive to the needs and desires of its sustaining society.

At no time in the recent past have flexibility and creativity been needed more in rethinking and retooling the models of the relationship between universities and society. Higher education is facing a reconceptualization by society perhaps more radical than any in its history since salaries were introduced at Oxford University to replace the earlier model of letting students pay faculty for tuition directly (so that nowadays 'tuition' refers to what students pay instead of what the teaching faculty offer them). The new conception includes at least the demands that education must be socially useful and that the providers of higher education negotiate with their consumers – their students – on the best path toward that utility. If we fail to respond and innovate effectively, we may preside over our own obsolescence. The only question is whether the adaptation to this new reconceptualization should be incremental, as is academic tradition, or will require a sudden seismic shift in perspective and practice. Governing boards of academic institutions are already pressuring administrators for quick solutions. The tension grows tauter by the day.

The changing views of higher education throughout history have arguably been motivated by the simple fact that society wants value for its investment, as it has since the first disciple paid the first master. But what is this socially sanctioned value? It includes at least that the average college graduate will be a more informed and better thinking citizen, better able to live a personally satisfying life because of their higher education experience – to be a *prepared* citizen. This in itself does not seem so different from past aspirations, except that now 'value' includes the idea that the practical knowledge produced by the higher education experience should be measureable in the short-term and of sufficient magnitude to justify the expense of that experience to students, parents, and governments. The evidence suggests that society is growing restless on this score.

The mounting criticisms of higher education are numerous and serious. Both within and outside of the academy, we hear from a growing chorus ideas such as 'tenure is an outdated and unhelpful practice,' 'the methods and form of instruction are behind the times,' and 'the content of the average degree program is largely irrelevant by contemporary standards.' We especially hear the objection that the rising costs of the undergraduate experience are outstripping the return in value for the time and money invested. At the far extreme are those who argue that the entire college concept needs to be rethought, perhaps abandoned – that 'college' as it is currently manifested is a relic of the past, like the flying-buttress cathedrals that have gone from vibrant centers of worship to objects of tourist curiosity in many countries.

We see the concept of value and practical knowledge expressed most keenly in undergraduate business education. Business, after all, is all around us, in every society. It's the mechanism by which we create value and transfer it to others, as old and simple as selling your grain to the baker so he can make and sell bread, and as modern as creating a low-cost phone app that delights millions and makes you suddenly rich.

The reactions of university leadership to such criticisms have ranged from simply ignoring them to worrying that they are harbingers of the impending collapse of the business model of the education industry. In this period of crisis, we are encouraged by the authors of this book, *Shaping the Future of Business Education: Relevance, Rigor, and Life Preparation in a Changing World* (SFBE). They have produced an outstanding collection of ideas and evidence for the value of higher education generally and, particularly, for business education infused with a deeper understanding of arts and sciences. The intellectual power and uniqueness of a business education infused with arts and sciences is a powerful model that, we believe, takes back control of the debate about the nature and value of a combined liberal-arts + business education. Business education, alone and by itself, is not enough. It can make someone efficient at the practical matters of effecting transactions, but it doesn't by itself create anything. Business is a mechanism and a means – by all means crucial, but insufficient. What is needed is both business knowledge and the creativity, connection, and ability to invent that the arts and sciences convey.

SFBE develops one of the most important ideas for improving the current educational model by combining the best elements of two ancient traditions of practical and theoretical learning in a *crucial educational fusion*. (This phrase was coined by Daniel Everett in several publications, first mentioned in his inaugural address as incoming Dean of Arts and Sciences at Bentley University in 2010.)

A fusion that leads to a *well-rounded education* that neither professional education nor liberal arts education alone can provide in preparing a learner for professional, social, and intellectual success. If you can master the complicated thinking and mathematics of accountancy you might be a good accountant. But accountancy alone will not prepare you to think across the range of contexts that the successful citizen will need to navigate. Likewise, if you learn to find, interpret, and build ideas about the past on primary sources and become a superb historian, what is it that you know about the business behind the stock news that signals boon or bane to your career prospects? The way forward is to help students to master both liberal arts and professional ways of thinking and foundations of knowledge. The idea that you cannot do both is based on a false dichotomy – or so this book argues – namely, that professional education and liberal arts education represent a disjunction rather than, as we believe, the optimal conjunction. To us, therefore, Thoreau failed to get beyond the artificial dichotomy that colored his thoughts about the possible and the desirable in the business of life. A failure that he shares with most who have been responsible for establishing the dominant business education model that is so aptly criticized by Ghoshal (2005, pp. 75, 88) when articulating that 'many of the worst excesses of recent management practices have their roots in a set of ideas that have emerged from business school academics over the last 30 years' and that 'the only alternative to any form of ideological absolutism lies in intellectual pluralism, which is likely to lead to better research and broadened usefulness.'

The liberal arts college environment has always been an excellent place to 'find yourself.' Many students want just that from college, that is, they want their college to offer them a series of exploratory experiences. On the other hand, there are students who already feel a strong sense of purpose and want an educational experience that fits their plans and priorities. Can't we serve them both? We should. Yet educators can only serve both groups of students and their interests by developing curricula and pedagogy based on a clear understanding of the concerns of the enveloping society as well as a well-argued philosophy of the goals, methods, and calibration of their enterprise. Universities need curricula that are neither too theoretical nor too applied. Innovative curricular planning need not slavishly follow the most recent trends as presented by the press, nor base itself on a 'Mt. Olympus plan' – where intellectuals dictate to society what it needs.

Is a business education worthwhile?

Many popular writers these days argue that business education is a bad investment (e.g. Glenn, 2011). Lynn O'Shaughnessy in TheCollegeSolutionBlog.com has been one of the most outspoken critics of business education, in statements such as: 'Contrary to conventional wisdom, students don't need to major in business to succeed. Frankly, I believe students often enjoy a better chance at landing good jobs if they major in a liberal art like economics, history, chemistry, a foreign language, English lit or philosophy.'

Such criticisms usually contain a kernel of truth. However, we would go further and say that attending college or university never *guarantees* success. No one *need* to major in anything to succeed in life, whether you define success financially or in terms of personal satisfaction – Bill Gates is one of many examples of financial success without college and there are many indigenous peoples around the world who lead satisfying lives without having even been to kindergarten.

Though there are indeed valid criticisms against business education, we nevertheless believe that an undergraduate education in business is an excellent choice, if it is offered in the right way. It is absolutely right to sound an alarm over the lack of broad learning that is the hallmark of some business programs, and we could not agree more with the suggestion made by many that the discipline of philosophy perhaps teaches one how to think critically as much if not more than any other course of study. But the fact remains that many people do not want to major in liberal arts and sciences, not even in philosophy, even though avoiding these fields may result in failing to develop some of the skills most needed in one's life and career. That is why data from the Social Science Research Council are so alarming: 'Students majoring in liberal arts fields see 'significantly higher gains in critical thinking, complex reasoning, and writing skills over time than students in other fields of study.' Students majoring in business, education, social work and communications showed the smallest gains...' (p. 11). It might even be correct that if students failed to take Arts and Sciences courses at all during their undergraduate careers, because, say, they only wanted business courses, that such avoidance could dumb-down American society more generally.

But this is an artificial concern based once again on the false dichotomy of liberal arts versus business. The crucial educational fusion we envisage combines the best of business and arts and sciences – developing critical thinking, cultural literacy, and professional acumen in a single course of study.

The fusion we have in mind integrates the arts and sciences with business in a model wherein philosophy, science, math, history, English, modern languages, visual arts and so on work in tandem with professional courses to provide a novel type of education, one in which professional education and the arts and sciences each enhances the value of the other. (In fact, business is but one professional area that could profitably be better integrated with the arts and sciences in a new educational model.) The arts and sciences should be encountered in a place of learning where culturally important knowledge, contexts of learning, critical thinking, complex reasoning, and communication skills are developed simultaneously with rigorous mentoring and training in professional learning. We say 'place of learning,' because the dialog and need for encounter to achieve this fusion cannot be duplicated entirely online.

Bentley University offers one example of this new educational fusion. The report of the Carnegie Foundation, *Rethinking Undergraduate Business Education: Liberal Learning for the Profession*, offers many other examples of strategic work on blending liberal arts with professional education, highlighting the specific innovations of many US universities in this regard.

A solid foundation in the liberal arts supports a cognitive dexterity that professionals need to perform well across a fluid range of contexts and challenges. That this cognitive conditioning and personal integration is important for the long-term is underscored in what many business executives often tell us: 'The basic business skills are what get you a job at our company. But to advance, you need the broad background of the liberal arts.'

Thus it would be misguided to portray any part of the current crisis in American education as professional education versus the liberal arts. All of us in higher education recognize our responsibility to contribute to our students' quality of mental, social, and professional life. And we are all concerned that the costs are getting out of hand.

Majoring in business is one of the best choices any student could make. But so is philosophy. That is why this book makes the case, from various angles and in many different contexts, that combing the liberal arts and business in a single course of study is a wise and prescient move.

This is not to deny that students who choose business may not take the same long-term, integrated perspective urged by their faculty and administrators. We recognize that undergraduate business programs can struggle to sell the humanities, in particular, and the liberal arts overall, to students. As we meet regularly with students at Bentley and elsewhere we encounter what is almost surely a general problem, namely, that some students see general-education requirements in literature, philosophy, and so on as irrelevant consumers of their precious time to master as many professional skills and bodies of knowledge as possible. Students have asked, for example, why on earth they have to take English composition – because 'this is a business university.' This honest question takes us to our next concept in building our larger idea of an educational fusion, the business university: just what would a business university be?

The business university

The etymology of the modern word 'university' comes from a Latin phrase for a community of teachers and scholars, a *universitas magistrorum et scholarium*. A business university is an inclusive group of scholars. It is a community of business professionals, scientists, humanists, social scientists and artists, at the very least. This is what distinguishes a business university from a business college (from 'collegium': a group of people living together under a single set of rules) or business school. In a university the community of teachers and scholars or, as we prefer to think of them, teacher-scholars, will each contribute their talents, interests, and teaching to programs, research, and curricula that draw upon the abilities of the community as a whole. A business university is a diverse community of teacher-scholars who dedicate themselves to the development of business professionalism while pursuing diverse majors across business or the arts and sciences, developing cognitive abilities and knowledge in the complementary contexts of the various liberal arts and business courses. At a business university everyone studies business, even though not all need major in business. All students should graduate with a firm professional foundation in business, intellectually grounded in the liberal arts. Modern societies run on business. How business is understood, its ethical commitments, objectives and so on, will therefore deeply affect the society in which it operates. And the stability and quality of life in any country is closely related to the economic success of the country. We believe that to fail to understand the basis of this part of modern culture and society is as serious a cognitive deficit as not knowing anything of the poetry of Shakespeare.

A business university will include business and other disciplines offered as part of a single community. This is how such a university stands out from a 'normal' university that contains a business college. In a normal university, the business teacher-scholars form their own community and liberal arts faculty another distinct community, with very little interaction between the two communities. But at a business university, there is also a single integrated community and an integrated curriculum at the heart of all teaching.

The dilemma of the humanities and the liberal arts

The crucial educational fusion the authors of SFBE expound and exemplify offers a possible solution as well to a more specific crisis – the future of the humanities. We hear these days of the 'crisis of the humanities.' The number of majors, jobs, and student interest in these subjects is dropping. *The Boston Globe* offered one report on the worries of the humanities in a 2010 article about the new Mandell Center at Brandeis University in Waltham, Massachusetts. The *Globe* asserted:

> At college campuses around the world, the humanities are hurting. Students are flocking to majors more closely linked to their career ambitions. Grant money and philanthropy are flowing to the sciences. And university presidents are worried about the future of subjects once at the heart of a liberal arts education. (A.1)

Such gloom must be placed in context. Doubts about the humanities have been around at least since Aristophanes wrote *The Clouds*. Taking a closer look, the humanities don't really seem to be experiencing a crisis, though perhaps they have a chronic illness. Bachelor's degrees in the humanities have held relatively steady since 1994 at roughly 12 to 13 percent of all majors. While such figures demonstrate that the health of the humanities is not robust, as measured in terms of student preferences, one cannot conclude either *crisis* or *terminal decline*.

What has been the response of university and college leaders to the ill health of the humanities? It has been to declare to applicants, students, faculty, and the public that these subjects are important. It has included more investments in humanities, from new buildings to hiring more faculty and publicizing the humanities energetically. Dartmouth College's recent president, Jim Yong Kim, recently offered the hortatory remark that 'Literature and the arts should not only be for kids who go to cotillion balls to make polite conversation at parties.'

We couldn't agree more with the idea that the humanities are important. But this type of approach is overly moralizing. Students do not take classes because adults tell them they'll be morally superior if they do. Today students are far too pragmatic for this.

The twofold difficulty in the humanities is the erosion of the number of majors in the humanities – thus threatening their existence – on the one hand and the long-feared 'closing of the American mind' on the other, produced in part by the growing number of students taking what some regard as easy majors.

In confronting these difficulties, it is vital that the humanities not claim for themselves a uniqueness they do not possess. For example, it has become nearly a truism to say that the humanities teach 'critical thinking skills.' This is correct, in broadstroke, of humanities instruction (though certainly not universally so). But critical thinking is unique neither to the humanities nor to the arts and sciences more generally. A good business education, for example, teaches critical thinking in management, marketing, accounting, finance, and other courses. More realistically and humbly, what we can say is that the humanities and sciences provide *complementary contexts* for reasoning and cultural knowledge that are crucial to functioning at a high level in the enveloping society. All that we think and are, even how we use our bodies, according to some research, derives in large part from our cultures and societies. Without an appreciation of this tacit, dark matter of the mind, we become less able to evaluate, discern, and predict – abilities crucial for all professions.

Thus, admitting that critical thinking can also be developed in professional schools, we realize that it is enhanced and further developed when the thinker learns to develop analytical skills in history, different languages, philosophy, mathematics, and other contexts. The humanities offer a distinct set of problems that hone thinking skills, even if they are not the only critical thinking game in town. For example, at Bentley and other institutions where most students major in professional fields, English develops vocabulary and clarity of expression while, say, marketing builds on and contributes to these. Science requires empirical verification and consideration of alternatives. Accountancy builds on and contributes to these. Science and English make better business students as business courses improve thinking in the humanities and sciences. Business people conversant in science and language are going to know what the scientists, book editors, moviemakers, technologists and other 'product producers' and 'innovators' are doing! It is the humanities experts that are at the forefront of new artifacts that delight, inspire, and are useful to people. Business thrives on innovation, not in business practice alone, but in producing and selling something of value to individuals – something not produced by business alone.

The late Steve Jobs of Apple could not have been a brilliant marketer without also recognizing brilliance in design – and that comes in large part from the humanities. Take Jobs's work on iTunes, for example. As a businessman, he said, 'we can deliver music easily and with zero incremental cost' and 'the way people get music sucks.' As an artist, he said, 'current MP3 players suck.' He saw you needed a) a better machine, b) an explore-and-purchase environment that kept the elements of sharing and discovery, and c) a way to force music publishers to see the new model was their only chance of survival. This is what we mean by 'fusion.'

The problems of the humanities are not going to be solved by lamenting the change in culture and exhorting folks to get back on course. Thinking like this could mean that new buildings dedicated to the humanities will wind up as mausoleums rather than as centers of engagement with modern culture and the building of futures in contemporary society.

So how do we harness the power of culture to revive and heal the influence of the humanities on future generations? We fuse the humanities, along with all the other liberal arts and sciences in innovative curricula with business. Programs that take in students without proper concern for their future or provision for post-graduate opportunities – how they can use what they have learned in meaningful work – need to think about the ethics of their situation. They are borderline Ponzi schemes. Today's students need to find gainful employment in which to apply all the substantive things they learn in college. Society no longer assumes that just because a particular subject may be good for you to take that the financial commitment and apprenticeship between student and teacher is thereby fully justified.

Again, the cultural zeitgeist requires of education that it be intellectually well-balanced and focused but also useful. Providing all of these and more is not the commercialization of higher education. Rather, the combination of professional education and the humanities and sciences is an opportunity that at once (re)engages students in the humanities and realizes Dewey's pragmatic goal of transforming education by coupling concrete objectives with abstract ideas, general knowledge, and theory.

About this book

We need an educational fusion if both professional education and a liberal education are to thrive. A symbiotic relationship in nature is stronger than an individual living alone. But how does this work in practice? The authors of SFBE develop these ideas in exciting detail.

In Chapter 1, the first chapter of Part I, Patricia Peknik does an outstanding job of setting the context for many of the remaining contributions in the book. Her discussion of the American foundations of practical business education provides a perfect framework for understanding the dominant current debate that pits liberal education against applied/professional training while making the case for fining an optimal fusion of both to produce responsible and engaged citizens who actively engage as innovative, wealth-generating professionals.

The chapter by Mark Davis (Chapter 2) targets a particular aspect of the broader canvas painted by Peknik by highlighting the current dominant criticisms of business schools and the programs they offer. He argues that the source of much of these identified weaknesses relates to development of and incentives provided to faculty who develop the business curricula and who are the principal teachers. His contention that management education needs to engage outside professionals (practitioners) is, we believe, entirely consistent with our contention that more diversity of thought and approach is required when engaging with the minds of the students – diversity of thought and approach that can also come from other disciplines outside the traditional scope of business.

A global perspective arguing for the need to expand our conception of the purpose of modern business is provided by Anders Aspling (Chapter 3). Anders's role as a key contributor to the development of the *Global Responsibility Leadership Initiative* and to the *Principles for Responsible Management Education* is clearly evident throughout the chapter and we could not agree more with his belief that we have an obligation to ensure that students develop a greater understanding of their individual responsibilities as future business leaders – responsibilities that are better developed as a natural outflow of the fused education that this book proposes.

In Chapter 4, the first chapter of Part II (that examines the fusion imperative through the eyes of authors traditionally identified with a business perspective), Catherine Usoff presents a compelling case for integrating the traditional techniques of liberal learning into accountancy programs. She makes the case that the challenges facing business today and the role expected to be played by accountancy graduates require far more comprehensive abilities in critical thinking, communications, and intellectual engagement than in the past. Developing these is better achieved through an integrated education that requires students to simultaneously engage with the *method* of liberal learning and the method of accountancy.

In a number of ways, Richard Cleary and Jay Thibodeau (Chapter 5) deepen the ideas introduced by Usoff by demonstrating how an understanding of mathematical sciences and accountancy, particularly in the form of the *sub-fields* of audit and statistics, can greatly assist the professional auditor in understanding the sampling challenge of audit procedures. They also demonstrate how quantitative techniques of pattern recognition can help effectively identify the presence of fraudulent practice. They further argue that independent courses in the two disciplines cannot and will not realize the maximum benefit for the student that an integrated and related engagement with the topics will bring.

Lest we fall into the trap of our education fusion argument being seen as having benefit for business students only, something we have already argued against, Emily Roth, Nicole Belmonte, and Nick Komissarov (Chapter 6) transpose the argument presented by Cleary and Thibodeau somewhat in making the case for how actuarial science is, and needs to be, enhanced by broadening the education through the inclusion of business courses and perspectives. They argue that business schools that understand the value of integrating soft skills into technical education are uniquely equipped to develop students for careers in the actuarial sciences.

The June 2011 *Economist* Intelligence Unit report 'Big Data: Harnessing a Game-Changing Asset' indicated that most business executives surveyed believed their organizations were dealing with increasing amounts and complexity of data. Dominique Haughton (Chapter 7) confirms this and makes a strong case for business analytics as an essential arrow in a business's quiver of techniques that will allow it to survive and compete. This being the case, she further argues strongly for a more significant inclusion of analytics, traditionally a discipline within the sciences, across the business curricula.

Heikki Topi (Chapter 8) brings together the business-side argument presented in the second section of the book by clearly demonstrating how business education can be transformed through disciplinary integration. As an internationally recognized scholar and contributor to information systems education, Topi is well positioned to articulate how information systems is intentionally integrative in nature and an excellent vehicle for introducing arts and sciences capabilities into business education. He further argues that the connections embedded in the field provide a feedback loop that can enrich the debate taking place across other more discipline-specific courses.

Part III develops a perspective on fusion from the vantage point of the arts and sciences.

Christopher Beneke (Chapter 9) uses an innovative and insightful two-dimensional taxonomy to argue for history's importance for professional students. First, studying history develops the ability to 'drill down' and develop insight into the origins of beliefs and practices that might otherwise be naïvely presumed to be universal truths rather than culturally determined and continually evolving perspectives. Second, reading history is intellectually broadening and cultivates one's ability to derive meaning from the seemingly distant and unfamiliar. Beneke makes an exceedingly strong case for the study of history being integral to developing cultural sensitivity and respect for difference, two characteristics considered crucial to executives operating effectively in our global environment.

The ability to immerse oneself in a body of text, whether fiction or non-fiction, is an essential building up for critical thinking – a point that Joan Atlas makes in 'The Need to Read' (Chapter 10). In particular, she makes a clear and convincing case for the need to hone one's ability to read without distraction, an ability made all the more difficult among today's youth who so value the ideals of multi-tasking. It is only through focused attention that a reader fully engages with literature and makes the connections to their personal experiences.

Elizabeth Brown (Chapter 11) makes a strong case for the inclusion of law in business curricula. Business executives in small, medium, and large companies cannot escape the need to understand multiple facets of law. All organizations face questions related to their legal status, employment conditions, consumer liability, and intellectual property issue, to name just a few. Being thoughtful and informed about these issues reduces the probability of legal error and allows one to better time when to seek professional advice.

Few could argue against the contribution of behavioral economics and 'irrational behavior' to the Great Recession despite the initial dismissal of predictions by Robert Shiller (2000) and others prior to the events that began in 2007. Gregory Hall (Chapter 12) builds on this new recognition in arguing that students need to develop insight into psychological theory. Only by doing this can they fully appreciate that rational economics and choice provides only a partial understanding of how businesses and societies respond to rapid economic and technological transformation.

The growing number of companies significantly engaged in research and development to both obtain and sustain competitive advantage makes it increasingly imperative that business leaders have a more than passing understanding of science and technology. Frederick Ledley and Eric Oches (Chapter 13) convincingly argue that 'business leaders need to have a pluralistic, integrative, and interdisciplinary knowledge of science and technology' and that the appropriate threading of these fields into business curricula, particularly at the undergraduate level, lays the needed foundation for this knowledge.

While most contributors to SFBE demonstrate the benefit of fusing liberal arts and business for business education, Gregory Farber (Chapter 14) makes a convincing case for the benefits that an immersion in aspects of a business curricula has for liberal arts programs. Furthermore, he suggests a 'blended' approach creates a more cohesive experience for the liberal arts student rather than an 'artificial bridge.' As such it offers a significantly higher probability of sustained benefit for the artist over their subsequent career.

Part IV examines current and future trends that will affect business education. Following the enormous amount that has been appearing in the popular press extolling the virtues of technology as the panacea of all our education woes, William Schiano (Chapter 15) gives a refreshingly insightful critique of the opportunity technology provides for business education in particular and for education more generally. His articulation of the different opportunities current technological platforms offer and his arguments for the continuing convergence of in-person and online experiences provide a far more nuanced picture of the future: a future that will require significant innovation by many but a future of technology-mediated learning that is far richer and diverse than current popular expressions suggest.

An important, perhaps insurmountable, challenge for those seeking to expand the role of ethical decision-making as a crucial element of management education is presented by Robert Frederick (Chapter 16). He contends that only a fraction of what happens when making ethical choices can be taught using cases and illustration. When called upon to make choices, context is inescapable and rational decision-making must partially give way to the 'private domain of emotion and intuition.' The philosophical position he takes in arguing that 'emotions are inextricably bound to ethical decision and can't be eliminated' amply demonstrates the potential of an understanding of philosophy to developing business leaders for tomorrow who appreciate the limitations of business theories and who consequently appreciate the ambiguities they will inevitably encounter professionally and privately.

Although the call to expand student capabilities for innovative and creative thinking has almost become deafening in recent years, achieving the goal lags significantly. Andrew Aylesworth (Chapter 17) presents a model for achieving the goal that offers real potential for business schools that break down internal and cross-faculty barriers in their curricula and thereby expand the opportunities for students to learn how to 'connect disparate dots' and create interesting new opportunities – opportunities through which successful innovations emerge.

Samir Dayal's (Chapter 18) call for an aesthetic renewal in American higher education is exceedingly timely. He raises the real danger that immediate employment, career-focused education, and 'hitting the ground running' in the job market will drive out elements of academic curricula that develop skills, talent, and insight for longer-term career growth.. Dayal's call reminds us that there is still a 'need for an education for its own sake' and that such aesthetic aspirations also reinforce the needed pluralist approach to business education that creates citizens who will continue to grow and enrich society throughout their lives.

Service-learning is well established within the U.S. tertiary education sector with students from business and liberal arts engaging in community work that both leverages and expands their classroom learning. Edward Zlotkowski (Chapter 19) argues that the full benefits of service-learning in developing civically engaged students and responsible citizens is best realized through combining liberal arts and professional education. Furthermore, he suggests that reciprocal benefit exists whereby engagement in service-learning helps embed the benefits of an academic program that fuses liberal arts and professional education.

Diane Kellogg's (Chapter 20) discussion of experiential learning programs that are substantially service-learning oriented provides a personal and powerful glimpse of how these programs call upon insights gained through arts and sciences and business curricula, inducing students to deepen their questioning of the experiences they have. The chapter adds a rich flavor to the insights provided by Zlotkowski.

Although the argument for transforming business education is by no means won, Dan LeClair's (Chapter 21) contribution brings together the threads of our contributing authors when making his case for fusion. He argues that the international community of business schools is beginning to develop solid foundations for this transformation and calling for greater engagement by other disciplines across the education spectrum. We concur with his perspective that we have grounds to be hopeful and conclude that these hopes flourish within 'the context of social purpose.'

Conclusion

Higher education is a mutual responsibility of the state and the citizen. Without it the individual has little chance of being an equal partner in the state. A state without an educated citizenry has no chance of being an equal partner in world affairs. The crisis of education in the West is one of the most important in our history. If social forces are allowed to denigrate it in such a way as to lead to the weakening and devaluation of higher education, the societies that allow such forces to run unchecked are severely weakened.

Yet at the same time higher education itself has responsibilities: it must provide value, both during the student experience and afterwards in the business of life. As the humanities and sciences produce graduates without meaningful careers in the students' chosen fields, they will become less relevant and all will lose.

This book makes a strong case for a new model of education, a crucial educational fusion, in which professional education, the humanities, and the sciences are integrated into a single pragmatic and cognitive whole that enables the leaders of tomorrow to understand the world and pursue their life's aims with the highest abilities possible that can be transmitted from the lessons learned by their fellow inhabitants of this world. It is this ambitious goal that all of us in higher education strive for. And it is the objective of this book to lay out one roadmap toward that goal.

References

Arum, Richard, Roksa, Josipa, and Cho, Esther (2011) *Improving Undergraduate Learning: Findings and Policy Recommendations from the SSRC-CLA Longitudinal Project* (Social Science Research Council), p. 11.

Everett, Daniel (2012) *Language: The Cultural Tool* (New York: Pantheon).

Economist Intelligence Unit Limited (September 2011) *Big Data: Harnessing a Game-Changing Asset.*

Ghoshal, Sumantra (2005) 'Bad Management Theories Are Destroying Good Management Practices,' *Academy of Management Learning & Education*, 4(1), pp. 75–78.

Glenn, David (2011) 'The Default Major: Skating through B-School,' *New York Times*, April 14.

Jan, Tracy (2010) 'Colleges Aim to Revive the Humanities: New Buildings and Focus Combat Dip in Enrollment,' *Boston Globe*, November 8, A.1.

Jim Yong Kim, quoted in Everett, Daniel (2011), 'The Broccoli of Higher Education,' *Inside Higher Education*, August 30; http://www.insidehighered. com/views/2011/08/30/essay_on_how_humanities_can_be_strengthened_ by_embracing_ties_to_professional_education

Shiller, Robert J. (2000), *Irrational Exuberance* (Princeton, NJ: Princeton University Press).

Part I
Background

1
The Rise of Business Education in America

Patricia J. Peknik

The debate over the role of a traditional liberal arts curriculum in the education of students focused on professional development has storied antecedents. Some of America's greatest intellectual figures have struggled with the question of how best to provide students with an education that was both intellectually rigorous and but also practical. It is a debate that continues today.

In colonial days, there was little debate. Long before the creation of modern political parties, the modern banking system, and our modern system of trade and commerce, the nation's oldest colleges had established a curriculum of classical history, classical languages, ancient literature, and theology. Over time, these institutions gradually added courses in 'practical' subjects, but at its core American higher education remained committed to the European model of classical learning.

Harvard was the nation's first college, created in 1636 and offering a curriculum in philosophy, history, mathematics, physics, and literature. The liberal arts curriculum at the nation's first colleges reflected the visions of colonial theologians, merchants, and planters to develop a sound and prosperous society of educated tradesmen, ministers, teachers, and public servants. The College of William and Mary (1693) educated Virginia's planter class in logic and rhetoric. Yale College (1701) offered courses in languages and civil policy, and graduates bound for careers in medicine, law, and commerce were equally required to master Latin, Greek, and Hebrew. At the College of New Jersey (1746), later Princeton, the sons of the colonial mercantile class read Homer, Cicero, Shakespeare, and Milton.

Primary among the goals of colonial colleges was to educate students in the classical tradition as well as in theology, and to train students to develop the critical faculties essential to a liberalism of spirit. Many of the founding fathers who led the revolutionary generation were first-generation college graduates who had received their training in rhetoric and oratory at colonial colleges. Despite regional differences in the economic, political, and religious life of the colonies, the curriculum at William and Mary (Jefferson's alma mater), King's College (where Alexander Hamilton was educated), and Harvard (the college John Adams attended) provided the revolutionary generation with a common intellectual vocabulary and a dedication to the liberal spirit.

In the decades after the Revolutionary war, colleges became more liberal in both curriculum and more demographically inclusive, offering courses in modern languages, political science, and practical sciences, and educating an increasing number of students from middle class families.

The question of whether, or how, to integrate a liberal arts curriculum and professional degree programs first arose significantly in 1819, when former president Thomas Jefferson founded the University of Virginia. Long before the creation of modern political parties, the modern banking system, and our modern system of trade and commerce, the nation's oldest colleges had established a curriculum of classical history, classical languages, ancient literature, and theology, and then gradually added courses in 'practical' subjects. Jefferson designed the curriculum of his beloved university to include courses in law, medicine, and science, believing that institutions of higher learning should provide highly specialized professional training. Students were able to choose from elective courses rather than follow the prerequisites of a set curriculum, in the belief that the spirit of liberty was integral to the intellectual development of an engaged citizenry. In his 1818 'Report of the Commissioners Appointed to Fix the Site of the University of Virginia,' Jefferson argued that one of the purposes of higher education was 'to harmonize and promote the interests of agriculture, manufactures and commerce... and give a free scope to the public industry' as well as 'to develop the reasoning faculties of our youth... and to form them to the habits of reflection and correct action.' Jefferson knew that his commitment to training students for 'the various vocations of life' was unorthodox: 'Some good men, and even of respectable information, consider the learned sciences as useless acquirements,' he noted, lamenting the reactionary view that 'what has ever been must ever be, and that to secure ourselves where we are, we must tread with awful reverence in the footsteps of our fathers.' Yet the country was full of 'real and living examples' of Americans who had made 'wonderful advances' in science and technology, Jefferson said, because they had the opportunity to focus on the acquisition and application of useful, practical knowledge (Jefferson, 1856, pp. 435–436).

Several decades later the debate played out most famously at Harvard College, when Charles W. Eliot, President of Harvard from 1869 to 1909, insisted that Harvard had a responsibility to integrate the goals of liberal and career education. Eliot designed an elective system under which students were free to choose their course of study rather than follow the traditional classical curriculum. He argued that students who had already decided on their professions should be able to choose courses which 'are related to, or underlie' their professional objectives, (Eliot, 1898, p. 125) and he advocated for the right of students to have the opportunity to 'win academic distinction in single subjects or lines of study' (Eliot, 1898, p. 139). Eliot was a staunch supporter of the laboratory and the case study method as essential pedagogical corollaries to the lecture and the textbook, believing that students were more engaged and curious when theory was married to practice, and he urged colleges to develop courses in new disciplines: 'A university, while not neglecting the ancient treasures of learning, has to keep a watchful eye upon the new fields of discovery, and has to invite its students to walk in new-made as well as in long-trodden paths' (Eliot, 1898, p. 143).

By the time of Eliot's reforms of the Harvard curriculum, then, colleges had been expanding their offerings, first incrementally and then in a wave of reform, to include courses intended to provide professional training to young Americans who wished to become engineers, scientists, and educators. Some critics worried that the study of agriculture or military science might compromise the traditional liberal arts mission of American colleges, but in an age of rapid technological innovation and economic development, the focus on scientific and practical education was of national consequence.

Throughout the nineteenth century, the federal government funded the building of roads, canals, and railroads, and crafted tax and legal policies designed to encourage private commerce. The Morrill Acts of 1862 and 1890, which granted federal land to state governments for the founding of colleges, created new institutions that taught from a broad, practical curriculum and trained the engineers and technicians who would oversee the country's dramatic expansion.

Faculty at traditional liberal arts colleges often criticized the move towards a practical curriculum and the loss of the classics as the foundation of higher education. A faculty committee at Yale College produced The Yale Report of 1828, an institutional memorandum that became an influential treatise arguing for the retention of the classical curriculum. The report, referring to the university's recent addition of courses in the sciences and political economy, was written in response to suggestions that American colleges, in order to thrive, needed to adapt to 'the spirit and wants of the age' by being better accommodated to the business character of the nation. The report's authors argued that a college's mission is to provide a solid education in the liberal arts and sciences, not to teach particular professional skills, because the study of ancient literature, classical languages, English language, and rhetoric and philosophy is the basis for the learning of professional skills.

The liberal and comprehensive study of arts and sciences, the authors said, makes a contribution to the learner's acquisition of professional skills because 'Every thing throws light upon every thing.' An understanding of literature and science will not 'grow up spontaneously, amid the bustle of business' later in life, the faculty argued, and self-educated men who can train themselves to think rigorously across disciplines – the Benjamin Franklins – are the rarest exceptions. The time for professional training was after a thorough liberal arts education:

> The young merchant must be trained in the counting room, the mechanic, in the workshop, the farmer, in the field. But we have, on our premises, no experimental farm or retail shop; no cotton or iron manufactory; no hatter's, or silver-smith's, or coach-maker's establishment. For what purpose, then, it will be asked, are young men who are destined to these occupations, ever sent to a college? They should not be sent, as we think, with an expectation of *finishing* their education at the college; but with a view of laying a thorough foundation…. In either case, the object of the undergraduate course, is not to finish a preparation for business, but to impart that various and general knowledge, which will improve, and elevate, and adorn any occupation … (Yale Report of 1828)

Not all older liberal arts colleges rejected this focus on a vocational curriculum. In his 1850 *Report to the Corporation on Changes in the System of Collegiate Education*, Francis Wayland, president of Brown University, sounded the alarm that American higher education had been out of touch with the demands of an energetic, industrial society, and that young people were looking to colleges to educate them for 'the productive professions.' Wayland echoed Jefferson's advocacy of an elective system of learning and emphasized the need for colleges to offer practical training to 'the agriculturist, the manufacturer, the mechanic, or the merchant.' Courses should be arranged so that 'every student might study what he chose, all that he chose, and nothing but what he chose.' Wayland, noting that mercantile and manufacturing interests had led the country's economic development, argued that colleges could remain vital and relevant only by offering programs of study in the professions: 'Every man has a special right to that *kind* of education which will be of the greatest value to him in the prosecution of useful industry' (Wayland, 1850, pp. 51–57).

Curricular reform that emphasized the need to include vocational training gradually became the rule over the course of the nineteenth century, transforming higher education. The industrial revolution made it necessary for colleges to train students in the professions, and this focus on practical education and marketable skills inspired the founding of the Massachusetts Institute of Technology (1861), a 'polytechnic' institute of industrial sciences which would train students in the habits of observation, reflection and analysis and produce a generation of inventors and industrialists devoted to national progress. Founder William Barton Rogers believed that an exclusive focus on classical learning could not help the nation advance in an age of rapid technological change and industrialization, that science and technology were 'legitimate foundations of higher education,' and that professional education should be introduced at the undergraduate level 'combined with the basic elements of a liberal education.' This new form of university education, combining the traditional elements of classical liberal arts learning with practical training, represented a form of higher education 'indigenous to American soil and American culture,' and colleges had the imperative to offer the kinds of courses that would prepare students to work in a more economically and socially complex society, Rogers said (MIT, 1949, pp. 8–10).

In the great age of nineteenth-century American industrialization and economic development, university-educated executives and managers were needed to run complex business organizations, including railroads and manufacturing industries, and courses in banking, bookkeeping, and management had to replace the old system of apprenticeships and inherited occupations. Joseph Wharton, a Philadelphia merchant and industrialist who had started as an apprentice bookkeeper and risen to become a prominent industrialist, donated $100,000 to the University of Pennsylvania in 1881 for the founding of a school of commerce and finance dedicated to providing a liberal education to future business leaders.

The case study method, which had become a prominent feature of scientific education at American colleges, became the hallmark of pedagogy at Wharton and in the business programs founded in the twentieth century. The case study approach was perfectly suited to an America described by psychologist and philosopher William James as wholly pragmatic, focused on practice over theory and instrumental learning over an allegiance to historical texts or abstract concepts. Only through concrete instances of practice and performance could students learn analogical reasoning or make sound ethical decisions, and the essence of the American experience is action and the lessons of experience, James said. In keeping with this belief in practical experience, the case study, the laboratory, and fieldwork became hallmarks of the American college during the early twentieth century.

But the relationship between a liberal arts curriculum and a curriculum devoted to professional training remained a subject of great academic and public debate. Harvard itself abandoned its elective system when Charles W. Eliot's successor, Abbot Lawrence Lowell, concluded that even students who wanted the academic freedom of the elective system and the professional training offered in specialized courses should still be required to engage in a broad, liberal course of study: 'The best type of liberal education in our complex modern world aims at producing men who know a little of everything and something well' (Lowell, 1909).

Throughout the past century, the basic questions have persisted. Should professional preparation be left in the province of technical colleges, or was there a way to combine the best of liberal arts education with the foundations of professional training? Was there an intellectually rigorous way to integrate the study of the humanities with vocational coursework? Each generation has had its own reasons to pose these questions, prompted by events as different as the entrance of women into American colleges in the 1920s to the rise of government-funded scientific research at state universities in the 1950s, and from the post-Second World War expansion of universities to accommodate the children of the Baby Boom to the culture wars of the late twentieth century in which liberals and conservatives debated the integrity and relevance of the new, expanded college curriculums.

The debate over how, and whether, to combine liberal arts learning and professional training is not new. The mission to educate students to be responsible, engaged citizens as well as productive and innovative professionals is as old as the country itself, and the question of how best to balance the teaching of philosophy and literature with the teaching of chemistry or accounting is a question college presidents, faculty, students and the public have been asking for centuries. What has changed is that with the dramatic expansions in enrollment and the increasing complexities of a technologically sophisticated and economically advanced society, the answers are more urgently needed, and of greater consequence than at any time in our past.

References

Eliot, Charles, W. (1898) 'Liberty in Education' (February 1885), in *Educational Reform: Essays and Addresses* (New York: Century).

Lowell, A. Lawrence (1909) Inaugural Address, Harvard University, October 6.

Jefferson, Thomas (1856), in *Early History of the University of Virginia, As Contained in the Letters of Thomas Jefferson and Joseph C. Cabell, Hitherto Unpublished...* (Richmond: J.W. Randolph).

Reports on the Course of Instruction in Yale College (1828) ; by a Committee of the Corporation and the Academica Faculty (New Haven, CT: Hezekiah Howe).

Report of the Committee on Educational Survey to the Faculty of the Massachusetts Institute of Technology, Cambridge, Massachusetts, December 1949 (Cambridge: The Technology Press of the Massachusetts Institute of Technology).

Wayland, Francis (1850) 'Report to the Corporation of Brown University on Changes in the System of Collegiate Education,' Read March 28, Brown University.

2
Challenges Facing Today's Business Schools

Mark M. Davis

The education that today's business schools provide is being severely criticized by their various stakeholders. These include current students, teachers, and alumni, as well as the companies and organizations that ultimately employee their graduates. Many of the issues brought forth are worth examining. While the root causes are many, the fundamental challenges facing business schools are two: (a) how do we educate business school students so that their education is more relevant when they enter the workforce, and (b) how do we make their education more affordable?

Challenges

The first challenge, in an era of rapid business, technological, and societal change, is one of *relevance*. In many cases, entire curricula as well as individual course content in business schools are not directly applicable in today's constantly evolving business environment because the topical coverage is either outdated, too theoretical, or a combination of the two.

Cost is the other major challenge. The escalating costs of a higher education in general, and business schools specifically, continue to outpace virtually every other segment of the U.S. economy with the possible exception of healthcare (healthcare.net, 2010). The U.S. Department of Education now publishes a list of the most expensive schools (Lewin, 2011) and is starting to ask these schools to justify future increases, because many students now receive federal loans to pay for their education. In his January 24, 2012 State of the Union address, President Barack Obama emphasized the need for institutions of higher education to better manage their costs: 'We can't just keep subsidizing skyrocketing tuition,' he said. 'We'll run out of money. States also need to do their part, by making higher education a higher priority in their budgets. And colleges and universities have to do their part by working to keep costs down.'

Those who manage and teach in business schools must reexamine how they educate their students so the result is more relevant and more affordable. In doing so, we need to look at both the *content* of what we teach as well as the *process of how* we teach. We need to be more effective in identifying what we teach so that it has more real-world application; at the same time, we need to be more efficient in how we teach in order to better control our costs without sacrificing quality.

Root causes of curricula irrelevance

Why is the education provided by today's business schools not giving students the proper tools to succeed in the workplace? Some institutional factors contribute to this problem, notably:

- emphasis on research and theory;
- lack of curriculum integration;
- misaligned reward structure;
- increasing rate of new knowledge.

Emphasis on research and theory

Today's business schools continue to emphasize faculty research in order to improve their rankings, often at the expense of teaching. This practice tends to encourage disciplinary rigor over practical relevance in the classroom. In addition, because significant portions of these rankings are based upon the number of articles that a school's faculty publishes, faculty are encouraged to publish a significant number of articles, often at the expense of quality. (Here quality is defined as how much an individual article contributes to extending the research envelope. Faculty therefore will publish several articles, each making a minor contribution to research, which is often referred to as 'creeping incrementalism' rather than publish just one article with a major contribution to research). 'Rankings' within the education industry by certain national and international publications are a top priority at most of the better business schools, and a significant part of these rankings is predicated on the number of articles that a school's faculty publish and the quality of the journals in which they are published. For example, in calculating the Bloomberg *Businessweek* rankings of MBA programs, 10 percent of a school's final score is based on the number of academic journal articles found in 20 publications (*Businessweek*, 2006). Higher rankings, as suggested by Figure 2.1, provide the justification for higher tuition costs.

As a result many schools 'buy their way into the top rankings' by offering well-published researchers very high salaries (often in the form of endowed chairs), even when their ability to teach in the classroom is questionable. (In contrast, good teachers are typically viewed 'as a commodity,' and therefore easily replaceable.) In addition, these well-recognized, highly paid researchers are typically assigned very few courses to teach (which can be a good thing if the researcher is a poor teacher!), thereby contributing to the cost of educating today's students while making little, if any, contribution to the educational benefits gained by the students.

In addition, as Bennis and O'Toole (2006, pp. 96–104) state, business schools have adopted a 'scientific model' to increase their respectability in the academic community. This model encourages faculty to focus more on theory and the rigor of the analysis that often has little connection or relevance to real world business issues and problems. Consequently, when this type of research is introduced into the classroom (as professors tend to do with their favorite topics), students lose interest because they cannot see how learning this material will improve their ability to compete in the workforce.

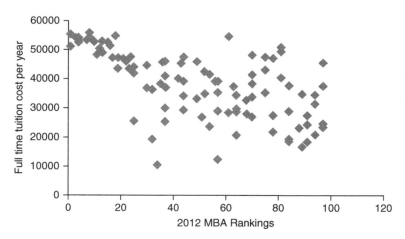

Figure 2.1 The relationship between MBA program rankings and tuition costs
Source: US News & World Report 2012.

Lack of curriculum integration

Companies today demand a new, larger skill set from business school graduates that extends significantly beyond that are learned in the traditional business school disciplines. This is especially true at the graduate level. This gap between the education that business schools provide and what businesses and organizations need was clearly articulated by Matthew Booth, Vice-President, Operations, Boston Financial Data Services: 'We employ a number of individuals with newly minted MBAs,' he notes. 'Although they have gained in-depth knowledge in various specific subjects I observe that they struggle to integrate their knowledge and apply it in the workplace' (Booth, 2005).

The need for tomorrow's managers to have a broader education is being acknowledged by a few business schools that have launched initiatives to integrate liberal arts into the business curriculum. For example, IE Business School in Madrid, Spain, has partnered with Brown University in Providence, Rhode Island to develop an executive MBA program that 'brings liberal arts to the MBA.' Another example at the undergraduate level is the liberal studies major (LSM) at Bentley University, which allows an undergraduate student to double major, one major being in a traditional business discipline and the other in arts and science. Unlike traditional arts and sciences majors that tend to drill deep within their respective areas, the LSM identifies common themes such as ethics and social responsibility that cuts across these traditional majors and that also have implications for business.

The lack of a truly integrated, applied curriculum in many programs is consistent with the larger problem at business schools: that a significant gap continues to exist between the skills that business schools are providing their students, and those skills that companies and organizations need (Mintzberg, 2004; Carnevale et al., 1990). This deficiency in business education was also recognized by Bennis and O'Toole (2005), who suggest that business schools need to provide more relevant curricula to prepare their students to be successful business professionals. To accomplish this, they suggest that business schools should partner more with companies and organizations that can provide students with internships that provide them with hands-on experience and actual real world projects that they need to have solved.

Peters (2006) suggests that undergraduate-level curricula should focus on discipline-specific content, while MBA and other business-related graduate programs emphasize integrating the traditional business disciplines because that is what is occurring in businesses today (Peters 2006;

Smith 2005). One approach for achieving this integration is to require faculty teaching in these programs to have some managerial experience either through consulting or actually working in companies and organizations. Integrating across courses and introducing students to real-world problems should be essential components of a graduate business school education (Latham et al., 2004). However, without this practical experience, it is difficult, if not impossible, for faculty to truly teach integrated courses that cross the traditional functional disciplines.

A few top-rated business schools are making progress in developing an integrated approach. These include the University of California – Berkeley, Stanford (*Stanford Business* magazine, 2006) and Yale (Weisman, 2006). Nevertheless, most business schools today still teach primarily the traditional, long-established functional courses with little or no integration.

When schools do attempt to introduce truly integrated courses into their curricula, they are often the first to be dropped or dramatically changed because they have no official home in any of the traditional business discipline-aligned departments. This lack of department commitment also often results in junior and adjunct professors teaching these integrated courses, further contributing to a poor quality experience in the classroom.

Misaligned reward structure

While students do have a choice, in terms of selecting elective courses within a given curriculum, discipline-centric curricula and the functionally focused courses within a given curriculum do not provide students with the opportunity and associated challenges of working through complex, interdisciplinary problems. Nor does this approach require students to evaluate which discipline or function offers the best solution to a problem. In contrast, business school education typically segments problems by functional areas, forcing students to view them from the relatively narrow perspective of the discipline in which a specific course resides. Consequently, students usually apply singular, one-dimensional functionally focused solutions to very complex problems. The notable exceptions to this are the typical capstone course or consulting project course in which students, out of necessity, are required to apply multiple perspectives to a complex business problem (Hubball and Burt, 2004). However, this one course, which is typically taught in the senior year, does not, by itself, sufficiently prepare students to enter the workforce and begin immediately making a substantive contribution.

Another factor causing this educational gap is the misaligned rewards structure that currently exists in academia. The processes associated with faculty career advancement tend to encourage and reward the perpetuation of what has been previously done, the result being to stifle and, in some cases, even punish creativity and innovation. This is especially true with respect to transdisciplinary research and teaching. This desire to hold onto the past recalls the words of Maurice Maeterlinck, the Belgian Nobel Laureate in literature, who wrote that 'At every crossway on the road that leads to the future each progressive spirit is opposed by a thousand men appointed to guard the past' (Christensen et al., 2011, p. 112). These processes can be divided into three major categories that are sequentially related to a faculty's career: the PhD process, the publishing process, and the tenure process.

The PhD process

The PhD or DBA process at most colleges and universities usually requires that the doctoral candidate choose a dissertation topic that is of interest to his or her faculty adviser. Often, the topic is an extension of the adviser's own specific area of research, which in turn is usually a continuation of the adviser's dissertation (which was based on the adviser's area of interest, and so on back).

Therefore, as a starting point in this process, the doctoral candidate must become familiar with the same body of knowledge that the adviser is acquainted with so they can share a common platform for developing a research topic for the dissertation that will extend the 'research envelope' for that particular body of knowledge. The dissertation, in turn, provides an initial research platform or springboard for the candidate in his/her initial years as a tenure-track professor, and so the cycle repeats itself.

An important part of this process encourages the candidate to develop a high level of expertise in one very specific, narrow area within his or her discipline. Rarely is one encouraged to cross discipline lines, as this would require venturing into an area that the adviser is not familiar with. Being transdisciplinary is also a challenge in finding a job at a business school, as virtually every school seeks to hire individuals for discipline-specific departments.

The publishing process

As one might expect, the vast majority of the top rated academic journals tend to focus on specific functional areas. For example, if you looked at the top 45 academic journals listed in the *Financial Times* of

London, which are considered by many to be the most prestigious and respected in their fields, you would not see any that are truly transdisciplinary in nature (ft.com).

Consequently, while some of these journals do accept transdisciplinary articles, they usually concentrate on publishing articles that fall entirely within their own disciplines. Faculty at those schools that require publication in top-tier journals as a major criterion for tenure (because, as noted earlier, it affects their schools' rankings) would therefore tend to avoid publishing transdisciplinary articles. As a result, in their quest for top ranking in *BusinessWeek* or *U.S. News and World Report*, business schools tend to perpetuate this problem.

Editors of these academic journals also have significant difficulty finding faculty to review transdisciplinary articles (Herschauer, 2006). Reviewers usually have a background in one particular area within a functional discipline, and consequently do not feel that they are qualified to review an article that attempts to integrate several disciplines.

The tenure process

The tenure process also encourages new faculty to develop a very high level of expertise within a very narrow area. When a tenure candidate's published articles are sent out for external review and evaluation, which is part of the tenure appointment process at many schools, the reviewers often will not comment on those aspects of the candidate's articles that extend beyond their own area of expertise, for the same reasons cited in the publishing process. As a result, the tenure evaluation committee often receives only partial reviews on the candidate's research, which it can misinterpret as the reviewer having a level of discomfort with the quality of the tenure candidate's publications.

Increasing rate of new knowledge

New knowledge within every academic discipline is being introduced every year. Yet the number of courses required for an undergraduate degree or graduate degree remains constant, or even, in some cases, is decreasing. Thus we have, at best, a zero-sum game: if we want to introduce new material or a new course into the curriculum, existing material or courses must be dropped. However, faculty are most reluctant to drop existing material or courses, because that is what they are most familiar with (and which have 'withstood the test of time') and are unsure about the long-term viability of this new knowledge.

Recommendations

The easiest, most obvious solution for closing the gap that exists between the skills that business school graduates receive and those required to succeed in today's business environment would be to place the responsibility totally on the shoulders of the business academic community. However, business schools cannot accomplish this alone. Rather, it requires an ongoing partnership between the two primary stakeholders involved: the academic institutions that educate individuals and the businesses and organizations that subsequently employ them.

The responsibility of the business community

Business firms and organizations in every sector of the economy should engage in a 'demand pull' strategy with respect to hiring business school graduates. They should clearly state/identify the skill sets they require and the various job opportunities that are associated with these skills, both now and in the future. Only by articulating these skills and perspectives can the case then be made for the academic community to take the necessary actions to change curricula and courses. At the same time, this demand pull strategy creates student awareness of which academic programs and/or courses are most likely to provide them with these skills.

In addition, it is generally recognized today that the education and development of individuals does not end when they complete their formal higher education. Given the pace of change, if individuals are to be successful throughout their careers, education must be viewed as a lifelong learning process. The business community therefore needs to provide the proper incentives and reward structures that encourage their employees to continually seek additional/new knowledge and skills. At the same time, businesses can have a significant influence on the structure of these post-graduate programs, to where they can even be custom designed to meet individual organizational needs. As businesses work with academics to develop these new programs, both sides will gain from the experience, with the results informing the more formal degree programs that academic institutions offer.

The responsibility of business schools

There are, of course, many things that business schools can do to provide their graduates with a better education that will increase their opportunities for success.

Develop integrated curricula and courses

Business schools need to develop truly integrated curricula. However, integration cannot be accomplished by simply waving a wand over a set of courses and saying 'integration' as is often the case; it requires commitment on behalf of both academic institutions and professors. Recognizing that the number of courses in any given degree program is a zero-sum game, each functional area must be willing to concede some of its current 'territory' of required courses to allow integration to take place in the form of standalone course(s). For example, Bentley University's revised part-time MBA program, which started in fall 2007, reduced each of the functional areas by approximately 30 percent to allow not only for an integrative module but also to reduce in total the number of required 'business fundamental' courses. The integrative module consists of four classes, each of which is team taught by faculty from two different disciplines. This provides the students with different perspectives in addressing/solving a complex business issue/problem.

In addition, a new organizational framework is necessary that permits 'structure to follow strategy.' As a starting point, all required core business courses should have a common designator rather than those of the traditional functional departments. For example, at Bentley University the undergraduate business core courses are all designated 'GB' for General Business and the graduate core business courses are designated 'BF' for Business Fundamentals. As such, individual departments no longer have the primary responsibility for designing course content; rather this is now done at the college level to ensure proper coverage of material across the entire set of core courses and that integration takes place among these courses.

A major weakness with this approach is that these courses tend to be treated as 'second-class citizens' by the functional departments, and, as such, are often taught by junior faculty or even adjunct faculty. To rectify this problem, these core courses should come under the responsibility of a 'general business core' department that consists of faculty from all of the participating disciplines. Such an approach was adopted at the University of Auckland Business School following the introduction of a new undergraduate degree program in 2001, and has proven both to be very effective and also well received by participating faculty (Carrie and Brodie, 2007).

Another approach to encourage integration in the classroom is to introduce material and cases that mandate students take a transdisciplinary approach. These courses should be team-taught with individuals from different functional areas so that several perspectives can be presented. While the faculty costs will increase with team teaching, these costs can be offset to a large degree in several ways. Class sizes could be increased. (For example, if a business school faculty is paid $180,000 per year, including benefits, and teaches a 4–4 load, or with a 2–2 load we assume 50% of the faculty's time is devoted to teaching, then the incremental faculty cost per course is $22,500.) Assuming tuition per year is $30,000 then the additional number of students needed to offset the cost of team teaching would be less than ten (with ten courses per year). Another approach to reducing the cost of team teaching is to limit the amount of classes that are actually team taught. Using adjunct faculty as one of the faculty in team taught courses also reduces costs significantly. Having said all that, if in fact team teaching does provide students with a much better education because of the different perspectives that are presented on a topic (and which industry needs to properly obtain solutions to complex problems), then tuition costs could be increased by some amount that reflects the incremental cost of having a second faculty teaching the course.

In addition, the academic community needs to develop materials that show students how to exploit both structured and unstructured knowledge. Examples of structured knowledge include that which is learned from organized databases, threaded emails, and minutes of a meeting; examples of unstructured knowledge include impromptu meetings with colleagues, post-it notes, and telephone calls (scribd.com). Both are important in solving complex business problems.

Developing relevant teaching materials in a timely and continuous manner is an ongoing challenge for academia. To facilitate such activities, faculty should:

- engage in communities of practice;
- have incentives in the form of internal, institutional grants for material and case development;
- share materials across institutions;
- visit world-class organizations on a continuing basis.

It is incumbent upon senior faculty who are actively engaged with industry through consulting and/or executive education programs to take a leadership role in promoting these activities.

Unfortunately, sharing best practices is not a common characteristic among academics. However, the sharing of information in the form of newly developed materials and cases leads to continuous improvement. It also ensures consistency in delivery through effective pedagogy. Building a sense of trust and collaboration is important, which can be facilitated through its inclusion as a component of an individual's evaluation and promotion.

Engage with businesses

The academic community needs to overcome the mindset that it needs to maintain a healthy barrier between itself and the 'real world.' In fact, just the opposite is true. Academia at both the organizational and individual levels needs to actively engage in partnerships with industry to develop curricula. These can be accomplished in several ways,

- field trips to companies;
- guest speakers from industry in the classroom;
- student internships at companies;
- student opportunities to undertake real-world projects as part of a course.

Such interactions with the 'real world' reinforce concepts presented in the classroom, introduce both students and professors to current business practices, and provide companies with an opportunity to learn more about potential employment candidates.

Just as businesses have recognized that the customer can play an integral role in the creation of value, a similar model can be applied to higher education in the form of a partnership between academia and business. Such a partnership would include:

- joint curriculum development and course delivery;
- opportunities for developing transdisciplinary course material;
- student internships;
- research partnerships that focus on specific needs of business.

This partnership would encourage businesses to take a more active role in the education process, hopefully shifting the emphasis from the current short term focus on annual rankings to a longer term perspective of creating real value for students in the classroom. This would ultimately have a positive impact on a school's ranking, as companies, because of their relationship with a school and knowledge of individual students through intern programs, etc., would offer graduating students higher starting salaries, which is one of the factors that is considered when school rankings are developed.

Focus on cost reduction

In the 30-year period between 1980 and 2010, the average annual cost of tuition, room, and board for a four-year college in the United States increased more than 900% (U.S. Department of Education, National Center for Education Statistics, 2011), in comparison the Consumer Price Index, which 'only' increased a little more than 250% (U.S. Dept of Labor, 2012). At the same time, student loans in the United States now exceed more than $1 trillion (Martin and Lehren, 2012). Clearly the cost of obtaining a college education is getting to the point where an ever increasing segment of the population can no longer afford it.

So how can colleges get a better handle on controlling costs? The most obvious answer is to just increase class size, but for many educational institutions, class sizes, especially in the required undergraduate courses, are already huge. (One colleague in England complained to me that his undergraduate class had more than 400 students.) Larger classes also affect the quality of education, in terms of the ability of students to interact with the professor.

Another, more viable, solution might be to learn from the private service sector (after all, education is a service). Faced with increasing competitive pressures to reduce costs, many services, from fast food, to hotels, to gas stations are turning to self-service, where the customer does a significant portion of the work, thereby reducing costs to the service provider. Similarly, a significant portion of the undergraduate courses could be taught through self-service. Every undergraduate course can be divided into two major areas: (a) basic or core knowledge about the subject and (b) critical thinking about the topic that involves applying the basic knowledge to solve real-world problems. Basic knowledge is probably better learned through self-service, if the course is properly designed. The technology is now available to permit and even encourage it, and in many cases the students actually learn the material better, because it is at their own pace, rather than at the pace set by the teacher in the classroom. For example, the Khan Academy (www.khanacademy.org) now has more than 3,000 videos available online free on subjects including arithmetic, physics, history, and finance. Using this approach, colleges could introduce self-service courses to students and then test them on their knowledge of the material without having them attend classes taught by professors. This would free up college resources both in terms of classrooms and teachers, thereby allowing for more students to be admitted without additional expenditures for either of these two resources.

Conclusion

Every stakeholder has a role in closing the gap that currently exists between the education that business school students receive and what they need to succeed in the marketplace. Business schools need to 'practice what they preach,' looking outside academia to identify best practices in other service industries, to identify and meet the needs of their customers. Similarly, business schools need to do a better job of identifying what their customers want and need – both the students who are receiving the education and the employers who are hiring the students.

Curriculum reform is a key element, but it will not be easy. At the same time, organizational changes are needed so that the organization is better aligned to support these changes in curriculum. And these changes cannot take forever to implement or else they will run the risk of always being outdated. Fast curriculum reform is critical (just like fast time-to-market for new goods and services is a critical element in the success of businesses).

Again, taking lessons for practitioners, business schools need to actively engage their two major groups of customers in the co-creation of value. Education is no longer a top–down process where professors lecture and students take notes. Rather, because of today's technology, it is an open process where all are engaged in value creation.

These changes will not take place overnight, but we must start now to ensure that in the not-too-distant future business school students will be able to look back and truly understand and appreciate the value of the education they received.

References

'The Rising Cost of College in America,' December 7, 2010. (http://www.health-carecolleges.net/blog/college-tuition-increases-the-rising-cost-of-college-education-in-america/), accessed February 13, 2012.

Bennis, W. and J. O'Toole (2005) 'How Business Schools Lost Their Way,' *Harvard Business Review* 83(5), pp. 96–104.

Booth, Matthew (2005) Comment made during the First Annual Conference on the Art and Science of Services, Bentley College, June 3–4.

Businessweek (2006) 'How We Come Up with the Rankings,' Bloomberg *Businessweek*, October 26 (http://www.businessweek.com/magazine/content/06_43/b4006008.htm), accessed April 11, 2011.

Carnevale, A. P., L. J. Gainer, and A. S. Meltzer (1990) *Workplace Basics: The Essential Skills Employers Want* (San Francisco: Jossey-Bass Publishers).

Carrie, D. G. and R. J. Brodie (2007) 'Service Science in Undergraduate Business Education: An Evolving Model for Integrating Business and Information Management,' *Proceedings of the Decision Sciences Institute MiniConference on Service Science*, Carnegie Mellon University, Pittsburgh, PA.

Christensen, C. M., M.B. Horn, and C.W. Johnson (2011) *Disrupting Class: How Disruptive Innovation Will Change the Way the World Learns* (Ney York: McGraw-Hill), p. 112.

Ft.com (www.ft.com/cms/s/2/bd9e8b74-fd17–11dd-a103–000077b07658.html). Accessed February 20, 2012.

Herschauer, James (2006) Based on conversation with James Herschauer, former editor of Decision Sciences, at the Annual meeting of the Decision Sciences Institute, San Antonio, TX, November.

Latham, G., S. D. Latham, and G. Whyte (2004) 'Fostering Integrative Thinking: Adapting the Executive Education Model to the MBA Program,' *Journal of Management Education* 28(1), pp. 3–18.

Lewin, Tamara (2011), 'What's the Most Expensive College? The Least? Education Dept. Puts It All Online,' June 30 (http://www.nytimes.com/2011/06/30/education/30collegeweb.html), accessed February 13, 2012.

Martin, Andrew, and Andrew Lehren (2012), 'A Generation Hobled by the Soaring Cost of College,' *New York Times*, May 12.

Mintzberg, H. (2004) *Managers, Not MBAs: A Hard Look at the Soft Practice of Managing and Management Development* (San Francisco: Berrett-Koehler Publishers).

Peters, K. (2006)'The Four Stages of Management Education,' *BizEd*, pp. 36–40 (May/June).

Scribd.com: (http://www.scribd.com/doc/50829720/27/Structured-vs-Unstructured-Knowledge), accessed April 12, 2012.

Smith, G. F. (2005) 'Problem-Based Learning: Can It Improve Managerial Thinking?' *Journal of Management Education* 29(2), April, pp. 357–378.

Stanford Business magazine (2006) 'Rising to the Challenge,' *Stanford Business* magazine, November.

Weisman, R. (2006) 'Rewriting the Business Plan,' *Boston Globe*, October 30, Higher Education, E1, E3.

U.S. Department of Education, National Center for Education Statistics. (2011). *Digest of Education Statistics, 2010* (NCES 2011–015), *Chapter 3*.

U.S. Dept of Labor (2012), Consumer Price Index, Bureau of Labor Statistics, Washington, DC, July 17.

3
Business, Management Education, and Leadership for the Common Good

Anders Aspling

We have more than half a century of business school history behind us – the first ones formed in the 1930s in the US and France, and they have their origin even further back in time. During this time the world has undergone big changes. In my more than 30 years of active engagement in management development they certainly have developed and gone through changes. However, during this time they have not changed to the extent needed to meet the challenges of the twenty-first century.

Some of the statements in this text may be provocative and they may even be exaggerating certain cases. It's all done with the aim of addressing burning issues as effectively as possible, and with the sincere belief that we need to apply critical thinking and hands-on action to resolve challenges we collectively face.

The global context

Today's world is characterized by interconnectivity between people, organizations, cultures and nations; between economies and within financial systems; between spheres of society – civil, public, political, and business; between the man-made and the natural environment; between technology, economic, social and natural systems.

This interconnectivity also means interdependency. So, the world of today and its development are driven and forged by interdependent dimensions – emerging economies, population growth, health development, a resource-based consumerism, a deepening divide between rich and poor, failing states, and more. All are inter-related in a systemic and complex way.

Furthermore, this interconnectivity and interdependency urgently and explicitly introduces a new kind of responsibility.

Since the turn of the century a new vocabulary has emerged. We talk and read about responsible business, a globally responsible leadership and about responsible management education. 'Taking responsibility is a way of taking ownership in our lives, of acknowledging our own hand in the shaping of destiny. Responsibility is the antidote for victimhood' (Visser, 2011).

We certainly live in an interconnected world. It's a small and fragile world that faces many man-made threats. We need a strong sense of urgency for deep change, and an awareness of the impact of our actions as individuals, learning institutions, as businesses, and as societies.

Some of today's global challenges include the following.

- Complexity abounds and is the normal state of affairs.
- Management is not a mechanistic science; multidisciplinary approaches are needed in facing the challenges of business and the role of business in society.
- The interdependence between business, politics, and civil society is increasing and so is the awareness of this interdependency.
- The global interconnectivity of the entire system is fully recognized.
- A one-nation/region economic hegemony is for the time being over; the world is being shaped by the development of a complex system of inter-related dimensions and forces, where the emerging economies play an increasingly important role.
- The stresses we are placing on the environment present the specter of large-scale adverse impacts on human society within the lifetimes of those being born today.
- Financial and economic systems regularly experience upheaval and turmoil.
- Unclear political developments abound in many societies, at all stages of economic development.

The interconnectivity of the world calls for a holistic and systemic view of the natural and man-made world and how different spheres of society interact (see Figure 3.1).

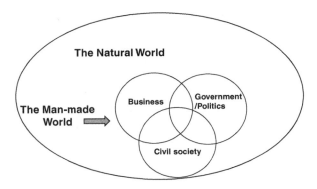

Figure 3.1   Interconnectivity: a holistic and systemic view

International organizational response

In July 2000 the United Nations created the UN Global Compact (UNGC) as a 'strategic policy initiative for businesses that are committed to aligning their operations and strategies with 10 universally accepted principles in the areas of human rights, labor, environment and anti-corruption.' Three years later the European Foundation for Management Development (EFMD), which sets standards for international business and management education, launched an initiative on global responsibility and the integration of sustainability and responsibility issues with the future of management education. Later in 2003 the two organizations formed a joint venture on how to develop a next generation of globally responsible leaders, allowing the EFMD to reach the UN's large corporate audience while also bringing the UNGC's 10 principles to EFMD's global network of learning institutions.

In 2004 and 2005, 21 organizations – companies and business schools and learning institutions – met for six work sessions to organize international standards for responsible leadership and management education. Their 2005 report resulted in the formation of the Globally Responsible Leadership Initiative (GRLI), a group dedicated to a continuous effort of responsible business conduct, management education, and leadership. Qualified companies and learning institutions were invited to join. Today the GRLI embraces some 70 learning institutions and companies from all parts of the world. It is an exclusive, selective, and dedicated group of organizations engaged in new practices, thought leadership, and advocacy.

Through the GRLI, organizations learn how management development, responsible leadership, and sustainability are expressed in different parts of the world and through the lens of different cultures. They learn a great diversity of approaches and the profound differences that different parts of the world have on issues of responsible leadership and sustainable development. They act and set examples for others to follow.

GRLI is today also explicitly engaged in shaping the management education of the future.

Different approaches

Large parts of the western and northern hemisphere have a history of separating businesses from societal responsibility and sustainable development. Business is mainly considered responsible for driving economic growth and development. To make up for this separation, many societies in the West have a strong tradition of charity and of philanthropy, from both individuals and organizations.

At the same time there are nations and regions in the western and northern parts of the world with traditions of collaboration between business and other sectors of society. In parts of Europe and North America there is a history of dialogue and common agreements between different spheres of society on shared responsibility for economic, social, and environmental development.

Many emerging economies represent cultures based on a holistic view of the world, though there is a wide diversity in the details. Both a collaborative and a holistic approach can have positive effects on the economic, social, and environmental challenges of the future. The complexity, connectivity, and systemic interdependence of the world seem to be in need of a more collaborative and holistic approach than what's been dominating during the different phases of western industrialization.

Russia has its history and its heritage, so does China, so does India, so does Latin America, so does Africa, so do the different parts of the Asia-Pacific region, so does the Middle East, and so does Japan. Many of the eastern philosophies represent collective interests and some argue that egoistic approaches should not have any influence on the way the world is being shaped; process engagement replaces the importance of personal intervention. In ancient Chinese and Indian philosophy there is no recognition of man taking independent action from the environment he inhabits. Some of them and many indigenous cultures display a strong relationship between people, their environment, and planet Earth. These approaches are in many cases fundamentally inclusive and holistic, and they offer alternatives to perspectives of the West. One critical issue for the future of business and management is whether it will continue to largely follow the western model? Or will the diversity of the world's different cultural approaches remain, and will we find ways of collaborating with respect for the prevailing differences and with a capacity to learn from our respective uniqueness? Or third, will a new global model emerge – where the differences and the diversity of world will blend, where an interdisciplinary and holistic approach will become mainstream, and where a combination of intellectual capacity, social, and emotional competence, even spirituality, personal growth, and refinement will define the learning?

Any of these three approaches is possible. In a globalised world, however, the second and third approaches are most appropriate. For the richness of the world's diversity to remain, the dominating accreditation systems of the world need to adjust. There is a growing insight of this need, which will be commented on later.

A diverse and changing world

We are better informed, we travel, we communicate and develop relationships across the world to an extent never known before. An increasing number of people are becoming more aware of the responsibility to care for our common future.

My own lived experiences over the past year include:

Shanghai – the boiling cauldron of ambition, change, strong tradition, obedience, modernization, and internationalization. A fascinating and historically unique development is taking place.

Lima, Peru – where a presentation of how a national company has changed its business model over the past five years from a traditional financial institution to a social institution explicitly contributing to the welfare and development of the country and its people is being finalized.

South Africa – a South Africa that is challenged by signs of derailing from the heritage of collaboration and reconciliation that shaped the 1994 transition, a South Africa with a democratic constitution, economic growth and positive social development. How will the responsibility as a leading African nation be fulfilled?

USA – its position in the world slowly but clearly changing, its economic and political issues not solved.

Europe – which so clearly represents the old world, for good and bad; how will it resolve its current problems, and what role will it play in the shaping of our global society?

All these issues and questions belong to the agenda for the education of future business managers and leaders, as they affect all enterprise and the role of business in society.

The role of business in society

The long-term success and survival of any business corporation depend on the successful development of society. Businesses, after all, need paying customers, and development is what creates them. This should imply that each business has an interest in contributing to a sound societal development – economically, socially, and environmentally.

A key question (explicitly approached by Milton Friedman) concerns the allocation of responsibilities for such a sound development. As noted above, in many parts of the western world, we have separated the responsibility between business and other spheres of society. Today, many would argue that, given the rapid pace of globalization and economic interdependence, the responsibility for sound development is shared by all of us and by the different institutions of society in collaboration. From an ethical perspective one may argue that those sectors/actors with most power and influence should have a more profound and immediate responsibility of contributing to a sound development of society as a whole and to the common good.

Recognizing that long-term successful business development depends on a sound development of society, including environmental concerns, the question becomes, 'shouldn't contributing to societal progress be integrated into a business's mission?' And consequently, shouldn't it be supported by clear strategies and actions, just as short-term market and economic goals are? And finally, is the financial and economic market system we have refined over more than 200 years able to host such long-term and widened business missions?

There are many conceptual frameworks for developing responsible businesses (Carroll, 1991; Visser, 2003 etc.). One model was presented in the EFMD magazine *Forum* in 2006 (Aspling, 2011). It identifies three phases or levels of development of the firm and how to integrate global responsibility with the strategy of the organization (Figure 3.2).

The first level is identified as *risk management*. This is about avoiding mistakes, but it also includes engagement in philanthropy. Initiatives are not fully integrated with the business model of the organization, but rather separate and stand-alone actions.

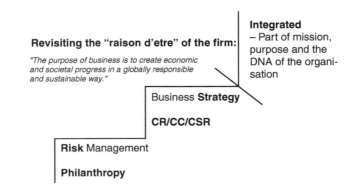

Figure 3.2   Three levels of responsibility – a conceptual framework

The first level is where the 'compliant' business would place itself. It follows regulations and it reports when compulsory. It often has a view on sustainability where it seems to have it all in place, and where it monitors its matrix regularly. It could very well also engage in philanthropy of different kinds.

The second level recognizes responsibility and sustainability as *issues of strategic importance* for the business development and operations of the organization. This is where concepts and actions regarding Corporate Social Responsibility (CSR), Corporate Responsibility (CR) or Corporate Citizenship (CC) have emerged.

The second level is where the 'strategists' would place themselves. They report voluntarily, follow and strive for rankings, use matrixes to integrate with business operations, communicate regularly and explicitly, follow customers and other stakeholder's positions closely.

The third level indicates that the organization has entered a different mode of operation and 'being,' where *responsibility and sustainability become part of the mission, the purpose and the DNA* of the organization. This is where 'The purpose of business is to create economic and societal progress in a globally responsible and sustainable way' (EFMD, 2005). The way the world has developed since the first GRLI partners defined the 'raison d'etre' of teh firm in such as way, it could just as well also include words such as 'serving the global common good.'

The third level represents the 'futurists.' They reinvent their business models, innovate, engage in responsible action for the common good as an explicit part of their mission and engage actively in stakeholder dialogues. They address systemic changes – financial, social, political,

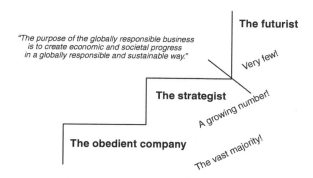

Figure 3.3 Where are we at? A general global view

technological, and environmental, envision a different, new and better world, and they advocate and lead in action.

The vast majority of businesses globally are to be found on the first level. There is a growing number of companies on the second level – and very few on the third (see Figure 3.3).

The business and management education of the future: key questions

The mainstream business school has until today been a servant of the corporation of the twentieth century. The challenges of today and the future call for a different approach – one where business education fosters businesses and business systems that work on the 'third level' described above. It is an approach where the role of business and management education is to develop the managers and leaders and create the businesses and business systems we need for the twenty-first century – on behalf of society. The GRLI, UNGC, PRME (Principles for Responsible Management), and others engage in finding the route towards this new role. There are at least three key questions to be answered in finding the route – and they have to be answered in the right order.

1. What kind of world and society do we want to create with the immense, but nonetheless finite, resources at our disposal?
2. What characterizes the corporations and organizations serving this goal?

3. What education and learning are needed for the leaders and managers serving this society and these corporations/organizations?

Although the dramatic global development of the past 25 years has influenced the way we educate, train and prepare managers and leaders, in most cases schools introduce issues regarding ethical behavior, responsibility, and sustainability in separate electives or add-ons to the regular and traditional curricula.

Very few schools have attempted or succeeded in integrating these issues with their full operations – their mission, management, curricula, most programs, teaching, and research. Examples of schools trying are Bentley University in the US, Exeter University in the UK, Griffith University Business School in Australia, CENTRUM Católica, Pontificia Universidad Católica del Peru and Fundação Dom Cabral (Brazil) in Latin America, to mention a few from different parts of the world.

A growing number of schools have founded institutes and centers that focus on global responsibility and globally responsible leadership. Examples are Audencia, Nantes, France and its Institute for Global Responsibility, China European International Business School (CEIBS) in Shanghai with its Centre for Leadership and Responsibility, and University of Pretoria and University of Stellenbosch Business School in South Africa with their respective Centre for Responsible Leadership and Centre for Business in Society.

So, there is a new approach in the making. But is a real paradigm shift about to happen? Is a new world view emerging where business graduates will see things differently, and accordingly think and act differently? (See Figure 3.4.)

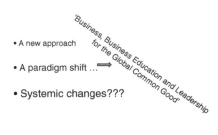

Figure 3.4 Shaping the business education of the future

The business and management education of the future: some thoughts on the current state of development

Does the business and management education of today meet perceived needs?

Does the education contribute in a focused and direct way to developing knowledge, skills, and competence for meeting today's perceived needs? Are some of the challenges introduced in this text being addressed? Is the role of business in society, i.e. the very foundation for the competence needed by future managers and leaders, being discussed thoroughly and in depth? The answer is, generally speaking, no.

It is possible to speculate on many reasons why this is so. Business schools are often limited regarding their knowledge base – focused on business issues according to the tradition of the twentieth century. They are often traditionally organized and activities comply with the division into different disciplines.

The broader knowledge and cross-disciplinary understanding that have been requested for a long time in many schools are in most cases not reflected in the way they are organized or operating. Instead, special projects may address issues of immediate importance cutting through different disciplines – often piecemeal and ad hoc – based on the history, culture, and specific focus of the school, and what members of the faculty represent regarding engagement and commitment, and what they take initiatives on.

Business courses at universities where other additional knowledge is available should be more able to offer a broader and richer education. There certainly are examples of this happening, but it is no rule. Many can attest to the minimal interaction that occurs between different parts of very well-known and prestigious universities.

However, it is important to note that there are examples of – especially smaller – schools where activities are organized on the basis of the challenges facing businesses and other organizations, rather than according to the taxonomy of business administration and academic disciplines. In these cases, cooperation and collaboration across traditional disciplines is a necessity and becomes a reality. The education is issue-oriented rather than disciplinary or functionally arranged.

Does the education meet the need to develop capabilities to actively and with insight participate in the debate about the development of our society and the role of business in this context?

Does the education meet the need for businesses to actively and constructively being able to act in synergy with other sectors in society? In most cases, no.

It is surprising that a larger number of schools have not already expanded their business programs to include wider knowledge of society and sectors other than business. Steps have been taken in a few areas, including politics and political science; but, more often, the steps address the 'third sector,' i.e. voluntary organization, NGOs, and not-for-profit organizations. There are multiple examples of how schools and individual programs engage in and learn from social projects locally and internationally – often promoted, initiated and even driven by students.

Does the education respond to the need for developing global citizens with a clear moral compass and respect for and knowledge of other cultures and the global development?

In most cases, no. But, here we find many good and explicit exceptions. Partnerships with colleagues in other parts of the world and efforts in developing countries provide an experiential learning for faculty/teachers and students/pupils.

For example, this is practiced extensively and compulsory at Babson College; and the mission of the school reads as follows: 'Babson College educates leaders who create great economic and social value – everywhere' (www.babson.edu).

There are also examples of schools and training programs in which the degree is supplemented by a certificate related to leadership. There are MBA programs with a recurring theme regarding the individual student's personal development and leadership. During these programs, with the support of a mentor, participants develop a guide for how to exercise a globally responsible leadership. The participation is mandatory and the document must address a pre-specified number of issues, and each participant formulates a vision of his/her own leadership after graduation and for the future.

Does the education meet the need for entrepreneurship, creativity, and innovation?

Yes, at a growing number of schools.

Does the education meet the need for refinement, cultivation, character, and self-knowledge as a basis for personal leadership?

With great variation. It is primarily post-graduate and executive education and development that accommodates applications where character, self-awareness, personal development, and leadership are in focus. An increasing number of MBA programs address these areas. This broader and deeper education could to some extent be introduced as an important part also of undergraduate education.

Most schools respond to the above-mentioned challenges, issues, and needs with individual and specific efforts. Individual programs – often offered as free choice – are available regarding, as examples, ethics, responsibility, globalization, sustainability, leadership development and personal growth. Few schools succeed or attempt to integrate key future issues not related to the traditional business education curricula through-out their programs – and in their operations. Individual programs can be found almost in every school with self-respect or self-esteem, and is also part of what is being reviewed in international accreditations. However, no consistent or revolutionary change has taken place either when it comes to integrating ethics, responsibility, or sustainability issues (economic, social, and environmental) all through the education of a school.

Again, this can be explained by the limited scope and the tradition that business and management education still fundamentally are built on. Despite lengthy discussions and explicit needs of complementary skills, new disciplines and interdisciplinary collaboration, there has been relatively little happening in reality. What is being seen, as said earlier, is rather additions or 'bolt-ons' supplementing traditional programs of the educational system rather than integration. The need for deep change is rarely reflected in the offerings and learning.

The business and management education of the future: proposed solutions

At the 2011 annual conference of EFMD, Thomas Sattelberger (a former executive officer of Lufthansa, Continental and Deutsche Telekom and Vice Chairman, EFMD) offered an inspiring presentation entitled 'Management Education 2025.' He noted these aspects of the challenge:

- to train managers and leaders for 2025 is an ideological task;
- it is as much about reason and emotion as intellect;
- diversity of thought and action must be regained as key for innovation and progress;

- economic and social value creation must go hand in hand – for the best of the whole community;
- voluntary cooperation between people and organizations of different types must be developed and supported;
- reflection and self-knowledge are required for personal development.

Sattelberger suggested the following for our business schools:

- Managing companies must build on the stakeholder model; the pure shareholder model is out-dated.
- Schools must move from classroom teaching to learning through experience.
- Research should concentrate on practical grounds.
- The map and the terrain are one and the same. There is no urgent need for developing more maps. More important is to learn to hands-on navigate the actual terrain. How is this reflected in the training?
- Diversity of perspectives, knowledge, and experience among faculty, staff, students, and clients.
- Training must include the knowledge of the environment and environmental threats, and how to create a society in harmony with the planet.
- Schools should develop partnerships with a wide variety of organizations to seek new ways to solve problems and meet challenges.

For businesses and future heads of recruitment, he argued that:

- interruption of careers need not necessarily be valued as negative, quite the opposite, as they offer different and complementary opportunities for learning and personal growth;
- non-linear careers must be encouraged, as we are in need of wide and cross-disciplinary competencies and experiences;
- employability will be based more on character than intellectual knowledge and practical skills, as values and beliefs will play an equally important role as intellectual excellence and practical skills;
- leadership is about serving people and giving them the opportunity to develop and perform to the best of their abilities; this service capability will be highly valued in the future as we need to develop through collaboration and co-creation, where many can contribute in shaping our common future.

From the learning and experience within GRLI, it could be said that at the business school of the future:

- disciplinary boundaries will be bridged in different ways than we see today – due to real-life issues and challenges being (often urgently) addressed;
- the challenges of the business world will drive the growth of intellectual capital to a larger extent than today – as it is an agent with power and ability to contribute to change for the future of our world, within current systems or as a driver for systemic change;
- the role of business in society will be addressed repeatedly with a holistic global perspective in mind;
- leadership, personal growth, and refinement will be explicitly on the agenda, as will statesmanship (see section 'Leadership for the Future', page 54) and the capability of participating in and contributing to the societal dialogue; both this and continuously reviewing the role of business in society ask for managers representing and exercising a leadership which is integrated with and addressing the shared challenges we face as part of a larger society and a changing world;
- learning is enhanced in line with the concept of 'Whole Person Learning' (Taylor, 2007);
- partnerships between civil society and business should be developed further – to meet the need for transcending boundaries, enhance collaboration, and enable co-creation;
- the school's mission is to deliver clear and explicit value to all stakeholders, taking externalities into account – a truly inclusive and holistic approach to learning and the role of the school of the future.
- the vision of a better local, regional, and global future is driving each and every part of its development – ultimately and explicitly contributing to the global common good.

Accreditation agencies

To encourage this new model of business school, the dominating accreditation systems of the world also need to adjust:

- They need to embrace the diversity of the world to a larger extent than today.
- They need to encourage innovation, experimentation and diversity, while keeping quality standards high. This may include redefining what quality entails for business and management education.

- They need to be open to new models and ways of learning, sourcing, organization, management, research, and knowledge creation.

The European Quality Improvement System (EQUIS – see www.efmd.org) has recently reviewed their way of approaching these issues. A former chapter on 'Contribution to the Community' has been revised and enhanced and is now labeled 'Ethics, Responsibility and Sustainability.' These issues should be looked at across mission and strategy, programs, research, faculty and staff resources and development, organization and management of the school, etc.

Different contexts have to be recognized especially when evaluating research and development and assessing internationalization.

The Association to Advance Collegiate Schools of Business – AACSB International – with its accreditation system stemming from the US tradition, likewise, is putting more emphasis on sustainability and responsibility issues in its quality mentoring and accreditation and also taking into account the different contexts around the world, which shape and to a large extent determine the appropriate education.

Our mental maps shape the way we see the world. Different cultures place themselves differently along a continuum of global economic development and its relationship to the environment. We might call this continuum the 'comprehensive versus fragmented' approach – in other words, 'integration versus segregation.'

It is difficult to place each culture along this continuum; let's just conclude that the western world and the industrial tradition embrace less of integration and a holistic view than many emerging economies.

Today's complex, globalized economies compel us to undertake some basic practices in order to shape and build a holistic view of the world:

- We need cross-border understanding, knowledge, and experience regarding regions, countries and cultures.
- We need cross-border cooperation and collaboration between different sectors of society to meet the current and future challenges of the world.
- We need interdisciplinary research and learning across academic disciplines and subject areas.

Change will come one way or another. Taking these steps will allow us to achieve systemic change in an orderly manner, rather than seeing change forced upon us by coercive and traumatic events.

Leadership for the future

In 2007 GRLI was one of the co-conveners of the UNGC's Principles for Responsible Management (PRME). GRLI explicitly serves as an advanced laboratory for the implementation of the six principles (see Appendix) and of a leadership for the future.

Regarding an appropriate leadership, some comments can be made.

First, *a true global understanding* is of fundamental importance. It comes from having hands-on experience of the rich diversity of our world. A large part of the learning that takes place within GRLI comes from experiencing the diversity and differences within a global community of peers.

Second, *a capability and capacity for innovation and entrepreneurship* is of fundamental importance to any society. To contribute with this capacity of innovation is one of the most important roles of businesses and free enterprises.

The third principle involves *personal values, considerations and decisions*. Responsibility goes beyond compliance, and is dependent on who you are as a person, and what kind of leadership you represent, exercise, and fulfill.

A core aspect is the degree to which the individual has developed his or her own level of consciousness and awareness of both the external global context and the inner dimensions of themselves. This is the starting point which defines the extent to which they are able to determine, with others, right action in a global setting. ('Globally Responsible Leadership: A Call for Engagement,' 2005)

Fourth, *statesmanship* represents the ability to actively participate in the societal debate and to take action to contribute to societal progress.

Fifth, the leader of the future must be *fully ethically grounded* and act with integrity.

And, finally, *a systemic awareness and understanding* is of greatest importance. Insights and knowledge of how systems affect mind sets and action and how they interact will become a much needed ability.

The globally responsible leader:

- embraces a global view and global ethics such as those reflected in the principles of the UN Global Compact and the Millennium Development Goals;

- recognizes that business has the creativity and resources to address, and make a big contribution to, many of the most important social and environmental challenges before us;
- has a global consistency in his/her general principles and standards, yet is sensitive and flexible to each local context;
- accepts that international policies are failing to keep up with the pace of globalization and that there are additional responsibilities above and beyond the law, since legal requirements often trail global development and practice;
- actively engages stakeholders not only to communicate how an organization or business is demonstrating its globally responsible leadership, but also to understand their expectations and concerns and to identify solutions to problems, challenges, and opportunities;
- recognizes that, beyond his/her responsibility for creating value at organizational or company level, he/she also has responsibility to contribute to a broader common good – locally, regionally, and globally;
- is driven by a vision of the future rather than pushed by the past.

Now it is required that we all take responsibility – in practice, as individuals and for the organizations we represent – for the development of a sustainable and prospering global society and for planet Earth. Is there a better place to do so than at institutions around the world where we are responsible for orchestrating education and learning?

Appendix

The Principles for Responsible Management Education – PRME

As institutions of higher education involved in the development of current and future managers we declare our willingness to progress in the implementation, within our institution, of the following Principles, starting with those that are more relevant to our capacities and mission. We will report on progress to all our stakeholders and exchange effective practices related to these principles with other academic institutions:

PRME Principle 1

Purpose: we will develop the capabilities of students to be future generators of sustainable value for business and society at large and to work for an inclusive and sustainable global economy.

PRME Principle 2

Values: we will incorporate into our academic activities and curricula the values of global social responsibility as portrayed in international initiatives such as the United Nations Global Compact.

PRME Principle 3

Method: we will create educational frameworks, materials, processes, and environments that enable effective learning experiences for responsible leadership.

PRME Principle 4

Research: we will engage in conceptual and empirical research that advances our understanding about the role, dynamics, and impact of corporations in the creation of sustainable social, environmental, and economic value.

PRME Principle 5

Partnership: we will interact with managers of business corporations to extend our knowledge of their challenges in meeting social and environmental responsibilities and to explore jointly effective approaches to meeting these challenges.

PRME Principle 6

Dialogue: we will facilitate and support dialog and debate among educators, students, business, government, consumers, media, civil society organizations, and other interested groups and stakeholders on critical issues related to global social responsibility and sustainability.

We understand that our own organizational practices should serve as example of the values and attitudes we convey to our students.

Websites

www.unglobalcompact.org, for the ten principles and PRME
www.babson.edu, for their mission statement
www.50plus20.org, general reference
www.grli.org, general reference
www.efmd.org, general reference
www.aacsb.edu, general reference

References

Aspling, A. (2006) 'EFMD and the Globalisation Process – Our Responsibility,' *EFMD Forum Magazine*, No. 3.

Aspling, A. (2009) 'En generation globaltansvarstagandecheferochledare – nu!' ('A Generation of Globally Responsible Managers and Leaders – Now!'), in De Geer &Trollestad (eds), *Etikiarbetslivochaffärer* (*Ethics in Work Life and Business*), (Stockholm: SNS Förlag).

Carroll, A. B. (1991) 'The Pyramid of Corporate Social Responsibility: Toward the Moral Management of Organizational Stakeholders,' *Business Horizons*, July–August.

Carroll, A. B. and Schwarz, M. S. (2003) 'Corporate Social Responsibility: A Three-domain Approach,' *Business Ethics Quarterly*, 13(4).

deWoot, P. (2006) *Should Prometheus be Bound? Corporate Global Responsibility* (Basingstoke: Palgrave Macmillan).

EFMD (2005) the European Foundation for Management Development (2005), Globally Responsible Leaders; a Call for Engagement, published report.

GRLI – the Globally Responsible Leadership Initiative (2008), The Globally Responsible Leader – A Call for action, published report first presented at the first UN Global Forum for Responsible Management Education at the UN Headquarters in New York, December 2008.

GRLI, World Business School Council for Sustainable Business and PRME (2012). The 50+20 Agenda – Management Education for the World.

Sattelberger, T. (2011) Management Education 2025, presentation at the EFMD Annual Conference.

Taylor, Bryce (2007) Learning for Tomorrow – Whole Person Learning (The Oasis School of Human Relations: Oasis Publications).

United Nations Global Compact Office (2008) Principles for Responsible Management Education – PRME.

Visser, W. (2011) The Age of Responsibility – CSR 2.0 and the New DNA of Business (London: Wiley).

Part II

The Business Education Perspective

4

Integrating Liberal Learning into the Accounting Curriculum

Catherine A. Usoff

In a field that may seem as far away from liberal arts as possible, accounting educators are using techniques and content from the arts and sciences to prepare students to succeed in a complex, global, technology-based business environment. The accounting profession, for the most part, has changed dramatically in the past 30 years. Where the focus may have been on recording transactions on green columnar ledger paper, almost all accounting is done today in information systems. The skills needed by students entering the profession are more sophisticated than they once were. There is still a requirement to understand the basic accounting model (assets equal liabilities plus equities), but accounting students need to know and understand so much more.

The new requirements for educated accounting professionals are dependent on knowledge, skills, and capabilities that most naturally result from an arts and science background. A strong understanding of the fundamental accounting concepts, as well as an understanding of business environments and transactions, are necessary to identify the appropriate accounting and reporting treatments. Accountants must exercise judgment to first ascertain the relevant options for recording an economic event and the associated disclosure, choose the best option, and then justify to stakeholders why that is the best option. The justification has technical requirements to it, but can also have ethical, global, and societal considerations. So, in addition to learning the standard debits, credits, accounting rules, and other components of a core body of accounting knowledge, students must also learn how to think critically, to be able to compare and contrast and consider several different perspectives, and to apply ethical decision making.

The importance of, and desire for, an arts and science foundation is not a new phenomenon in accounting education. When accounting was first added to college curricula, it was widely believed that students should have at least two years of arts and science courses followed by two years of accounting courses. More recently, accounting educators have incorporated liberal arts concepts and techniques directly in the accounting courses they are teaching. Here is a brief history of accounting education, the justification for why it is important to incorporate liberal arts concepts and approaches into accounting courses, specific examples of this integration, and recommendations for the future of accounting education.

History

In articles in succeeding issues of the journal *Issues in Accounting Education*, Van Whye (2007a, 2007b) provides a two-part history of accounting education in the United States. He relates how accounting education started in the 1880s at Wharton. At first, accounting teachers provided the fundamental technical aspects of accounting, with a focus on balance sheets. As the accounting profession developed in the later 1800s, the American Association of Public Accountants was formed. The association pushed for a more theoretical basis to accounting education, to align it with other areas of study in college. Requiring a college education was considered imperative to establish the legitimacy of accounting as a profession, similar to medicine and law.

The early years of formal college accounting education at New York University were marked by a tension between instructors who developed a theoretical foundation for accounting and others who emphasized the importance of practical, laboratory-like experience. In the late 1930s, as accounting associations were trying to influence curricula, they mandated a significant amount of accounting content but also required two years of liberal arts education. There was recognition from the very beginning that the liberal arts component was important to the formal education of a professional accountant but it was not expected to be integrated with the technical accounting content. In light of the New York State college education requirement for accounting certification, McCrea and Kester (1936, pp. 106–117) explained the type of education that was most suitable for professional accountants. In addition to general business and technical accounting courses, aspiring CPAs should have 'a sufficiently broad knowledge of the so-called arts and sciences to give him a proper appreciation of present-day civilization' (McCrea and Kester, 110). Similar to other professions (engineering, law, and medicine), McCree and Kester prescribed a two-year liberal arts program that would provide the foundation for the business and then technical accounting coursework (112).

Although initially dominated by public accounting, professional accounting education branched out in the early 1950s to include 'industrial' or 'managerial' accounting (Van Wyhe, 2007a, 169). There were consistent and early concerns about the lack of certain skills of professional accountants such as writing, oral communication, and analytical thinking. The later history of accounting education was marked by constant battles for increasing legitimacy of accounting as a profession, rather than a trade. Arguments were made for the need of a fifth year of education, consistent with graduate education requirements for the other learned professions. It is not clear that there was ever a curriculum imperative for the fifth year, only that such a requirement was expected to elevate accounting to a similar professional level as law and medicine (VanWyhe 2007b).

More recent history of accounting education included calls for improving the quality of the education. In 1989 the American Accounting Association formed the Accounting Education Change Commission (AECC) to identify the required skills and knowledge for the accounting profession broadly speaking (public accounting, corporate accounting, nonprofit accounting, and tax). The AECC's goal was to provide guidance to accounting educators as they pursued improvements in the curriculum. The view of the AECC reinforced the idea that liberal arts were important in preparing students to become professional accountants. 'Accounting classes should not focus only on accounting knowledge. Teaching methods that expand and reinforce basic communication, intellectual, and interpersonal skills should be used' (AECC, 1990, p. 310).

Relationship between accounting and liberal arts

Technical knowledge is critical for maintaining the credibility of any business degree. The foundation of professional preparation is typically the technical knowledge that is required to understand and execute the primary responsibilities of standard entry level positions. For example, an accounting student must know how to create an income statement and balance sheet.

This base knowledge, however, is not enough anymore to ensure a successful start to an accounting career. The pace at which the world changes today requires that the accounting graduate has this knowledge but also much more. For a student who wants to be a valuable professional with potential for advancement, he or she must have highly developed reasoning ability. It is this broader capability that allows the business student, later accountant, to know when to apply the proper tools of the trade, how to interpret results, and what decisions to make.

The arts and science education primes the pump for many students to enable them to accept and flourish in an educational experience that pushes them to not only learn the technical knowledge but to understand the implications of that knowledge in different contexts. The arts and science curriculum provides both a foundation and reinforcement for the well-educated business professional. The frequent criticism of the profession that students did not possess good communication and critical thinking skills (Accounting Education Change Commission, 1990; Albrecht & Sack, 2000; American Accounting Association, 1986; American Institute of Certified Public Accountants, 1999; Arthur Andersen & Co. et al., 1989) implied, however, that requiring a general education component to the accounting degree was not the entire solution. Students did not seem to naturally integrate the skills they learned in liberal arts to bear on the applications required in upper-level accounting courses or on the job.

So, although there was very early recognition that a formal education for professional accountants should include a liberal arts foundation (Van Wyhe 2007a, Merino 2006), it is only more recently that accounting academics have emphasized the need for more explicit inclusion of liberal learning within the accounting courses themselves (Sangster 2010, for example). This is consistent with the AECC's position that teaching methods within accounting courses should be expansive, rather than narrowly focused on accounting knowledge. According to Fogarty (2010, 409), 'The proposed solution is to extract the desired skills from their liberal arts context and reset them in business and accounting coursework.' Likewise, Willits (2010, p. 23) prescribes that '...accounting faculty must determine ways to accomplish the shared objectives of a liberal education via the part of the curriculum they can control: accounting courses.' Such an approach is supported by Resnick (1987): 'One cannot reason in the abstract; one must reason about something.... As knowledge in the discipline develops, the base on which effective problem solving can operate is naturally available' (p. 36).

By explicitly reinforcing the communication, multiple perspectives, and thinking skills in the accounting courses, students are made to demonstrate the necessary integration and will be better prepared for the work place. Many business courses have evolved to include interactions with real companies in an attempt to expose students to the complex, messy problems they will have to deal with in their professional careers. Most, if not all, accounting faculty emphasize the reality that there is rarely only one right solution to a problem. The approach to accounting education has to become more consistently like the approach taken in many arts and science courses. There must be an increased emphasis on critical thinking, problem definition, analysis, and the creation of well-reasoned and data-driven arguments.

Typical accounting students have been known to have characteristics that might be resistant to attempts to broaden their focus, to expose them to deeper learning (Boyce et al., 2001, pp. 37–60). Many students are drawn to accounting because they perceive that there is a 'right' answer. They appreciate the fact that there is a structure to accounting, a way of proceeding that leads to a 'bottom line.' The business environment, however, is much more complex than it used to be, and as such the application of accounting rules is not as straightforward. Accountants must make judgment calls and be able to see the big picture as well as the details. They must be able to deal with some uncertainty – to be able to apply basic concepts to produce a treatment that is defensible, and to be able to clearly articulate that defense.

Today the accountant will have to explain why he or she approached something in a particular way. The answer is not going to be clear cut. Employing typical arts and science techniques within accounting courses can help students to better deal with the ambiguities and complexities they will encounter in their future jobs. Boyce et al. (2001) call on accounting educators to utilize strategies and assessment techniques in their courses that will challenge students' natural proclivities to help achieve deeper learning.

Examples of integrating arts and sciences techniques into accounting education

There are several examples of accounting faculty who have taken it upon themselves to either teach or reinforce learning approaches that are more common in arts and science courses. Some of the examples provided here are from personal conversations with colleagues, and others are documented in the accounting literature. After discussing specific examples, two recommendations for programmatic efforts are presented.

In a graduate accounting program at Bentley University, one of the required courses is 'Professional Accounting Research & Policy.'

In this course, students learn appropriate methods for researching accounting issues, analyze accounting research to assess its relationship to accounting policy, identify and discuss ethical issues, and study how accounting policy is made. The foundation for the skills required to master the concepts in this class are taught in the course. For example, in a section about applying critical thinking to accounting problems, the instructors present Bloom's Taxonomy of Thinking Skills (Abdolmohammadi and McQuade, 2001, 193). The explicit incorporation of liberal arts content in an accounting course is more likely to result in the students' successful attainment of the required higher order thinking skills. Careful integration is important so that students don't separate out the acquisition of the skills from the content (Gabriel and Hirsch, 1992, pp. 243–270). Instructors in the course ask students to apply critical thinking skills in a very deliberate way by using cases throughout the text.

One example used in the course asks students to identify the specific professional ethics principle (e.g., integrity, competency, objectivity) that is represented by a particular narrative explanation of a situation. The exercise requires the student to identify that there is an ethical issue, and more specifically what that issue is. The student must connect the abstract concept (e.g., integrity) to a specific scenario. On the surface, one would say that this is not an 'accounting skill,' but rather a skill generally attained through a liberal arts education that is invaluable to the ability of the accounting professional to successfully do his or her job. The student may not, on his own, connect his or her liberal arts learning to the accounting context. Reinforcement of the skills in direct proximity to the accounting context, by virtue of including explicit instruction in the accounting courses results in stronger preparation for the requirements of professional practice.

As traditional accounting tasks are being outsourced to lower wage countries (Milliron, 2008, pp. 405–419), young auditors in the US are increasingly required to apply higher level thinking skills than in the past. At least one of the Big Four public accounting firms, KPMG, has made materials available to students and professors to help develop professional judgment capabilities in young professionals. An auditing professor at Bentley University introduces the KPMG monograph to his students at the beginning of the semester. He then relies on the framework throughout the semester, drawing on it each week as they grapple with auditing concepts and issues. In addition to learning the psychological basis for biases that can hinder effective professional judgment, students are required to write and orally present arguments to support their applications of professional judgment to evaluate specific situations. Students are developing skills that have typically been taught and reinforced in liberal arts courses by learning the foundation for those skills and applying them directly to an auditing (public accounting) context. Unlike the past, when auditors were expected to grow through on-the-job experience, the KPMG framework is an attempt to structure the acquisition of professional judgment before graduation, so that new auditors are prepared to face the more challenging profession that awaits them.

Another typical liberal arts technique is the use of debate to foster critical thinking skills. Camp and Schnader (2010, pp. 655–675) describe their use of debate in two different accounting courses. In a tax course, students are asked to debate over the extension of a tax credit. The instructor sets up the debate to mimic congressional debate on the issue, with both sides presenting their positions (to extend a specific credit or to let it expire), rebuttals, questions from the audience, and then finally a vote. Camp and Schnader (2010) provide detailed guidance for creating a similar learning experience in a tax or financial accounting course, but also give enough background information to allow an accounting professor to incorporate this technique into any accounting course where there is value in looking at different perspectives on the same issue. The requirement to debate an issue necessarily includes the requirement to do background research to truly understand the issues and the assigned constituent's viewpoint. The students must also develop coherent arguments to support their stated views. The second example described in Camp and Schnader (2010) asks student teams to identify a particular constituency that is affected by the Sarbanes–Oxley act (e.g., publicly traded companies, auditors, the SEC (Securities and Exchange Commission), investors). Each team was to draft an amendment to the act and argue their position to support it.

Nelson et al. (2003, pp. 62–75) demonstrated that teaching formal logic theory to auditing students improved their ability to identify flaws in logic in several descriptions of real-world scenarios. By contrast, untrained students and audit professionals did not perform as well as the trained students. This quasi-experiment provides convincing evidence, albeit in a small sample, that integrating specific instruction that would normally be found in a philosophy course can improve audit decision making. The authors did not compare the effect of their treatment with the alternative of having students learn formal logic theory in a philosophy class that they might later apply to decisions in an auditing class (or in practice), but the effect of the imbedded instruction was compelling enough to consider the value of such embedding.

Hayes and Baker (2004, pp. 231–250) report on their use of a folk story about Buddhist monks to illustrate the concept of substance over form. Varying interpretations of an event in the story represent the potentially different perspectives that parties can have on a particular economic event. The recording of the event should reflect the substance of the transaction rather than the legal form of the transaction. The folk story presents a way for students to understand the concept without introducing the complexity of financial transactions. Once they understand the underlying concept, they can apply it more clearly to the accounting context.

Kimmel (1995, pp. 299–318) explains that in order to include the critical thinking components necessary to prepare successful future accountants, one needs to take into account both the developmental stages of college students and the components of developing critical thinking skills. He presents a typical accounting curriculum (304) and identifies specific types of activities to include in each course so as to systematically build students' critical thinking skills over the entirety of the accounting program. Kimmel (1995) recommends that accounting professors be very explicit about the need for, and incorporation of, critical thinking activities in their courses. Students may be less resistant to such content if they see the explicit connection to their success as future accounting professionals. One implication of Kimmel's suggested approach to the accounting curriculum, which is reinforced by others writing about the requirement to include liberal arts techniques in accounting courses, is that the doctoral programs in accounting should be preparing future accounting faculty to effectively provide the instruction that today's accountants need.

The preceding examples should be helpful to accounting educators who wish to integrate liberal arts techniques with accounting context to help their students gain the skills required for today's business environment and more highly evolved accounting function. Kerby and Romine (2009, pp. 172–179), like Kimmel (1995), take a more programmatic approach to the integration. They describe a longitudinal approach to improving students' oral communication skills. Kerby and Romine (2009) report on a case study of a particular accounting program where the same rubric was used for oral communication assignments in three different years. Students' progress could be tracked to determine whether they had achieved effective oral communication skills prior to graduation. This approach is commendable as it not only demonstrates the willingness of accounting faculty to integrate necessary non-accounting skills into the accounting curriculum but it shows how a program holds itself accountable for ensuring that students attain these skills.

In addition to using liberal-arts techniques in accounting contexts, accounting faculty could use the same rubrics that English composition faculty use in the general education courses. In this way, students would clearly see that what they are learning in their liberal-arts courses is important to, and integral to what they are learning in their accounting courses. A consistent approach to evaluating oral (and written) communication would convince students that the first two years of their undergraduate education, usually the general education core, is not just something that they need to get through so they can get to the 'important stuff,' namely their accounting courses.

Many accounting instructors are perhaps not inclined to include liberal arts techniques in their courses because their own introduction to the field has shaped their way of thinking (Boyce et al. 2001; Nelson 1995). There are, however, fairly detailed examples that should help accounting instructors who have the will to better prepare their students for a profession that is very different from the one for which they were trained.

The way forward

Today, it is imperative to integrate liberal arts approaches into accounting education. This approach is supported by calls from the profession and by the reality that the intellectual demands on entry-level accounting professionals are more advanced than they were in the past. Although students take arts and science courses as part of their accounting degrees, they tend to compartmentalize the knowledge and skills gained there. It is important for accounting faculty, therefore, to explicitly hold students accountable for applying the knowledge and skills in accounting contexts. In addition to providing instruction and opportunities for the application, accounting faculty must also consider the appropriate developmental approach for achieving effective results. They should also use assessment techniques to determine whether their approaches are successful in preparing students for the types of analysis and decisions they will need to make in their future careers.

This demand on accounting educators requires thoughtful consideration in accounting doctoral programs. Suggesting that accounting faculty integrate more liberal learning techniques in their courses implies that they should be adequately prepared to do that successfully through their own professional preparation.

References

Abdolmohammadi, M. and R. J. McQuade (2001) *Applied Research in Financial Reporting: Text and Cases* (New York: McGraw Hill/Irwin).

Accounting Education Change Commission (AECC) (1990) 'Objectives of education for accountants: Position Statement Number One,' *Issues in Accounting Education*, 5(2), pp. 307–312.

Albrecht, S. W. and R. J. Sack (2000) *Accounting education: Charting a course through a perilous future, Accounting Education Series 16* (Sarasota, FL: American Accounting Association).

American Accounting Association (AAA) Committee on the Future Structure, Content and Scope of Accounting Education (The Bedford Committee) (1986) 'Future Accounting Education: Preparing for the Expanded Profession,' *Issues in Accounting Education*, 1(1), pp. 168–195.

American Institute of Certified Public Accountants (1999) *Core Competency Framework for Entry Into The Accounting Profession* (New York: AICPA). Available at: http://www.aicpa.org/edu

Arthur Andersen and Company, Arthur Young, Coopers and Lybrand, Deloitte Haskins and Sells, Ernst and Whinney, Peat Marwick Main and Company, Price Waterhouse, and Touche Ross (1989) *Perspectives on Education: Capabilities for Success in the Accounting Profession*. (New York).

Boyce, G., S. Williams, A. Kelly, and H. Yee (2001) 'Fostering Deep and Elaborative Learning and Generic (Soft) Skill Development: the Strategic Use of Case Studies in Accounting Education,' *Accounting Education: An International Journal*, 10(1), pp. 37–60.

Camp, J. M. and A. L. Schnader (2010) 'Using Debate to Enhance Critical Thinking in the Accounting Classroom: The Sarbanes–Oxley Act and U.S. Tax Policy,' 25(4), pp. 655–675.

Fogarty, T. J. (2010) 'Revitalizing Accounting Education: A Highly Applied Liberal Arts Approach,' *Accounting Education: An International Journal*, 19(4), pp. 403–419.

Gabriel, S. L. and M. L. Hirsch, Jr. (1992) 'Critical Thinking and Communication Skills: Integration and Implementation Issues,' *Journal of Accounting Education*, 10, pp. 243–270.

Hayes, R. S. and C. R. Baker (2004) 'Using a Folk Story to Generate Discussion about Substance Over Form,' *Accounting Education*, 13(2), pp. 231–250.

Kerby, D. and J. Romine (2009) 'Develop Oral Presentation Skills Through Accounting Curriculum Design and Course-Embedded Assessment,' *Journal of Education for Business*, 85, pp. 172–179.

Kimmel, P. (1995) 'a Framework for Incorporating Critical Thinking into Accounting Education,' *Journal of Accounting Education*, 13(3), pp. 299–318.

KPMG Monograph. 'Elevating Professional Judgment in Auditing and Accounting: The KPMG Professional Judgment Framework,' Accessed March 24, 2012 through the faculty portal at KPMG.com https://clients.amr.kpmg.com/facultyportal/faculty/Curriculum+Materials/Audit/Audit.htm#profjudge

McCrea, R. C and R. B. Kester (1936) 'a School of Professional Accountancy,' *Journal of Accountancy*, February, pp. 106–117.

Merino, B. D. (2006) 'Financial Scandals: Another Clarion Call for Educational Reform – A Historical Perspective,' *Issues in Accounting Education*, 21(4), pp. 363–381.

Milliron, V. C. (2008) 'Exploring Millennial Student Values and Societal Trends: Accounting Course Selection Preferences,' *Issues in Accounting Education*, 23(3), pp. 405–419.

Nelson, I. T. (1995) 'What's New about Accounting Education Change? An Historical Perspective on the Change Movement,' *Accounting Horizons*, 9(4), pp. 62–75.

Nelson, I. T., R. L. Ratliff, G. Steinhoff, and G. J. Mitchell (2003), 'Teaching Logic to Auditing Students: Can Training in Logic Reduce Audit Judgment Errors?' *Journal of Accounting Education*, 21(3), pp. 215–237.

Resnick, L. B. (1987) *Education and Learning to Think*. (Washington: National Academy Press).

Sangster, A. (2010) 'Making our Students More "fit for Purpose": A Commentary on "A Role for the Compulsory Study of Literature in Accounting Education,"' *Accounting Education: an international journal*, 19(4), pp. 373–376.

Van Whye, G. (2007a) 'A History of U.S. Higher Education in Accounting, Part I: Situating Accounting within the Academy,' *Issues in Accounting Education*, 22(2), pp. 165–181.

Van Whye, G. (2007b) 'A History of U.S. Higher Education in Accounting, Part II: Reforming Accounting Within the Academy,' *Issues in Accounting Education*, 22(3), pp. 481–501.

Willits, S. D. (2010) 'Will More Liberal Arts Courses Fix the Accounting Curriculum?' *Journal of Accounting Education*, 28, pp. 13–25.

5

Mathematics and Auditing: How Liberal-Arts Theory and Business-Practice Education Inform Each Other

Richard J. Cleary and Jay C. Thibodeau

College courses in mathematics and statistics, particularly those in the first years of the undergraduate curriculum, are increasingly being taught to emphasize conceptual understanding. The mechanical calculations that previously dominated such courses can now be readily and effectively done by technology, freeing instructors to develop each student's conceptual thinking and problem-solving skills. Statistics education, in particular, has seen a well-documented shift toward the teaching of concepts in the context of applications that matter in business or society.

Correspondingly, the concepts now being emphasized in statistics – traditionally considered a discipline in the arts and sciences – have important applications to the 'business side' subject of financial statement auditing. Yet despite this seemingly natural synergy between teaching mathematics and statistics in context, and the need for auditors to better understand decision-making with statistical data, surprisingly little has been done to integrate the teaching of these two important fields.

We believe that these two disciplines, when taught in an integrated manner, have positive impacts on each other. On one hand, students of math and statistics learn effectively when immersed and engaged within a real-world application such as financial statement auditing. On the other hand, business students studying auditing learn to make better professional judgments when they understand the principles of mathematics and statistics. What follows are some ideas for teaching mathematical and statistical concepts to the practitioner studying auditing, while simultaneously using the auditing context to reinforce the concepts for the more abstract thinkers that are studying mathematics and statistics.

Educating future auditors

Today's financial statement auditors work in a highly regulated, difficult environment where they must make professional judgments about the reliability of financial statement balances of the entities that they are hired to examine. They report these decisions in a very public way, a true real-world application with a tremendous impact on the proper functioning of the worldwide capital markets. As a result, auditors need to employ the very best tools at their disposal when completing their work.

The objective of a financial statement audit is to provide reasonable assurance that the financial statements prepared by a company comply with the set of accounting rules that exist in a particular jurisdiction (e.g., International Financial Reporting Standards, or IFRS). An auditor is required to gather enough evidence to determine whether the financial statements have been recorded in accordance with those rules. Having gathered and examined the evidence, the auditor will reach a conclusion and report an opinion about the correspondence of the financial statements with the prescribed rules. Simply put, through their examination, auditors add credibility to the financial statements of the company being audited (Abdolmohammadi and Thibodeau, 2007).

Auditing education starts with understanding this professional landscape. Before taking the auditing course, undergraduates first take courses that impart detailed knowledge about prevailing accounting rules. This gives them the background knowledge necessary to conduct a successful audit.

In our experience, most students in these courses see mathematics and accounting as closely related subjects. Both are quantitative fields that involve problem solving, and a student with an exposure to only entry-level topics in each area would very reasonably conclude that they have much in common. For example, a high-school algebra course and a first bookkeeping course each involve learning some algorithms that, when correctly applied, lead to a specific correct answer.

Beyond the apparent similarities in the classroom, there are also some surprising similarities in practice that have a synergistic effect.

For example, in both fields, advances in information technology have dramatically changed the way in which the field can be taught. In accounting and auditing, routine tasks are now handled by computerized information systems. Because of this, companies look for graduates skilled in critical thinking and the ability to consider multiple alternatives before making a final professional judgment. Interestingly, given the changes brought about by advances in information technology, it is more important than ever to provide auditing students with sound mathematical and statistical conceptual knowledge.

However, real-world barriers to this approach remain. When we look at the realities of the business statistics education and audit practice environments, it is easy to see how an audit manager might be reluctant to apply statistical concepts. For example, students in a first statistics course (typically the only course that a practicing auditor is required to take) gain experience in using hypothesis tests to make decisions. However, these courses do not usually discuss the ways in which those decisions have to be implemented in practice. For example, the first business statistics course might feature an example where the null hypothesis says that eight percent of transactions were improperly documented. The problem provides data that say in a sample of 60 such transactions, the auditor finds six, or ten percent, that are improperly documented. The statistics student can do the calculation to determine that this difference is not statistically significant, and the claim of eight percent is reasonable. Having the student stop at that point is a nice statistics application, but it omits the real-world decisions that linger in an actual auditing context. In practice, the auditor has just employed a hypothesis test to make a key professional judgment about the overall effectiveness of an internal control procedure that is conducted thousands of times per year with a sample of just 60 instances of that control. Is this sample size sufficient? Is the eight-percent rate in the null hypothesis the appropriate standard? What are the implications if the rate is really ten percent instead of eight percent? The statistical process is useful to the accountant, but the difference between the 'statistics problem answer' and the 'real world decision a word,' is striking.

This lack of alignment between the business curriculum and auditing practice has resulted in a reluctance to use hypothesis-testing techniques. So, how can the statistics and accounting curricula be integrated to provide students with the experience they need to translate a statistical result to an effective decision in the field?

Key math concepts and their connection to auditing

Four broad mathematical tools are typically listed among the learning objectives for the mathematics and statistics courses in today's business education. Traditional teaching has kept liberal arts and business courses separate, meaning that most business practitioners fail to realize that they already have mathematical tools that can help their decision-making. Teaching that emphasizes increased understanding of concepts, and reinforces the idea that good problem-solving is a general skill that can aid in any discipline, helps students make the connection to effectively apply them on the job. Here is a look at the four tools and their application.

Estimation. The first tool is *estimation*, the ability to have a sense of an approximate solution before a precise solution is developed. Mathematics teachers develop this ability in many ways. The great mathematician George Polya (1887–1985) was famous for using the phrase, 'Let us Teach Guessing.' This might sound to the layman as if he was suggesting picking solutions to problems at random, but of course it is quite the opposite. Polya's idea was that solutions to most hard problems begin with a vague notion of what the solutions might be, a guess in the best sense of the word. If the application is too daunting to guess, consider a simpler case. After making a guess, think about how to check whether the guess was correct.

Repeating a series of guess-and-check steps is a great way to solve many mathematical problems. In an introductory calculus course, we always include a section on optimization as an application of the derivative, a classic and beautiful mathematical approach that follows the principle of estimation. However, few business problems can be expressed in terms of a single function whose derivative is easy to find. By combining the classical approach with technology, we can make these problems much more realistic. Data can be introduced, a function can be chosen to model the data, and approximate solutions can be found using modern technology and compared to an idealized analytic solution.

As an example, consider the concept of materiality in auditing. The simple fact is that financial statement measurements are not flawless. In many cases, an amount on the financial statements is a function of a significant estimate made by the management team. For example, financial measurements are based on estimates such as the estimated depreciable lives (a guess?) of a fixed asset or the estimated amount of accounts receivable that are uncollectable (a guess?). In essence, when auditing such a balance, an auditor must think of the final net income not as the one 'true' figure but as one possible measure in a range of potential net income figures allowable under the rules. Some amount of inaccuracy is essentially permitted in the financial statements because small inaccuracies would not impact an investment decision. In addition, the cost of finding small inaccuracies would be too high and would ultimately delay the release of financial statements. The general rule is that the information is material if it is likely to influence a financial statement users' decision. The concept of estimation is therefore essential for auditors.

Pattern recognition. A second high-level skill that the quantitative portion of a business curriculum encourages is *pattern recognition.* In most business calculus courses this skill is developed through examples matching graphical and analytical information. A classic question might show four graphs and ask students to match them with four types of functions that have different growth properties, perhaps exponential, logarithmic, linear and cubic. The ability to toggle between graphical and verbal descriptions helps students to recognize the many different ways that real-world quantities behave.

Subsequently, in statistics courses we add the idea of *variation* to the model. Few pairs of real-world quantities are perfectly linearly related, but many follow a relationship that is approximately linear with some random noise. Identifying the individual points that are farthest from expectations is a powerful tool in understanding any real-world relationship. Patterns of expenditures in business, for example, often follow a somewhat surprising relation called Benford's Law (see the description below; for background, see Cleary and Thibodeau, [2005]). Deciding when a certain set of expenditures does not conform to this expectation is a powerful tool for auditors.

Mathematicians function as experts in pattern recognition. Similarly, at the beginning of every financial statement audit, auditors use their prior experience and the data available to look for the patterns of a healthy company. The end result of these processes may differ (a proof for mathematicians, a decision and a public statement from the auditor) but the intellectual 'habit of mind' is much the same. Bedard and Biggs (1991) found that auditors that were able to recognize basic underlying patterns in a set of data were also able to perform significantly better in generating and evaluating a hypothesis about a seeded error in the data. One of the important conclusions of this and related audit judgment research is that pattern recognition is important to auditor expertise.

Separating examples. Next we consider *separating examples.* Mathematicians and statisticians love the intellectual exercise of characterizing a key feature of a particular object that separates it from other similar objects. In a first-year calculus course, a well-known example would be the absolute value function. This graph, shaped like a V, is a continuous function because you can draw its graph without lifting your pencil. However, it is not a differentiable function because the sharp point means that we are unable to define the rate of change when x = 0. This example shows us that two sets that seem similar (continuous functions and differentiable functions) are not exactly the same. As a result, absolute value serves as a separating example.

How can this sort of abstract definition aid a practicing auditor? Auditors routinely have to make classifications. Is a particular internal control effective at preventing fraud? While the definition of effective may not be as precise as the definition of differentiable, it is still the case that the auditor must use available data and experience to make such decisions.

When a mathematician discovers a new object, it is compared to known cases, and then deviations from the known forms are studied carefully. Deviations lead to new classifications, and a search for generalization leads to decision rules about how to classify objects. Separating examples become a stock in trade, one that we expect students to learn even in first year courses in calculus. Similarly, external auditors looking at the internal control activities of a company have many details to consider, but at the core, they face a binary-choice problem: either the internal control activity is operating effectively, or it is not.

Models and model diagnostics. A fourth area of emphasis is *models and model diagnostics.* In a first mathematics course we tend to emphasize structure through topics in calculus and financial mathematics. For example, mathematical models using exponential growth and decay are typically shown to model phenomena from areas as diverse as biology (population growth models, radioactive decay) and business (growth of industries, depreciation of assets). In application, however, exponential growth models have physical limits. Biological populations run out of food, businesses saturate a market, and the models no longer apply.

In a statistics course we try to teach students to recognize that all models are based on assumptions. But what if the assumptions are wrong? Which of the assumptions are reasonable and which are unlikely to hold? Model diagnostics refers to the practice of using the available information to assess whether a particular mathematical model is a good fit to a real problem. Much as the biologist must recognize whether a certain population's habitat can continue to support it, the auditor must decide whether a particular business is a viable going concern.

Because of the use of samples to gather evidence about various populations, the process of gathering and evaluating audit evidence relies substantially on statistical theory. Unfortunately, auditors have limited knowledge and experience applying relevant statistical thinking. In addition, there are few, if any, useful quantitative guidelines to assist auditors during the execution phase of the audit process. Our work in this area has only reinforced our belief that more effective statistical practice can help improve an auditor's professional judgments and the entire auditing process.

Despite the importance of statistical thinking, many auditors have received very little training on statistical theory during their undergraduate education. Auditors have little subsequent training on using statistics to make good decisions. We believe that an opportunity exists to help auditors become far better consumers of statistical information and better producers of audit evidence based on established statistical practice. In our view, such grounding will also help the defensibility of audit work papers, a very important consideration for auditing firms seeking to mitigate their litigation risk.

One example: Benford's Law

Benford's Law is a counterintuitive probability result that suggests that first digits of numbers in many common situations are not uniformly distributed. It indicates that a first digit of one is more likely than a first digit of two, and this pattern continues. We find that when Benford's Law applies, a first digit of one comprises about 30 percent of all data points, while nine is first in only about four percent of all entries (Cleary and Thibodeau, 2005). Interestingly, it is worth noting that Benford's paper proposing this distribution appeared in 1938. It was nearly 60 years later that Nigrini and others in the field of accounting (e.g., Nigrini and Mittermaier, 1997) began to take advantage of the result. It is one of many wonderful examples of how a 'pure' research idea can prove to be an important 'applied' idea some time later.

We believe Benford's Law is a motivating example to help students make the connection between auditing and statistical theory. For example, say we have a new object, in this case a firm's financial records. Does this object conform to the expected pattern, in this case Benford's Law? If not, how do we classify the difference? Is it due to fraud, or is there an innocent explanation?

Students have some evidence to back the use of Benford's Law. Nigrini (1999) was the first to highlight the potential of Benford's Law as an effective fraud detection process. He outlined a number of practical applications where a fraud auditor could effectively employ digital analysis using Benford's Law, including accounts payable data, general ledger estimations, duplicate payments, and customer refunds. Importantly, Benford's Law has also been shown to be an effective tool for internal and governmental auditors as well. For example, Nigrini (1996) demonstrated the applicability of Benford's Law in a taxpayer compliance context, raising the possibility of its effectiveness as a tool for governmental auditors.

By around 2004, Benford's Law was incorporated into leading auditing software packages, though not always in a statistically sound way (Cleary and Thibodeau, 2005.) These drawbacks made applying Benford's Law in practice quite risky for many auditors. The well-documented successes in which such an analysis uncovered significant fraud were evidence of the technique's potential but, the fact remains that a Benford analysis does add to the overall cost of the audit. As a result, there are many auditors that have now deemed the technique too expensive to use in practice. Perhaps not surprisingly, this reaction only adds to the curiosity of trying to devise more efficient ways to execute a Benford analysis.

So how is Benford's Law useful as a tool? As an exercise, applying the law to auditing for fraud follows the cognitive process of looking for deviations from an expected pattern – just the process that we claim that mathematicians and auditors (and people in many other fields) share!

Challenges to an integrated approach

Although most students graduating with a degree in auditing are likely to have had courses in mathematics and statistics, such courses tend to provide an overview of the key concepts with examples from generic contexts and rarely, if ever, use audit examples. More interaction will give students practical tools based on fundamental mathematical concepts. As we explain, the stakes are high.

The Securities and Exchange Commission (SEC) requires an annual audit of the financial statements and related footnotes of publicly traded companies in the United States. In recent years, the work of financial statement auditors has received increased scrutiny. A significant number of high-profile financial statement frauds (e.g., Enron and WorldCom) that occurred around the year 2000 reduced confidence in the financial statements being reported by publicly traded companies. As a result, the US Congress passed the Sarbanes–Oxley Act of 2002 (SARBOX) in an effort to restore confidence in the capital markets.

One of most dramatic changes mandated by SARBOX is governmental regulation of the audit profession. Section 103 of SARBOX established the Public Company Accounting Oversight Board (PCAOB). Under the law, the PCAOB is required to perform detailed inspections of the audit process employed by each auditing firm. Overall, in executing its responsibilities related to inspections, the PCAOB has made it clear that the interests of the investing public will always come first. As a result, the financial statement auditor now operates in a highly regulated work environment and all of their professional judgments are being scrutinized.

While there are many benefits from these changes, it has almost certainly reduced the willingness of auditors to use data interrogation techniques like Benford's Law. Without statistical expertise, practicing auditors fear having to explain and justify choices they make on the basis of a statistical test. That is why exposure to statistics is so important for future auditors. Our current statistics and accounting curricula fail when they create barriers between the 'practical' hypotheses about a business operation and the statistical outcomes of a particular analytical procedure.

In addition, there are substantial costs to the auditing firm for the extra work done on identified risk factors that result in no audit findings. For example, 'false positives' have become a strong deterrent to the use of Benford's Law, as any such indication might perhaps necessitate an additional site visit by the auditing firm. Stated simply, the cost can be substantial. As a result, the judicious use of Benford's Law is likely to be the only way the tool's use will be encouraged.

Auditors must think hard about the situations where Benford's Law should be employed. For example, an auditor should use it only when the risk of misstatement is high due to the industry and/or financial health of the company being examined. In such circumstances, the auditor may wish to use Benford's Law on those accounts that represent the greatest risk of material misstatement. In addition, an auditor needs to know enough about statistics to minimize the number of false positives and, when they do occur, to quickly be able to root out the explanation.

The wording in the independent auditor's report makes clear that auditors provide reasonable and not absolute assurance that the financial statements are free of material misstatement. This auditing vocabulary can be readily translated into statistical terms. The term 'reasonable assurance' for an auditor is essentially the notion of 'confidence' for a statistician, and what auditors call 'material' difference is what a statistics text would call a 'practically significant.' Exploiting these parallels can improve audit efficiency. For example, an auditor with a firm understanding of practical significance would recognize that some differences are clearly inconsequential or immaterial to the decision context at hand. In this same spirit, when evaluating the magnitude of a misstatement discovered in the auditing process, an auditor must recognize that certain misstatements are so small, that they also are clearly inconsequential or immaterial.

Conclusions

What similarities exist between the cognitive processes of expert auditors and expert mathematicians? What are the opportunities for collaboration?

In curricular matters, applications from mathematics courses should appear in auditing courses. There are a number of application areas that can provide a mechanism to link the concepts learned in mathematics and statistics to the accounting curriculum. For example, we firmly believe that the concepts of confidence, practical significance, estimation, and pattern recognition can all be effectively integrated into the accounting curriculum in an efficient manner. Conversely, for students primarily interested in mathematics and statistics, auditing applications can provide easy-to-understand, real-world examples such as those noted above.

In the regulated public company auditing market, the auditor's responsibility to detect fraud during a financial statement audit has increased dramatically. Such added responsibility has placed a great demand on auditors to devise more effective and efficient processes to detect it. We believe that auditors can make greater use of Benford's Law and other statistical techniques that have been greatly facilitated by the use of modern technology.

One final advantage of incorporating a unit on Benford's Law into business statistics coursework is the extent to which it will differentiate a course from the standard liberal-arts statistics course. Many business statistics books focus far too much on techniques and computation and not enough on the big picture notions of how to think in a statistical manner. And sometimes there are very few examples from disciplines outside of business (in fact some statistics educators refer to business statistics texts as 'the liberal-arts books with the interesting material removed'). Including Benford's Law would help to counteract such complaints. Indeed since Benford's Law has intellectual merit and applications in so many areas, we believe it should be an important part of the statistics and auditing curriculum.

We will continue to try to combine sound mathematical thinking with business practice so that auditors can use analytical procedures with confidence. Given the real-world environment for auditors and the current curricular disconnect between statistical decisions and practical decisions, the task is formidable remains important.

References

Abdolmohammadi, M. and J. Thibodeau (2007) 'Auditing,' in *Encyclopedia of Business and Finance, Second Edition* (New York: Macmillan).

Bedard, Jean and Stan Biggs (1991) 'Pattern Recognition, Hypotheses Generation, and Auditor Performance in an Analytical Task,' *Accounting Review* 66 (July), pp. 622–642.

Benford, F. (1938) 'The Law of Anomalous Numbers,' *Proceedings of the American Philosophical Society*, 78, pp. 551–572.

Cleary, Richard and Jay Thibodeau (2005) 'Applying Digital Analysis using Benford's Law to Detect Fraud: The Dangers of Type I Errors,' *Auditing: A Journal of Practice & Theory*, (May).

Nigrini, M. (1996) 'A Taxpayer Compliance Application of Benford's Law,' *Journal of the American Tax Association*, 18(1), Spring, pp. 72–91.

Nigrini, M. (1999) 'I've Got Your Number,' *Journal of Accountancy*, May, pp. 79–83.

Nigrini, M. and Mittermaier, L. (1997) 'The Use of Benford's law as an Aid in Analytical Procedures,' *Auditing: A Journal of Practice & Theory*, 16(2), pp. 52–67.

6

Broadening the Profession: New Skills in Actuarial Science

Emily Roth, Nicole Belmonte, and Nick A. Komissarov

Actuarial science is receiving increasing amounts of attention at business schools and other academic institutions. Actuaries assess the likelihood of, and develop products to manage, the effects of uncertain events such as accidents, illness, or the timing of death. They are most often employed by insurance companies, but can also work on benefit and pension plans or risk management strategies for individual companies, or they can take on a variety of roles in the financial industry. And recently, actuaries have moved into new areas of expertise such as catastrophe modeling, enterprise risk management, and predictive modeling.

Actuaries also play important roles in state and federal government. As insurance is a highly regulated and complex product, actuaries at state insurance departments review companies' product filings and amendments to certify that insurance products are fairly priced and satisfy state regulations. Government agencies, such as the U.S. National Association of Insurance Commissioners (NAIC), hire actuaries to evaluate the solvency and the ability of insurance companies to pay future benefits to their policyholders, be it a death benefit provided by a life insurance policy or a payment to a nursing home provided by a long-term care policy. At the federal level, the United States Office of the Chief Actuary states that it 'plans and directs a program of actuarial estimates and analyses relating to Social Security Administration-administered retirement, survivors and disability insurance programs and to proposed changes in those programs' (ssa.gov). Naturally, actuaries also play vital roles in the development of new laws that would apply to a country's healthcare policy. They are also often called to testify and provide expert opinion on various topics before Congressional committees.

Becoming a credentialed actuary in the United States entails completion of a series of challenging exams and projects as well as Validation by Educational Experience (VEE) requirements in economics, corporate finance, and applied statistical methods. This combination of exams and courses certifies that actuaries acquire a unique skill set that encompasses a familiarity with many general business functions and an in-depth understanding of forecasting and managing risk.

A strong actuarial program at a college or university can help students complete one or more preliminary exams, the VEE requirements, and one or more actuarial internships. The path to becoming a credentialed actuary is clearly laid out and doesn't require completion of a particular major – one can find programs that are successful according to these metrics in either liberal arts or business colleges.

However, the path to becoming a *successful* actuary is less clear. As the role of an actuary is expanding, so is the required skill set. To help address this, the Society of Actuaries (SOA) – one of the major U.S. actuarial organizations – has published a 'Competency Framework' outlining skills expected of its members (*The Actuary*, June 2009):

- technical skills and analytical problem solving;
- communication;
- relationship management and interpersonal collaboration;
- leadership;
- strategic insight and integration;
- external forces and industry knowledge;
- results-oriented solutions;
- professional values.

Note that technical ability is only one of the listed competencies. The exam process can weed out candidates who are not technically sound, so companies today are focused on finding actuarial students who can communicate, manage teams, offer strategic insight, and demonstrate other skills.

To meet these multiple goals, professors in successful higher-education actuarial programs work on strengthening these qualities in their students without giving up any of the technical coursework that actuarial students must master. Professors around the globe are striving to achieve this balance. According to Dr. Adam Butt et al. (2011), a study of the quality of actuarial education in Australia revealed that 'the lack of teaching technical material in a business context and the lack of development of non-technical skills such as communication are the most significant defects of the current program' (Butt et al., 2011, p. 1). Butt et al. go on to say that 'A balance must be struck between educating the technical capabilities that are the key differentiator of the profession and the more general capabilities that are increasingly necessary in the actuarial workplace' (Butt et al., 2011, 15). Business schools are well positioned to offer the environment and training that balances these two needs.

Stephanie Martone, a senior actuarial assistant at John Hancock and a business school graduate of Bryant University, agrees:

> My college education gave me the foundation that I needed to enter the actuarial profession. I began at a liberal arts college unsure of what I wanted in a career. Once I determined that I wanted to take actuarial exams, I realized that this college did not have courses that would prepare me for the exams. I decided that it would be best to transfer to a school that, at the very least, had actuarial classes. I enrolled in Bryant University as an Actuarial Mathematics major. By the time I graduated, I had passed two exams, and was studying for a third. I was fortunate enough to be offered two jobs at major insurance companies in a very poor economy. I give credit to Bryant, because I know that I would have never been given these opportunities at my other school.

Here is a look at each aspect of the SOA standards and how business schools succeed in graduating well-rounded, technically competent, and business-savvy actuaries. (It should be noted that the SOA framework was used because this actuarial organization had clearly outlined standards available. They are not the governing body for all actuaries, as other organizations can provide actuarial certification in different areas of practice or other countries. However, the authors believe that these competencies can be widely applied to the actuarial profession.)

Communication, relationship management, and interpersonal collaboration

Interpersonal skills are critically important in the business world, but this is an area in which actuaries have historically fallen short (think of the classic green-eyeshade, socially challenged math wizard). In an interconnected, communication-intensive modern business environment, most actuaries can ill afford to conform to this stereotype. In addition to helping candidates through the interview process (candidates generally have to impress not only fellow actuaries, but also human resources and other less technically oriented professionals), the ability to communicate well adds value to their work throughout their careers.

So how do business schools offer an advantage in this area? Liberal arts colleges help students develop communication skills, but business schools focus on helping students develop *business* communication skills. It can be difficult to transition from writing papers with minimum page requirements to writing memos and emails for which brevity is critical. Business communications must be succinct, persuasive, and memorable. Business students learn to write executive summaries and short memos, conveying their message to an audience with limited time.

Verbal communication skills are equally important. Often in business, findings are communicated through presentations using software such as PowerPoint and Keynote. Actuaries need to be comfortable presenting in either a large group setting or a small meeting. They need to be able to present formally on a topic, and also handle unanticipated questions.

In addition to presentations, actuaries should be comfortable communicating in more casual business settings. Business schools like Bentley University have a strong focus on developing professional communication skills. In addition to embedding presentation work into many core courses, they offer courses specifically focused on presentation, communication, and negotiation skills. Graduates are therefore more prepared for the variety of presentation styles demanded of a professional – team and individual, formal and informal, small audiences and large.

Leadership

Great technical and communication skills will get an actuary only so far. Individual contributions may be recognized, but the next step for many professionals is management, whether it is managing projects, employees, or a book of business. For these, leadership skills are essential. In an insurance company, an actuary might lead teams of professionals from accounting, marketing, and other non-actuarial disciplines. In fact, many insurance companies hire interns and college graduates into actuarial 'leadership' development programs (Prudential, Travelers, Northwestern Mutual).

Management training is an important differentiator for a business school. As opposed to traditional liberal arts, business training gives a student an opportunity to learn how to become a successful leader of cross-functional business teams. This is a skillset that can be learned in a classroom setting through group work, where students are encouraged to consider different perspectives to enhance their projects. For example, in a Bentley general business course called Integrated Business Project, student teams comprised of individuals from various majors complete a semester-long project to create a business plan for an actual company. Since this single project spans a full semester, it teaches organizational, time management, planning, and prioritization skills. Since students from diverse backgrounds are working together, they learn resource management, matching tasks with skill sets, and delegation strategies. And since the project has to merge various components of a business plan, students develop strategies to involve everyone, and develop methods to evaluate each other's work. Students graduating from business schools are generally well-practiced at group leadership and know how to be valuable team members, not just strong individual contributors.

Sarah Linszner, an actuarial associate at John Hancock and a graduate of Bryant University, believes that the non-technical business skills that she picked up at Bryant helped her to be successful on the job:

> I truly believe that attending a business school, Bryant, has helped me transition faster and easier from college student to successful young professional than I would have experienced had I not gone to a business school. Most technical skills that the job requires, such as applications of Excel and actuarial software, I have been able to pick up quite quickly on the job. In contrast, I believe that non-technical skills such as communication, teamwork, and leadership must be developed through experiencing different business problems and attempting to solve them in the context of using these soft skills. While attending Bryant, I was presented with many real-life business problems that provided me the opportunity to develop my soft skills through experience, such as working with a group to create a business plan or managing a group to raise funds for charities. By having the opportunity to develop these skills in college, I entered the professional world much more prepared to deal with the 'human element' of every business problem that I have been presented with so far in my career.

Strategic insight and integration

Perhaps the most critical skill in the business world, and one that a business school is particularly well-equipped to pass on to students, is being able to view work in a business context. An actuary recently involved in entry-level hiring at Liberty Mutual Insurance, Peter D'Orsi (Bentley'03), cites this as the most important skill for an incoming actuary to exhibit. He describes the interview process:

> At Liberty Mutual Insurance we've been looking for candidates with undergraduate business degrees for our actuarial program over the last couple of years. Candidates from schools such as Bentley and Bryant tend to have a better 'big picture' view of the insurance industry ... as far as understanding how actuarial work needs to fit into the business. Actuaries at Liberty are deeply involved in common actuarial disciplines such as pricing and reserving, but are also involved in projects involving product development, underwriting, finance, and more. Many actuaries go on to be senior managers of business units. In fact, our former CEO was an actuary by trade. Actuaries work as managers of statewide operations, distribution, and claims. These jobs all require business skills that people can develop a foundation for in an undergrad education. The success of actuaries in positions such as these has led us to look for entry-level candidates who are 'business people with actuarial training.'

Christopher Cunniff, product manager of workers' compensation at Liberty Mutual Insurance, provides a similar outlook. Cunniff notes that the best characteristic an actuary can have is being well-rounded, emphasizing the necessity of using technical skills along with business acumen and strong communication skills to influence business decisions. He recalls many times when actuaries would give their opinions to senior management with no business context – they would provide an actuarial opinion and any considerations beyond that were out of their hands. But an actuary's work product is infinitely more valuable to a company if the actuary considers other business needs alongside the technical calculations. An insurance company has to weigh the actuarially sound rate with a multitude of other factors, such as retention goals, market conditions, and the regulatory environment. Successful actuaries understand all of these considerations, rather than being concerned exclusively with their calculations.

Strategic insight and integration is further defined by the SOA as the ability to anticipate trends and align work products with broader business goals (*The Actuary*, June 2009). The aforementioned Integrated Business Project course combines lessons in marketing, finance, and operational strategy and culminates with the writing of a complete business plan for a real company. This provides students with the opportunity to take classroom lessons and combine them with real-world market research. They must create, distribute, and analyze a survey for market participants, as well as research company and industry financial information in order to identify industry trends and create a business strategy. And, since many business school faculty members have real-world business experience, the feedback that the students receive on their work is invaluable preparation for their careers.

External forces and industry knowledge

Actuaries must also appreciate external forces and industry knowledge, including economic, social, regulatory, geopolitical, and business environments (*The Actuary*). Most of the technical work that an actuary completes when pricing insurance is based mainly on profitability and compensation for risk but sometimes includes assumptions about external factors. For the work to be truly valuable, actuaries must also understand how their work will be influenced by these factors.

Because forecasts are uncertain, there is always a range of fair and sound insurance rates. Business strategy starts with the actuarially sound range and determines precise actions based on other insurance principles. For example, the Casualty Actuarial Society (CAS) states that rates should 'promote ... availability for insurance consumers' (casact. org), so a company should consider affordability when setting rates. Companies may also face a difficult regulatory environment, and may choose to be less profitable in one line of business to remain in the regulator's favor when writing another, more profitable line of business in the same state. For example, the state of Florida has obliged insurers to keep the price of homeowners insurance so low that many companies face the risk of large losses should a big hurricane strike the state. However, companies writing business in Florida can also offer auto insurance, and this line is much less susceptible to hurricane risk. This creates a balance, or trade-off between risk and reward.

Other externals include business cycles and market swings, growth targets and economies of scale. All of these forces need to be considered when operating an insurance company. An actuary who performs his or her work in a bubble may provide one-dimensional information that the company needs, but an actuary who sees his or her work in a big-picture context is far more valuable as an employee.

Results-oriented solutions

The related competency that adds value to an actuary's work is the ability to produce results-oriented solutions, turning knowledge of the business strategy and external environment into actionable recommendations. Executing strategies is an important business skill, and business schools emphasize performance in this area. At Bentley for example, students work to creatively solve big, complex business problems. In one offering of the Honors Capstone course, students were given a semester-long task from State Representative Bosley to try to reduce energy costs in Massachusetts. The team spent the early part of the semester working to understand the current situation in the state, researching initiatives already in place, concerns, and theoretical solutions through academic papers, news articles, and interviews with stakeholders. Then they used the data and information they had gathered to create recommendations, and they presented their findings at the State House. As a result of this work and the issues raised, Dr. Charles Hadlock, who taught the course, has been involved in ongoing discussions with state personnel about the viability of alternative energy sources.

Professional values

Today the governing bodies of many professions pay close attention to educating their members on honesty, integrity, and professional values. In the U.S., the CAS, SOA, and American Academy of Actuaries (AAA) have codes of conduct and standards of practice to uphold the integrity of the profession. The actuarial societies mandate courses on professionalism that must be completed before a candidate receives associateship or fellowship designation. The International Association of Actuaries (IAA) states that the purpose of its professionalism committee is 'to encourage appropriate standards of professional actuarial education and practice internationally' (actuaries.org). Like CPAs, sometimes actuaries have to sign off on work products, such as reserving opinions in insurance company financial statements. However, while an accountant is signing off on the accuracy of real assets and liabilities, the actuary is signing off on the accuracy of a forecast that cannot possibly be perfect.

Therefore, an actuary relies on professionalism standards as protection from prosecution. These standards are guidelines for how a professional actuary should behave regarding documentation, methods used, and best practices.

As with any set of guidelines, actuarial standards of practice cannot address every possible situation an actuary will encounter. They are a starting point, but there are gray areas and varying interpretations. Therefore, while organizations strive to provide support for members, actuaries must be responsible for their own ethics and professional values in order to uphold the integrity of the profession. And the stakes are high – an actuary can be suspended or have their credentials removed if they are found guilty of breaking professionalism standards (Behrens, 2012). Actuaries also can be sued by clients relying on the veracity of their work.

Business schools pay close attention to these developments and understand their importance. Some examples from Bentley include the following:

- Students have the option to pair a business major with a liberal studies major (LSM) in ethics and social responsibility (Bentley.edu).
- Many business classes cover case studies that focus on business ethics and analyze what went wrong in a particular situation and how an ethical issue could have been resolved or avoided.
- In introductory accounting classes, much attention is given to cases of fraud in famous corporations.

A course called 'The Role of Community Service in a For-Profit Organization' includes group discussions and case studies on different ethical issues, and also puts social responsibility into practice. Students teach a class at a local high school on general business and social responsibility. Then, the high school class creates a non-profit business plan and presents it to a panel of senior managers from Boston-area companies. The college students are not just teaching these younger students – they are also serving as role models demonstrating how important it is to focus on school, go to college, and be mindful of social responsibility.

Being an ethical professional is a personal choice, but Bentley's curriculum ensures that students have some exposure to the importance of business ethics and the potential consequences of not upholding professional values. Students graduating from such a program are better prepared to deal with ethical issues and can help their employers avoid infamous situations such as those at Enron, WorldCom, and others.

Technical skills and analytical problem solving

The heart of an actuary's role is measuring and forecasting future risk, which requires great technical knowledge and the ability to analyze complex problems. For this reason, many actuaries have a background in either actuarial science, or a broader technical subject like mathematics.

It has been said that the value of a degree in mathematics is that the student is taught how to think. Most don't go into careers in which they regularly use the formulas and algorithms learned in class. Rather, they use their understanding of these concepts to interpret computer-generated results and to logically analyze different problems. Obviously a student can earn a mathematics degree at a liberal arts college, but the difference between that and a business school's math degree is that at a business school students learn to think analytically *in a business context*, which was one of the major deficiencies identified by the aforementioned Dr. Adam Butt in his studies of actuarial education. Business school courses are less focused on theory, and more focused on applying analytics to real-world situations. Coursework is practical and can reflect changes in the business environment. The theory behind the analytics might stay the same for many years, but translating that theory into practice is an ever-changing process; business schools are well-practiced at staying current.

Conclusion

Business schools are distinctively equipped to train students for a career like actuarial science not because they bypass technical education for soft skills, but because they understand the value of *integrating* soft skills into technical education. Skills like communication, leadership, and big-picture focus aren't taught in a lecture – they are honed through practice. A business school teaches the technical skills but also incorporates group work, presentations, and real-world context into the entire curriculum.

There is a school of thought that there is a need for two types of actuaries. One is the 'stereotypical' actuary, who is exceptionally technical, a master of statistical and mathematical methods. This is the type of actuary who will create ingenious new models to measure risk and will write papers that future actuaries will study. Perhaps a liberal arts school is better equipped to produce this type of actuary.

But there is a second type of actuary that is breaking the mold. This actuary still passes exams, and so is certainly technically capable and has an above-average understanding of math, statistics, and finance. But, this actuary is also a business person, and uses his or her understanding of complex concepts to influence business decisions. This is the type of actuary that a business school is exceptionally capable of training, and there is clearly a demand for that skill set, both in the insurance industry and beyond.

References

Actuaries.org, IAA website (http://www.actuaries.org/index. cfm?lang=EN&DSP=CTTEES_PROFESS&ACT=INDEX).

The Actuary (2009) SOA Competency Framework, *The Actuary* magazine, June vol. 6, no. 3 (http://www.soa.org/library/newsletters/the-actuary-magazine/2009/june/act-2009-vol6-iss3-framework.pdf).

Behrens, Nancy (2012) 'Up to Code: Types of Discipline,' Jan-Feb, Contingencies Online (http://www.contingenciesonline.com/contingenciesonline/2012010 2#pg19).

Bentley.edu (http://undergraduate.bentley.edu/academics/liberal-studies-major).

Butt, Adam J, Brian W. B. Chu, John A. Shepherd (2011) 'Actuarial Education: Theory into Practice.' 46th Actuarial Research Conference, August 11–13.

Casact.org Statement of Principles Regarding Property and Casualty Insurance Ratemaking, (http://www.casact.org/standards/princip/sppcrate.pdf).

Prudential (http://www.prudential.com/view/page/public/14408).

Ssa.gov (http://www.ssa.gov/oact/actuaries/index.html).

Travelers (https://www.travelers.com/about-us/careers/development-programs/actuarial-science.aspx).

Northwestern Mutual (http://www.northwesternmutual.com/career-opportunities/corporate-opportunities/Documents/actuarial_brochure.pdf?win_type=pdfform).

7
Business Analytics at the Confluence of Business Education and Arts & Sciences

Dominique Haughton

Business analytics, in simple terms, is data analysis applied to business problems. While its origins and history are closely tied to finance and other data-intensive areas of business, in recent years business analytics have moved into many more areas of corporate and social life. Along with this trend has come a closer connection to the traditional areas of higher-education arts and sciences. In this chapter we will explore the connection in three ways:

1. Business analytics techniques that are used to investigate arts and sciences topics, such as text analytics, music analytics, or living standards analytics;
2. How arts and sciences skills, such as good writing and creativity, are key to the skill set of a strong business analytics professional;
3. How business analytics, because of its close connection to statistics and computer science with overtones of social science, is arguably an art and science discipline in itself, as well as a business discipline.

What is business analytics?

The term *business analytics* was coined by corporations in the late 1980s to mean data analysis applied to business problems. Other now-common related terms include 'predictive analytics,' data mining and more recently data science. Typically, but not always, business analytics problems involve large data sets, of (for example) 1 million records. This state of affairs is due to the fast and widespread generation of all types of data from corporate client transactions, social networking sites, and other business data that, taken together, has given rise to the term 'Big Data.' The press provides a wide coverage of the phenomenon (see for example *The Economist* 2010 and 2012 for extensive discussion and coverage). IBM has centered its entire 'smarter planet' movement on data analysis considerations (IBM, 2012).

The explosion of interest in business analytics can be shown by a simple analysis: Figure 7.1 charts the sharp increase in use of the phrase 'business analytics' in all Google books between 1995 and 2008. By comparison, the term 'finance,' for example, over the same period, shows a slight relative decrease from about .0022% to .0020%.

But where are business analytics being used? Despite the growth in the term, many applicants to business graduate schools still seem to believe that quantitative methods are limited to financial applications. (Quantitative finance, which relies on advanced probabilistic and stochastic process ideas, addresses key problems in portfolio optimization and the management of financial assets. The field is dominated by strong schools of thought that are heavily represented in the financial industry centers of London, New York, and Paris.)

Of course, quantitative finance is critical for that purpose. However business analytics techniques are widely used in other financial operations – for example, in work groups that examine customer transaction data to help identify promising new products or to find cross-selling opportunities. And in insurance companies, the traditional field of actuarial science is now moving in the direction of business analytics, in large part because of the preponderance of

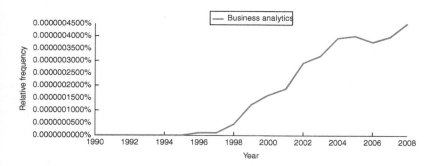

Figure 7.1   Rise in the relative frequency of the term 'business analytics' from 1990 to 2008

Source: books.google.com/ngrams

large volumes of claims data that must be understood and interpreted analytically.

Beyond finance and insurance, quantitative methods now extend to a much wider space. Covering a wide range of data analysis and modern data-mining techniques, business analytics now applies to marketing, management, operations, inventory control, sales forecasting, and fraud detection. Not all of these business analytics techniques are 'advanced'; in fact, a significant part of the work involves simple descriptive statistics, coupled with a good dose of common sense and critical thinking.

Origins of understanding: putting business analytics in context

The strong demand for analytics professionally, as well as interest in the press and academic and corporate circles about 'big data' and related issues has been fueled by, and continues to spawn, a considerable volume of publications, conferences, and workshops. A few important projects that identified the place of analytics in business and society include a path-breaking book, a key report by the McKinsey Global Institute (2011), and recent work by Hoerl and Snee on 'statistical engineering' (Hoerl and Snee, 2012).

The book *Competing on Analytics* by Thomas Davenport and Jeanne Harris (2007) is generally recognized as a launching pad for the explosion in interest in analytics. Their work caused many to appreciate that analytics capability is key to success in today's business environment. They explained how companies can and should compete on analytics, offered a map of the territory, and discussed the success of analytics in corporations such as Harrah's and Marriott International.

The extensive McKinsey report, 'Big data, the next frontier for innovation, competition and productivity,' included the most widely quoted figures concerning the shortage in the United States of employees with deep analytics capacity (140,000 to 190,000) and of data-savvy managers (1.5 million). In addition to these and other informative figures, the report gave a useful overview of the potential of big data in five domains: health care, public sector administration, retail, manufacturing, and personal location data, with implications for organizations and policy makers.

In the past few years, Roger Hoerl, manager of General Electric's Global Research applied statistics lab, and Ronald Snee, president of

Snee Associates (*Quality Progress*, June 2012, 5260), have published a series of papers and given a number of workshops on what they refer to as 'statistical engineering.' They defined statistical engineering as the study of how to use the principles and techniques of statistical science for the benefit of humankind. The inspiration for it arises from the Total Quality Management movement. Hoerl and Snee's work is an effort to help ensure that statistical projects have a high impact in organizations, and are not relegated to the land of 'nice to have but can be dispensed with' projects, and to provide statisticians (AKA analytics professionals) with an opportunity to become true leaders in their organizations.

Data analysis as storytelling: making data confess the truth

In the real world, where business analytics must be part of an overall business effort, data analysis is not a dry mathematical exercise. It is, in fact, a form of narrative – a story, told in the context of business activity. Here are a few examples of how data analysis can be seen as a type of storytelling activity with a detective component to it.

Trans-disciplinary collaboration across departments in a business university

In 2001, several initiatives were deployed at Bentley College (now Bentley University) to foster cross-department collaboration. Recognizing that important business problems are not confined within arbitrary disciplinary walls, the school made a deliberate effort to combine department activities in such a way as to offer a more holistic and realistic business education.

As in a number of analytics projects, a simple visualization of the data goes a long way towards unraveling what is going on. The story presented here lives in the analytics space, but is related to sociology, where the study of social networks originated.

Figures 7.2a and 7.2b represent the network of cross-department collaborations, as measured by the presence of co-published article(s) by teams of authors comprising at least one member of each department. While nothing much was visible from the raw data stored in the faculty publications database, it is quite clear from Figures 3a and 3b that cross-department collaborations have intensified since the implementation of the initiatives. Further discussion of this story can be found in Adams

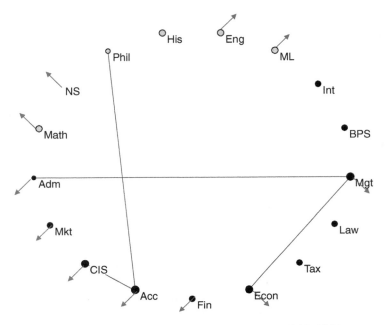

Figure 7.2a   Network of cross-department collaborations, 2000–2001

Notes: Gray vertices are Arts and Sciences departments, black vertices are Business departments (or Administration). The thickness of the lines is proportional to the strength of the connection; the size of the vertices is proportional to their degree. Arrows indicate that outside collaborators have also been involved. Note that Mathematics, Natural Sciences, Philosophy, History, English, Modern Language, International Studies and Behavioral and Political Science are Arts and Sciences departments.

et al. (2006). This finding was indeed confirmed by establishing that the densities of the two networks are statistically significantly different, but the main point is immediately visible to the naked eye.

These figures, in addition to illustrating how insights get extracted from looking at data with a particular twist, also offer a quick glance at a very important and current area of analytics: the analysis of social networks. In this field, links between two actors can represent many types of connection, from friendship, collaboration, and advice seeking to internet links (between websites, for example). Links can be directed or not. Key concepts include how central an actor is, as measured by his/her/its number of connections, but also by how much of a gateway a particular actor might be, in that shortest paths from any pair of two actors might pass through that particular actor.

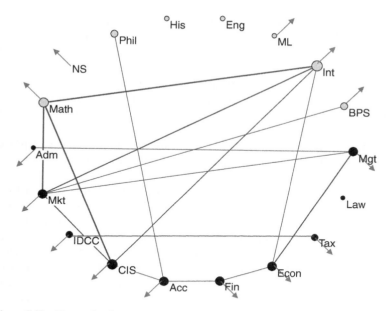

Figure 7.2b Network of cross-department collaborations in 2002–2003

Notes: Gray vertices are Arts and Sciences departments, black vertices are Business departments (or Administration). The thickness of the lines is proportional to the strength of the connection; the size of the vertices is proportional to the degree. Arrows indicate that outside collaborators have also been involved.

Interestingly, one of the major collaboration groups emerging from Figure 3b is that involving Math (and arts and science discipline in general), CIS (which can be considered as either an arts & science or business discipline), marketing and international studies.

Living standards and Location Impact Factors in Vietnam

This story takes place in Vietnam and is concerned with living standards, using the typical economic standard of annual household expenditure per capita. It is a story which lives in the realm of data analysis, geography, economics, and global studies, cutting across the boundaries between topics which might be considered as business topics (such as data analysis and economics) and topics which might be considered as arts & sciences subjects (such as geography and global studies). The study of living standards is related to explorations of business issues, since buying power is necessary for business activity to take place.

One challenge in this situation is that surveys that seek to evaluate household expenditures are expensive to run; as a result, sample sizes tend to be rather small, and in particular too small to estimate average living standards at the commune level with a decent level of precision. Techniques that combine administrative data (such as census data) with data from the survey can be pressed into service to obtain what is referred to as small area estimates of average living standards at the commune level. The result of this estimation is displayed for southern Vietnam on Figure 7.3a, where it is clear that communes in the Mekong delta region (in the lower left part of the map) tend to display modest living standards.

However, an interesting insight emerges from Figure 7.3b, which now displays Location Impact Factors (LIFs) for communes in the Mekong Delta that were covered by the living standards survey. These LIFs (Nguyen et al. 2012) represent the effect of the geographic location of the commune, when characteristics such as education, labor structure, household size, and other population factors are controlled for. The LIFs for most of the communes in the Mekong Delta on Figure 7.3b are at the high positive end of the spectrum, implying that the

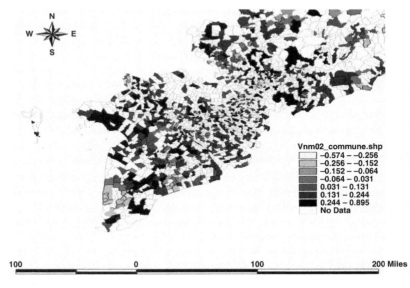

Figure 7.3a Small area estimation of living standards in communes in the Mekong Delta

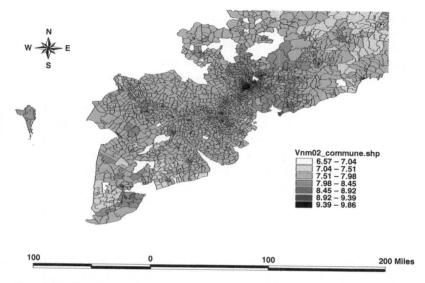

Figure7.3b Location Impact Factors (LIF) from communes in the Mekong Delta

Note: In Figure 7.3a, communes in the Mekong Delta seem to display low living standards, but the Location Impact Factors for these communes tend to be high (Figure 7.3b)

mere location of these communes is associated with a living standards upwards shift.

What is going on here is that the usual correlates of wealth, such as small household sizes, or a high level of education, are not favorable in the Mekong Delta. To some extent, they are moderated by the geographical location of the communes, probably by the presence of waterways and a reasonably favorable climate. Unraveling this insight involves some advanced modeling (Nguyen et al., 2012; Haughton and Haughton 2011), but fundamentally relies on looking at the data with a particular twist.

Authorship problems, literature fingerprinting, and visualization analytics

Another area in which analytics contribute to arts and sciences as 'detective work' is in the field of authorship. Occasionally in literature, authorship is suspect. Literature 'fingerprinting' uses a number of statistical measures in a text – for example, word frequencies and sentence lengths – to derive a 'fingerprint' for the text. Hopefully, this will help to decide whether (for example) the text was written by Mark Twain or Jack London.

Data mining techniques (Support Vector Machines) have been used to infer the authorship of the disputed Federalist papers (for example, Fung et al., 2003). A convenient reference for text mining concepts and tools is Davi et al. (2005).

It is interesting to note that algorithms used in firms such as Turnitin to examine whether student work is original are different from the data mining techniques which infer authorship via literature 'fingerprinting.'. In this case, the objective is to write an efficient algorithm to help identify whether portions of student writing have in fact appeared somewhere on the internet. The problem is a computer science and algorithmic one, but no data analysis per se takes place, to the best of our knowledge. We note in passing that the use of Turnitin is not without ethical and legal issues, for example that of questionable use of students' intellectual property, or a concern that the careless use of plagiarism detection devices such as Turnitin could stand in the way of good pedagogical approaches to teaching students how to avoid plagiarism in the first place; for more discussion of these issues, see http://cyberdash.com/plagiarism-detection-software-issues-gvsu/.

Music analytics; Zipf's Law

A large literature now exists on music data mining, including a volume edited by Li et al. (2012), which itself contains numerous references. A substantial body of work concerns techniques for classifying and recognizing music pieces, and the study of the social aspects of music. In many of these cases, data mining (AKA analytics), which is frequently considered as a business discipline, encounters the art of music.

One of the very interesting stories reported in the Li et al. volume is that Zipf's law, which applies to the frequency of words in natural text, and states that the frequencies of words ordered from the most frequent to the least frequent are proportional to 1/1, 1/2, 1/3, 1/4, etc. also applies to the frequency of notes, as well as the frequency of distances between repeated notes, in music. Even more interesting is the fact that 'most socially sanctioned music, across styles, exhibits near Zipfian distributions' (Manaris et al., chapter 6 in Li et al.).

An article by Collins et al. (2011) discusses the use of Markov chains to randomly generate music that resembles Chopin mazurkas.

Fraud detection

Fraud detection is a very common application of data mining in many areas. In order to predict fraud, it is very useful to have at hand a sample of cases that were fraudulent as well as cases that were not fraudulent. It is then a matter of fairly standard analytics to build a model that predicts whether a case is fraudulent or not on the basis of a number of predictive variables.

In the absence of a sample where one would know which cases are fraudulent or not, detecting fraud would involve identifying outliers, cases that are extreme in some measure or another.

A good source of reports on the use of analytics in fraud detection is the collection of SAS (Statistical Analysis System, a leading statistical software package) white papers, for example the Health Care fraud report by Julie Malida, as well as other SAS white papers on fraud detection, notably in the financial industry. See also Clauss et al. on the Madoff case (2009).

Training and mentoring the business analytics student

Bentley University has been training business analytics professionals at the graduate level since the early 1990s, first at the master's level and more recently at the PhD level, as a specialization in the Bentley Business PhD.

The focus at the master's level, and to some extent at the PhD level, is informed by close consultation with a number of business partners who are part of the analytics community at Bentley. The skill set currently taught in the analytics courses includes regression analysis (linear and logistic), factor analysis, cluster analysis, and decision trees, as well as a number of data mining techniques, and time series analysis (with the statistical package R, The R Project, 2012). In addition it is strongly recommended that candidates take a course in computer science that covers database management and SQL (Structured Query Language). All are strongly encouraged to certify one or preferably two levels of SAS. This regimen, established with the needs of corporate partners in mind, yields excellent placement of graduates at organizations such as Epsilon, EMC, Mullen, Bank of America, and so forth.

Further plans for graduate analytics programs at Bentley include the launch of a new master's program that will ensure that graduates not only are proficient in the techniques of analytics but are exposed to the frameworks that help analytics projects have an important impact on their organizations, following in the steps of the statistical engineering movement. Mastering these frameworks relies on a number of skills that one might call 'soft,' such as effective writing and creative thinking. Success in business analytics, a business as well as an arts and science discipline, relies on skills that are unequivocally arts and science skills. For example, in addition to effective writing and creative thinking, critical thinking is invaluable in helping the business analytics professional decide whether data analysis results make sense or not, or whether data can be trusted or not. It is another aspect of the detective behavior inherent in most good analysts.

Conclusion

This chapter has attempted to provide a flavor of what business analytics is about, its current trends, and how it is connected to the Arts and Sciences. It is of course by no means exhaustive, but reflects the point of view and taste of the author. To summarize, a Wordle of the content of the chapter is given in Figure 7.4. The graph is constructed with the help of an algorithm that takes into account the frequency of words in the document (www.wordle.net).

Essentially, the algorithm works by first sorting words in decreasing order of frequency of occurrence in the body of text, and then places words one after the other on the display, in such a way as to avoid

Figure 7.4   Wordle contents of the chapter

intersections of words. A brief description of the algorithm is given in Viégas et al. (2009).

Viégas et al. also point out that the use of Worldles has spawned a participatory culture which is interesting from the sociological and psychological point of view. In addition esthetic considerations in the creation of Wordles belong to the domain of art. So in addition to providing a summary of frequent words which can be seen as a exploratory text mining (an analytics activity) process, the Worldle reaches out to domains of Arts and Science such as sociology, psychology, and art.

References

Adams, S., N. Carter, C. Hadlock, D. Haughton and G. Sirbu (2006) 'a Recipe for Collaborative Research,' BizEd, 30–34, September/October.

Clauss, P., T. Roncalli and G. Weisang (2009) 'Risk Management Lessons from Madoff Fraud,' *International Finance Review*, vol. 10, ch. 17, J. J. Choi and M. Papaioannou (eds).

Collins, T., R. Laney, A. Willis and P. Garthwaite (2011) 'Chopin, mazurkas and Markov, Significance,' 8(4), pp. 154–159.

Davenport, T. and J. Harris (2007) 'Competing on Analytics,' Harvard Business School Press.

Davi, A., D. Haughton, N. Nasr, G. Shah, M. Skaletsky and R. Spack (2005) 'A Review of Two Text Mining Packages,' *American Statistician*, 59(1), pp. 89–103.

The *Economist* (2010), 'The Data Deluge,' http://www.economist.com/node/15579717.

The *Economist* (2012), 'The Ideas Economy; Big Data and the Evolution of Smart Systems,' http://ideas.economist.com/event/information-2012.

Fung, Glenn, Olvi Mangasarian, and John Jay (2003) 'The Disputed Federalist Papers: SVM Feature Selection via Concave Minimization,' in 'Proc. 2003 Conf. on Diversity in Computing,' ACM.

Haughton D. and J. Haughton (2011) *Living Standard Analytics*, (New York: Springer.)

Hoerl, R. and R. Snee (2012) 'Statistics Roundtable.' *Quality Progress*, June, 52–60.

IBM (2012), Smart Planet, http://www.ibm.com/smarterplanet/us/en/?ca=v_smarterplanet.

Li, T., M. Ogihara, and G. Tzanetakis (2012), *Music Data Mining* (Boca Raton: Chapman and Hall).

Manaris, B., P. Roos, D. Krehbiel T. Zalonis, and J. R. Armstrong, 'Zipf's Law, Power Laws and Music Aesthetics,' in Li et al. (eds), *Music Data Mining*.

McKinsey Global Institute (2011), 'Big Data: The Next Frontier for Innovation, Competition, and Productivity,' http://www.mckinsey.com/Insights/MGI/Research/Technology_and_Innovation/Big_data_The_next_frontier_for_innovation.

Nguyen, P., D. Haughton, I. Hudson, and J. Boland (2012), *Multilevel Models and Small Area Estimation in the Context of Vietnam Living Standards Surveys*, Preprint.

The R project (2012), http://www.r-project.org/.

Viégas, F., M. Wattenberg, and J. Feinberg (2009) 'Participatory Visualization With Wordle,' available at www.research.ibm.com/visual/papers/worldle_final2.pdf.

8
Transforming Business Education through Disciplinary Integration: The Case of Information Systems

Heikki Topi

It is easy to see business education as a domain governed by traditional business disciplines, such as accounting, economics, finance, management, and marketing. To make things even simpler, it is tempting to separate these from other professional disciplines (such as engineering, medicine, and law) and a very broad set of arts and sciences (A&S) disciplines. Business fields do, of course, acknowledge that A&S disciplines provide foundational knowledge (for example, psychology, social psychology, and sociology for management; mathematics and economics for finance). Ultimately, however, the core business disciplines have separate identities as the guardians of state-of-the-art theoretical and practical knowledge in specific areas of business. Business education, and particularly the power to make decisions regarding what belongs to business education and what does not, is seen as the prerogative of these disciplines.

The world is, of course, much more complex in practice. In addition to the disciplines that see themselves as pure 'business' and those clearly outside business, some disciplines have a boundary-spanning identity, one that intentionally brings together business and some other discipline(s) in a way that forms the core of the field.

One such 'integrative' discipline is Information Systems (IS). By its very nature, IS allows business and A&S disciplines to inform and transform each other, facilitating boundary-spanning and knowledge transfer between disciplines. By looking at how Information Systems does this, we can demonstrate the positive changes to business education that non-business disciplines bring.

Information Systems as an academic field

Information Systems is one of the five computing disciplines recognized by the three important professional and academic societies related to this area of study (ACM, AIS, and IEEE-CS; see Shackelford et al. 2005). In this context, IS is the discipline that focuses on the ability of information and computation to transform the way non-computing domains achieve their goals. It integrates content related to computing and at least one non-computing domain (see Figure 8.1, adapted from Topi et al., 2010). Historically, business has been by far the most common of the non-computing domains (Gorgone et al., 2003). The most dominant current work in Information Systems – whether research or teaching – takes place at schools of business/management. When IS researchers contribute to top journals outside their own discipline, these journals are very often in business (for example, in management, marketing, operations management, and accounting). The field has made a strong case for its critical role for business students (see, e.g., Ives et al., 2003).

At the same time, Information Systems clearly has an identity separate from business (Topi et al., 2010). This identity builds on capabilities that are most often associated with, on the one hand, computer science (particularly its focus on computational thinking) and, on the other hand, many social sciences, including psychology, social

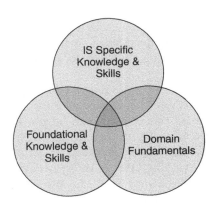

Figure 8.1　Integration of domain fundamentals with computing (IS) capabilities in Information Systems studies

Source: Adapted from Topi et al. (2010), © Association for Computing Machinery and Association for Information Systems.

psychology, and sociology. Figure 8.2 presents a framework that positions Information Systems in the context of A&S and business disciplines.

From the perspective of education, the Information Systems discipline is very clear about its integrative nature (Topi et al., 2010): educational programs in Information Systems always bring together core IS capabilities with a deep understanding of a domain (such as business, law, health care, government, etc.), applying IS capabilities with the purpose of advancing the practice within the domain. At its best, the relationship is symbiotic: Information Systems allows the domain to improve, while at the same time addressing the challenges of the domain forces Information Systems to push its own boundaries.

Key questions for IS academics

A large number of studies have analyzed the research in Information Systems to classify the discipline's core areas of expertise (for example, Alavi et al., 1989; Culnan, 1986; Swanson & Ramiller, 1993; Vessey et al., 2002; Sidorova et al. 2008; and Taylor et al., 2010). Sidorova et al. (2008) identify five core elements of the IS discipline:

- IT and organizations;
- IS development;

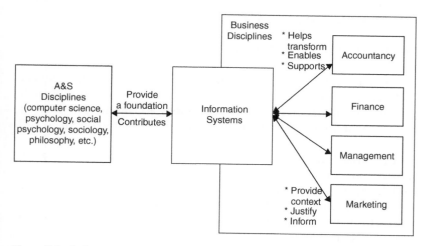

Figure 8.2   Information systems in the context of arts & sciences and business disciplines

- IT and individuals;
- IT and markets;
- IT and groups.

Taylor et al.'s (2010) analysis leads to a different three-category model of key themes within the discipline:

- research on development, implementation, and use of systems in various application domains;
- IS strategy and business outcomes;
- group work and decision support.

For our purposes, we will focus on three of these areas: IS development, IT and individuals (Sidorova et al., 2008), and the development, implementation, and use of systems (Taylor et al., 2010).

Sidorova et al. (2008) define IS development as an area that

> examines the information technology itself, and how it is developed. Here, the research tends to be more technical in nature, largely focusing on system functionality and/or the design of different types of systems such as decision support systems, expert systems, or databases. Also, development methodologies and approaches for performing IS development are examined, including prototyping, object-oriented methodologies as well as the use of programming and query languages. (p. 475)

They state that IT and individuals

> examines primarily psychological aspects of human-computer interactions; from its corresponding research themes, this research focuses primarily on individual technology acceptance, HR issues in IS, computer self-efficacy, end-user computing, and so on. (p. 475)

On the surface, these areas may seem the least directly linked to the business domain. However, they are the closest to other computing disciplines, and also depend on a number of 'reference disciplines' outside computing, including psychology, social psychology, and sociology. This helps to demonstrate the integrative nature of IS within the business/A&S matrix.

Information Systems attempts to address topics such as:

- the modeling of complex data and processes;
- using computational approaches for solving problems;
- designing architecturally solid concept structures;
- structuring, managing, and utilizing large amounts of stored data, information, and knowledge.

By definition, Information Systems is interested in applying these capabilities to the problems and opportunities within a real-world domain, such as business.

Reference disciplines of information systems

From its inception, Information Systems has depended heavily on a variety of 'reference disciplines' that have provided the field with theories, methods, and research practices. Culnan (1986) identified economics, political science, psychology, and sociology as 'underlying disciplines' and computer science, accounting and finance, management, and management science as 'related applied disciplines' (computer science would, in all likelihood, dispute this classification, but that is another story). Baskerville and Myers (2002, p. 3, Figure 1) suggested that the key reference disciplines for Information Systems are economics, architecture, engineering, computer science, and cognitive psychology.

The formal A&S field of 'computer science' (CS) is generally recognized as one of the most important reference disciplines of IS. Significant elements of IS content are closely linked to the formal discipline of CS, and IS education depends on it. The latest Information Systems reference curriculum (Topi et al., 2010) explicitly acknowledges that in areas such as programming fundamentals, algorithms and complexity, architecture and organization, and programming languages, IS borrows its body of knowledge from CS. In many areas (such as, for example, data management), IS has naturally also created its own, unique content, sometimes contributing to CS. In yet other areas of research, IS and CS have a very fruitful, symbiotic relationship (as suggested by Baskerville and Myers, 2002).

Computer science is not, of course, the only A&S reference discipline for IS. Many areas of IS are strongly dependent on theories and research methods of psychology, social psychology, sociology, and philosophy. This is true both for the content that is taught in IS courses and scholarly research in IS.

There are many examples of the close connection between IS and the A&S disciplines. For example, the Technology Acceptance Model (Davis, 1989; Davis et al., 1989), one of the best known and most often cited theories in IS, was originally presented as a variation of the theory of reasoned action (Fishbein and Ajzen, 1975) and benchmarked against it. Later technology adoption research has greatly benefited from the theory of planned behavior (TPB; Ajzen, 1991), innovation diffusion theory (Rogers 1995), and social cognitive theory (Bandura, 1986), as described by Venkatesh, Davis, and Morris, three leading IS scholars in the area of technology adoption (Venkatesh et al., 2007). IS research has, of course, modified and adapted these general theories to the IS/IT adoption context, but the foundational value of these core theories in key social sciences is undeniable for IS in general and for understanding IT adoption in specific.

In the area of information systems modeling, two highly prominent researchers, Yair Wand and Ron Weber, have built an entire research program on the foundation of Bunge's (1977) presentation of ontology in his groundbreaking *Treatise on Basic Philosophy*. They demonstrate how Bunge's concept of ontology can be applied in a useful way to areas as diverse as audit and controls of information systems, information systems design, review of the consistency and completeness of systems specifications, and decomposition of large-scale systems, among others (Wand and Weber, 1990). Overall, Wand and Weber have successfully utilized Bunge's work as a foundation for highest quality work in information systems for about a quarter of a century (from mid-1980s to the present day).

The relationship between IS and business education

There is a transformational symbiotic relationship between Information Systems and the traditional business disciplines, such as accountancy, finance, marketing, and operations management. IS data and process modeling, computational approaches, design science, and information management have had a profound impact on areas such as accounting information systems, computational/quantitative finance, database marketing, and service science and management. At the same time, the process of addressing business problems with IS tools has transformed our understanding of IS processes: modeling, computation, design, and information management.

In the same way, business education and information systems education are symbiotically connected. There are advanced areas in many core business disciplines that are very difficult, if not impossible, to understand fully without having a strong set of IS capabilities. Here are some key IS capabilities that are linked to recent advances in various business disciplines.

Computational thinking has received a lot of attention recently, not least because of the strong emphasis that the National Science Foundation (NSF) has given to it. Jeanette Wing, Jan Cuny, and Larry Snyder write that 'Computational thinking is the thought processes [sic] involved in formulating problems and their solutions so that the solutions are represented in a form that can be effectively carried out by an information-processing agent' (Wing et al., 2011).

A very important element in computational thinking is abstraction, which is a key component in developing capabilities for dealing with complexity. Computational thinking deals with abstraction of both processes (with algorithms) and data (with abstract data types). Students who are capable of thinking computationally are able to approach any complex problem effectively. They have a set of tools that allows them to separate essential from peripheral and express the essential so that it can be considered for automation and process transformation. A professional with a high level of computational skills and a deep understanding of a problem domain is well-prepared to contribute to positively transforming the domain.

In business, an example of this is quantitative or computational finance, a subfield of finance that integrates advanced computational methods, mathematics and statistics, and financial economics to create models for identifying trading and investment opportunities and for managing risk associated with those models. Despite the damage done to computational finance's reputation from the financial crisis of 2008, computational models continue to have a significant impact. Innovators in finance still need strong computational capabilities together with an excellent understanding of the domain itself.

Modeling complex systems is not only limited to traditional computational thinking. Information Systems continues to push the boundaries of knowledge in the modeling of complex systems at all levels of abstraction. For example, systems analysis and design focuses on understanding and transforming processes; data management focuses on understanding and representing the entities an organization is interested in and their relationships. Both can help businesses model and design complex organizational phenomena, expressing the models in a way that non-experts can verify them, and transforming the abstract domain models into a design model form that can easily be expressed with computing technology.

At the level of business processes, these modeling activities can be considered as part of any business professional's core skills set, as acknowledged by the emergence of business process design and management in business school curricula. The fundamental process management capabilities are essentially the same regardless of the level of the model's abstraction. A business professional skilled in systems analysis and design and conceptual data modeling is very well prepared for analysis and transformative redesign of business processes. This is particularly true because a professional with Information Systems education is particularly capable of understanding the opportunities that technology provides on the basis of her in-depth knowledge of the systems themselves.

Understanding and managing information. Information processing is an essential part of any functional business discipline. The recent phenomenon of 'big data,' and the need to make sense of it, has only intensified the need for professionals with strong skills in structuring and analyzing data. In a recent survey, the *Economist* described data as 'new raw material of business,' continuing that it is 'an economic input almost on a par with capital and labour' (*Economist*, 2010, pp. 3–5). Skills that improve an individual's capabilities in understanding, managing, and using information for analytical purposes are now highly useful for a business major, regardless of one's specialty.

Examples abound. Marketing analytics, for instance, have radically evolved due to the increased availability and systematic use of data. While 'database marketing' started in the 1980s (e.g., Cespedes & Smith, 1993), recent advances allow activities such as large-scale analysis of current, prospective, and prior customer behavior and preferences to drive marketing decisions. And of course, the advent of traceable online purchasing, customer engagement, and other modern marketing methods would not be possible without deep analysis and acting on data.

Accounting, and particularly auditing and forensic accounting (Janvrin et al., 2008), are highly dependent on in-depth understanding of how information is stored and structured in organizations. It is impossible to fully understand accounting in modern organizations without understanding the systems that are used for this purpose, and particularly the ways these systems store, secure, and disseminate data.

Designing and implementing functioning artifacts. One of the capability sets that studies in Information Systems intend to develop is the design and implementation of functioning artifacts based on a set of well-defined specifications. This may sound trivial, but building things that need to work is actually quite rare in business studies (and in higher education in general, except in engineering, architecture, and computer science). This set of experiences is very useful across the spectrum of functional areas in business. The experience of designing and building something new that needs to perform in a verifiable way gives an acute appreciation of the complexities related to creating things from scratch, compared to just reading about the construction process or only creating an abstract model. Almost invariably, core courses in Information Systems (including those in data management, systems development, and systems analysis and design) include both assignments and projects that require the students to build a software artifact according to a set of specifications. These exercises oblige the students to focus on details and verify operational logic in a way that is rare elsewhere in the business curriculum.

Building functioning systems is typically much more time-consuming than (particularly novice) actors in the processes expect. Also, it often comes as a total surprise to the actors how many different types of sources of errors exist as potential obstacles for making something fully functional, even in the case of relatively simple systems. Building a functioning system also illustrates how important it is to understand how the components of a system are interconnected and how a problem in one part of a system is quickly reflected elsewhere. Another lesson to learn from a system construction process is the difficulty of creating something based on (written) specifications.

One area of business that can greatly benefit from increased understanding of what it takes to build functioning systems is service science, management, and engineering (SSME). Within the business school context, SSME-types of initiatives in most cases take place in the operations management groups. According to Spohrer (2008), 'service research addresses the challenges of improving the quality, productivity, regulatory compliance and sustainable innovation of service systems.' Service science is not only focused on research but is an important area in education, too. For an aspiring practitioner, it is highly beneficial to experience the challenges of implementing a system with the potential to radically improve the quality and productivity of service provision.

Information Systems as an intermediary between A&S disciplines and business

Modern businesses are very complex. Understanding processes and concept structures through advanced modeling, solving challenging problems with computational methods, designing elegant architectures, and structuring information for use at multiple levels of decision making are all essential capabilities. The study of Information Systems develops all these capabilities (and many others); at the same time, they are all based on one or several A&S disciplines and integrated by scholars and professionals in IS. To summarize some of these A&S disciplines, computational thinking is largely based on computer science, mathematics, and logic; modeling complex systems has its foundations in philosophy and particularly ontology; mathematics, computer science, and philosophy underlie the principles of understanding and managing information; and the processes of designing and building functioning artifacts require a rich variety of creative, communication, and computational capabilities.

In education, one essential role of Information Systems is to integrate the areas in which it itself creates new knowledge with relevant areas from other fields of study (such as computer science), and then apply these integrated capability sets to practical problems from real-world domains. Business as a whole and functional business areas specifically are excellent examples of these domains, which not only have benefited from these capabilities but also have been, and continue to be, transformed by them.

Lessons to learn

Traditional core business disciplines are not sufficient for building a strong foundational set of capabilities for success in modern business. Problems in business are large-scale, complex, and integrative in nature, as are the emergent opportunities that create new ways of doing business. Solving the problems and benefiting from the opportunities almost invariably requires the use of capabilities that are based on A&S disciplines, either directly or through integrative disciplines such as Information Systems. Acquiring a strong background in A&S disciplines is, of course, important for a variety of reasons, many of which are entirely independent of preparation for business. Our claim is, however, that the capabilities that A&S disciplines provide are critically important for operating successfully in any business context. If one's intent is to identify what a good preparation for business needs, the capabilities created by the study of A&S disciplines should have a central role in the process.

Disciplines that are intentionally integrative in nature, such as Information Systems, are an excellent mechanism for introducing the A&S capabilities into business education. Information Systems creates opportunities for students to apply a large range of capabilities based on A&S disciplines in an integrated way to interesting and challenging business problems. Abilities to structure and solve problems computationally, to understand and find the information that is and is not available for decision making, and to work in groups to build functioning systems according to specifications are not esoteric technical skills; they are vital capabilities for building successful organizations.

It is essential that successful business education operates across traditional disciplinary and structural boundaries. This does not only consist of help and support that non-business disciplines provide to business but genuine desire for faculty members to engage their students in activities that require expertise from a rich variety of disciplinary backgrounds. Projects with an emphasis on Information Systems offer exciting opportunities for creating these trans-disciplinary processes. In them, the focus should not be on solving technical problems but on how the integrative and transformative capabilities of computation and data management can be used to address needs of organizations or individuals in a way that helps them achieve their business/organizational goals.

References

Ajzen, I. (1991) 'The Theory of Planned Behavior,' *Organizational Behavior and Human Decision Processes*, 50(2), pp. 179–211.

Alavi, Maryam, P. Carlson, and G. Brooke (1989) 'Ecology of mis Research: a Twenty Year Status Review,' pp. 363–375. Presented at the International Conference on Information Systems, Boston, MA, USA.

Bandura, A. (1986) *Social Foundations of Thought and Action: A Social Cognitive Theory* (Englewood Cliffs, NJ: Prentice-Hall).

Baskerville, R.L. and M. D. Myers (2002) 'Information Systems as a Reference Discipline,' *MIS Quarterly*, 26(1), pp. 1–14.

Bunge, M. (1977) *Treatise on Basic Philosophy: Vol. 3 Ontology I: The Furniture of the World* (Boston: Reidel).

Cespedes, F. V., and H. J. Smith (1993) 'Database Marketing: New Rules for Policy and Practice,' *Sloan Management Review*, 34(4), pp. 125–143.

Culnan, M. J. (1986) 'The Intellectual Development of Management Information Systems, 1972–1982: A Co-Citation Analysis,' *Management Science*, 32(2), pp. 156–172.

Davis, F. D. (1989) 'Perceived Usefulness, Perceived Ease of Use, and User Acceptance of Information Technology,' *MIS Quarterly*, 13(3), pp. 319–340.

Davis, F. D., R. P. Bagozzi, and P. R. Warshaw (1989) 'User Acceptance of Computer Technology: a Comparison of Two Theoretical Models,' *Management Science*, 35(8), pp. 982–1003.

The *Economist* (2010). 'Data, Data Everywhere,' *The Economist*, 394(8671), pp. 3–5.

Fishbein, M. and I. Ajzen (1975) *Belief, Attitude, Intention, and Behavior: An Introduction to Theory and Research* (Reading, MA: Addison-Wesley).

Gorgone, J.T., G. B. Davis, J. S. Valacich, H. Topi, D. L. Feinstein, and H. E. Longenecker Jr. (2003) 'is 2002: Model Curriculum and Guidelines for Undergraduate Degree Programs in Information Systems,' *Database for Advances in Information Systems*, 34(1), pp. 1–52.

Ives, B., J. S. Valacich, R. Watson, and R. Zmud (2003) 'What Every Business Student Needs to Know about Information Systems,' *Communications of the Association for Information Systems*, 11(1), pp. 467–477.

Janvrin, D., J. Bierstaker, and D. J. Lowe (2008) 'An Examination of Audit Information Technology Use and Perceived Importance,' *Accounting Horizons*, 22(1), pp. 1–21.

Rogers, E. M. (1995) *Diffusion of Innovations* (New York: Free Press).

Shackelford, R., J. H. Cross, G. Davies, J. Impagliazzo, R. Kamali, R. LeBlanc, B. Lunt et al. (2005) Computing Curricula 2005 – The Overview Report. Retrieved January 23, 2012 from www.acm.org/education/curric_vols/CC2005-March06Final.pdf.

Sidorova, A., N. Evangelopoulos, J. S. Valacich, and T. Ramakrishnan (2008) 'Uncovering the Intellectual Core of the Information Systems Discipline,' *MIS Quarterly*, 32(3), 467-A20.

Spohrer, J. (2008). Interview of Jim Spohrer, July 28. Retrieved January 23, 2012 from http://www-07.ibm.com/ph/ssmeconference/pdf/Open.pdf

Swanson, E.B. and N. C. Ramiller (1993) 'Information Systems Research Thematics: Submissions to a New Journal, 1987–1992,' *Information Systems Research*, 4(4), pp. 299–330.

Taylor, H., S. Dillon, and M. Van Wingen (2010) 'Focus and Diversity in Information Systems Research: Meeting the Dual Demands of a Healthy Applied Discipline,' *MIS Quarterly*, 34(4), pp. 647–447.

Topi, H., J. S. Valacich, R. T. Wright, K. Kaiser, Nunamaker, J. F., J. C. Sipior, and G. J. de Vreede (2010) 'IS 2010: Curriculum Guidelines for Undergraduate Degree Programs in Information Systems,' *Communications of the Association for Information Systems*, 26(18). Retrieved January 23, 2012 from http://aisel.aisnet.org/cais/vol26/iss1/18.

Venkatesh, V., F. D. Davis, and M. G. Morris (2007) 'Dead Or Alive? The Development, Trajectory And Future Of Technology Adoption Research,' *Journal of the Association for Information Systems*, 8(4), pp. 268–286.

Vessey, I., V. Ramesh, and R. L. Glass (2002) 'Research in Information Systems: An Empirical Study of Diversity in the Discipline and Its Journals,' *Journal of Management Information Systems*, 19(2), pp. 129–174.

Wand, Y. and R. Weber (1990) Mario Bunge's Ontology as a Formal Foundation for Information Systems Concepts. *Studies on Mario Bunge's Treatise, Poznan Studies in the Philosophy of the Sciences and Humanities* (p. 720). Amsterdam; Atlanta, GA: Editions Rodopi B V.

Wing, J., J. Cuny, and L. Snyder (2011) 'Computational Thinking – What and Why?' Retrieved January 23, 2012 from http://link.cs.cmu.edu/article. php?a=600

Part III
The Arts & Sciences Perspective

9
Change over Time: The Study of the Past and the Future of Business Education

Chris Beneke

Why would someone enrolled at a business school study history? The reasons may not be self-evident. On the surface, history is a manifestly impractical subject, earning a spot on a 2012 '13 Most Useless Majors' survey (Carnevale et al.; *The Daily Beast*, 2012). A student who completes a history course, a concentration in history, or even an entire history major, may not be well prepared to conduct an audit, trade stocks, build a house, repair an air conditioning system, or treat an ailing patient. Given such limitations, the professionally oriented undergraduate may perceive required history courses as a prerequisite leading to nowhere or even an obstruction on the road to a career in business. Tuition-wary parents may likewise view it as a vestigial piece of an outdated and prohibitively expensive educational ideal.

For their part, historians trained at traditional liberal arts institutions may be just as unenthused about the prospect of teaching at business colleges and universities. The fact that business schools require continual demonstrations of contemporary relevance – no small task for a scholar whose expertise resides in the study of non-contemporary people, events, and places – is an underlying source of aversion. Confronted by the demand to relate the past to the present, to convert the rich experience of those who lived before us into easily digested lessons for the modern manager, the history professor may be tempted to fall back on L.P. Hartley's dictum that 'the past is a like a foreign country: they do things differently there.' Of course, such rumpled musings might in turn prompt the thoughtful student to ponder why he didn't simply register for another international studies course where he would study actual foreign countries.

But history's presence at business universities is not as anomalous as skeptics on both sides of the lecture podium sometimes suggest. Consider this fact of post-graduate life: the early careers pursued by history majors from comprehensive university or liberal arts colleges fall into roughly the same patterns as those pursued by business majors at professional schools. While slightly more than one in ten history majors move directly into education, an overwhelming majority land in business (Carnevale, et al., 2012). In other words, even history programs with robust majors are generally not training students to teach or conduct advanced historical research. Like historians at dedicated business schools, they are mostly preparing students for professional careers, and, more often than not, business careers.

The question, then, is what kind of preparation does historical study offer to business students? Despite the protests of career-directed undergraduates and the misgivings of corporate-wary faculty, it may be the very best kind of preparation. Taught well, history students gain insight into the deep arts of cross-cultural negotiation, the alluring possibilities of revolutionary innovation, and the daunting obstacles to substantive change. History also enriches business education by safeguarding against excessive confidence in our abilities and with cautions against the transient certainties of the present. While these are important to a broad spectrum of pursuits, including good citizenship itself, they are critical to business education. The rigorous study of the past cultivates habits of thought that are vital for leadership in organizations where creativity must be continuously reconciled with constraint.

History's contribution to business education might be imagined along two axes. On the vertical axis, historical study allows students to drill down (especially through the use of historical texts, visual images, maps, and material artifacts) into the origins and trajectory of beliefs and practices that they take for granted. It allows them to see how change occurs, how the residue of decisions accumulates, how obstacles emerge, and opportunities subtly assert themselves. On the horizontal axis, history broadens intellectual and moral horizons by cultivating students' capacity to derive substantive meaning from the ever-changing and the unfamiliar, bringing into view the irreducible particularity of their own cultural situation and its tangled connection to other times and places.

In short, history involves meticulous attention to the mechanics of *change over time*. It points us to the sometimes inscrutable interaction of causal forces and human intentions, as well as the threads of continuity and nodes of discontinuity, that have woven our world into a complex tapestry of old and new. In the process, history offers training in grounded empathy – the ability to recognize something analogous in another community of people, coupled with an understanding of the social conditions and traditions that have made their experience so different. These are skills essential for the student who will go on to become a business professional, and a citizen.

The deep dive: historical change and contextual understanding

Few clichés are as enduringly mocked as the limp observation that 'The world is changing.' Yet a kernel of truth resides within that pedestrian husk. The world does often resemble a great, churning mass of technological, economic, social, political, and environmental adjustment. But this is itself nothing new. Almost any previous generation could have presented its own resume of social and commercial adaptation. History puts those earlier changes in context and, by doing so, lends cognitive order to otherwise unfathomable tumult. Historical study has particular value for those who need to tease out the underlying social, economic, and political currents that propel waves of disruptive change through the world. It offers models both for blunting their impact and capitalizing on the opportunities that emerge in their wake.

Just as it makes the velocity of global change more comprehensible, history can also point us to the unremarkable continuity of ordinary life. This too is essential for business education. Indeed, at nearly every turn in our daily existence we encounter mundane demonstrations of how cultural forms can be frozen or at least slowed to an apparent standstill. The ideas, practices, institutions that frame our choices and behavior are often quite sticky. Consider the 3.5-inch floppy disk symbol that represents electronic storage on most computer interfaces. One would be hard-pressed to squeeze more than a single digital music file on one of those old plastic disks. But the symbol persists, as does the imaginative residue of the technology itself. Or consider the dial tone sound that still reverberates from landlines and cell phones decades after the disappearance of the dial itself. The effect of these technological vestiges are minimal and innocuous but they nonetheless offer stark reminders of the past's grip.

Indeed, in countless grand and quotidian ways, our choices are framed by the changes that occurred – and the changes that did not occur – in the years that preceded us. This applies to the world historical impact of judicial decisions, military actions, and financial turmoil as much as it does the ephemera of 1990s computer interface design and handheld communications. 'The past is never dead,' William Faulkner observed, 'it's not even past.' History bears upon us every minute of the day. A business decision-maker who fails to appreciate the force of old habits and the ubiquity of economically irrational behavior is at a perilous disadvantage.

One of history's tasks is to foster an appreciation of what happens when innovative ideas and practices meet the inertia of ingrained habits. We need only consult the case of nineteenth-century feminists such as Elizabeth Cady Stanton and Susan B. Anthony, who confronted centuries of hardened gender norms. It was difficult for contemporaries to countenance women publicly addressing men, let alone addressing men in public on behalf of women's rights. The back-and-forth of argument, organization, and legal revision continued for decades before white American women first gained the suffrage in a handful of western U.S. states. Some aspects of this change were accretive and continuous, some disruptive and intermittent; some appear to have been promoted by the parallel cause of African American rights and some hindered by it. The process of reform was neither regular nor easily mapped, but it is precisely that bracing mixture of the abstract and the concrete, the known and the unknown, that makes history so instructive to a business student.

Moving from the study of the past to the anticipation of the future is no more straightforward. The *pro forma* stipulation that past performance is no guarantee of future results holds here as well. Despite the popular admonition that those who forget the past are doomed to repeat it, even a careful study of the past does not yield reliable predictions about the future. If anything, historical study reminds us how difficult the future is to anticipate, let alone shape. By tracing the contours of change over time, historical study allows us to take a measure of our broader situation and the possibilities for improving the past we have inherited. History helps us apprehend that the societies we encounter across the globe are moving 'targets,' ever-evolving and ever in need of reinterpretation.

Anticipating what lies ahead is another matter. History yields no certainties, unless we count the certainty that change will occur and that it will most assuredly be complex. Like the actuary, the historian works with multi-variables. But historical inquiry offers no algorithms and few useful estimates of risk or liability. Though the occasional treaty, election, congressional vote, executive order, natural disaster, or military victory has direct, traceable, and even partially quantifiable effects, the forces of history are too diffuse to serve predictive value. They provide wisdom rather than forecasts, projecting possible outcomes given the cumulative experience of human beings over a long period of time. Such an amassing of common sense may perhaps make it more likely that actual outcomes are aligned with projected outcomes. It will more reliably reinforce our awareness of the tendency that the projected and the actual invariably diverge.

Whatever the practical impact of strategic plans, historical methods should help professionals formulate them. Historian, business consultant, and former Sensitech CEO Eric Schultz observes that strategic planners and historians both 'sift through mountains of information, separate signal from noise, find a coherent pattern in the signal, and then tell a story about how it is all meaningful to the present' (Schultz, 2009). These empirical and narrative-oriented skills can be cultivated in other fields as well. But they represent a special area of historical expertise. Understanding how different conclusions can be drawn from the same evidence, how different forms of evidence can be selected depending on the end, and understanding how more persuasive interpretations developed, are essential parts of historical learning. Appreciating the causes and scale of the 2008 financial meltdown, for instance, is impossible without the ability to discern patterns of behavior and decision-making that took place over long spans of time by individuals with very different obligations, interests, and motivations – precious few of whom saw the crisis coming. Tracing the complex interaction of forces such as these is an especially powerful way to demonstrate both the possibilities for deliberate action and the limits of human apprehension.

The broad view: history as grounded empathy

If history deepens, it also broadens, both intellectually and morally. Again, the end is shared with other disciplines. It is the means that are distinctive. Poring over slave ship manifests or examining first-hand accounts of early modern witchcraft trials presents a stark picture of how the world could be lived and imagined differently. The very strangeness of these artifacts helps us appreciate that human expression is always inflected, if not determinedly shaped, by widely varying contexts. Only through rigorous historical study can we adequately

appreciate how the contemporary world emerged from a concate-
nation of circumstances, by accident and purpose in an unceasing
train of decisions that produced one unanticipated consequence after
another.

Sorting familiar aspects of the past from the unfamiliar provides a
sense of how, what scientist Robert Wright calls, the 'circle of moral
consideration' has expanded, and sometimes contracted, over time.
And it suggests how it might expand again (Wright, 2009, p. 26). The
notion that business is compatible with a robust sense of social responsibility dates at least to the nineteenth century. Andrew Carnegie's
influential *Gospel of Wealth* (1889) opens with a brief account of
western world's revolutionary transformation from widely shared
pre-industrial squalor to the generally improved, highly segmented,
and newly unequal conditions of the industrial age. For Carnegie, this
historically conditioned development imposed substantive obligations – especially to provide charity and cultural uplift – upon those
who found themselves at the top of the sharply inclined modern social
pyramid. A similar sentiment is conveyed by Jacob Marley's lament
on his narrow, pecuniary existence in Charles Dickens' *A Christmas
Carol* (1843). Assured by Ebenezer Scrooge that he was 'a good man of
business,' Marley's spirit bellows, 'Business! ... Mankind was my business. The common welfare was my business; charity, mercy, forbear-
ance, and benevolence, were all, my business. The dealings of my trade
were but a drop of water in the comprehensive ocean of my business!'
Once we get beyond the extravagant sentimentality here, it is not hard
to discern the salient point for business education, which is that the
full scope and responsibility of business practice manifests itself in the
reflective study of the past.

The notion that the 'comprehensive ocean' of your business should
take priority over the everyday workings of your business will no doubt
meet a cool reception from many students. A sizeable majority enroll
in a business college with the intention of earning prodigious sums of
money, or at least enjoying comfortable post-graduate lives. They are
generally not seeking moral redemption. But if they are to do good
work on behalf of their companies and avoid doing (at least direct)
harm to others in the process, they must appreciate the 'comprehensive
ocean' of their business. An historically enriched, contextual understanding of their business is critical to that end. Marley's lament might
seem like a way of restating the popular claim that arts and sciences
subjects prepare students for something called 'global citizenship.' The

point that this well-intentioned catchphrase misses – and the point that any education shorn of historical understanding misses – is that an acquaintance with current events and cultural particularities is a necessary but not sufficient condition for understanding global change and the burdens that the present imposes on the future. For that, they need history.

History as stakeholder theory

In the context of business education, historical study might be best conceived as an extended lesson in stakeholder theory. A chief task for historians is to survey the full circumference of consequences that past decisions produced, to account for the complex externalities of past choices and identify free riders (those who derive direct, uncompensated benefit from public goods). Like stakeholder theory, history identifies the cross-generational communities which must reckon with our decisions, while drawing attention to the potential lessons that future generations might draw from our own example.

Our business practices have illuminating precedents in earlier ages, as do our social concerns. The consumer who craves sleek electronics but is concerned about working conditions in the Chinese electronics industry has her counterpart in the antebellum U.S. social reformers who refused to purchase products made from slave-picked cotton or slave-harvested sugarcane. Both were/are conscious of how seemingly harmless consumer choices and business decisions affect distant others. Historical study draws these connections, accounting for the unpredictable residue of change, the unanticipated impact of decisions made, actions taken, and the haunting silence of those never heard from.

Among the core insights of behavioral economics is that we esteem those things we have lost more than we do those very same things we have gained. Most of the time (perhaps out of sheer psychological necessity) we proceed without an immediate cognition of what was lost or foregone in earlier ages. By bringing to view the changes that accrue to whole societies over time, history extends this fundamental psychological mechanism and thereby illuminates the intrinsic value of those 'inefficient' elements of social or natural life, such as landscapes, regional customs, and traditional work routines that present obstacles to short-term economic development.

All of this is to better appreciate that 'creative destruction' is still destruction. If history underlines the necessity of some kinds of change, it also cautions against change for change's sake. Some proverbial 'boxes' (outside of which we are dogmatically encouraged to think) are the residue of defunct ideas and outdated practices. Others make every-day work possible (*Inside Higher Ed*, 2011). Routine gestures and long-tried procedures are often essential for the smooth functioning of organizations, economies, and societies at large, even to a meaningful experience of freedom itself. We literally cannot cross the street without them. History helps the business student appreciate their humble efficacy.

That said, some considerations elude calculations of marginal utility entirely. It is possible, for example, to roughly calculate the economic costs of racial segregation in the U.S. for a century after the Civil War. It is much more difficult to estimate its symbolic and moral significance. Likewise, religious rituals and patriotic ceremonies are not preserved simply because altering them would be expensive. Maintaining or abandoning traditions cannot be usefully described in terms of gains or losses in exchange value. There are gains and losses that aren't measurable in any conventional sense. Some changes reverberate immediately in the soul, and some in the decades that follow. Some do both. The same caveats about predicting the future on the basis of the past apply to calculations of the remote (temporal and geographical) effects of our decisions. Nonetheless, as any environmental historian could attest, myopia, indifference, and sheer callousness have their greatest effects over long periods of time.

Such considerations may not, of course, yield immediate profit to individuals or businesses. The benefits of historical study, as with all elements of liberal education, clearly exceed their professional utility. There is a surplus of public value that results from the historically infused business education. We do not know in what fields our students will ultimately end up. What we do know is that they will all be citizens. As non-profit institutions, business universities also have an obligation to prepare students for responsibilities that lie outside the pecuniary, that is, for the 'comprehensive ocean' of their business.

History and the business school curriculum

If there is a compelling case to be made for history's essential contribution to a rigorous and morally responsible business education, how exactly should it fit into the curriculum? A student who took 40 courses in history over the course of his college career would not be especially welcome in an accounting firm. Yet nor would the student who took 40 accounting courses. Even the most pragmatic of students recognizes the need for some educational range. So do employers who regularly mention 'a diverse educational background ... as a requisite for promotion' (*Inside Higher Ed*, 2011). Conventional apologists for liberal arts education concede little, if anything, to professional preparation. They have their counterpart in the business colleges that offer little in the way of liberal arts education beyond some remedial training in social studies. Bentley's Liberal and Business Studies majors (discussed elsewhere in this volume) offer one viable model for bridging the gap between these antagonistic positions.

The question of how much history business-oriented students need to prepare themselves for lives as professionals and citizens can't be answered in the abstract. With more assurance we can say that history complements the training offered in other fields. Rooted in the intensive use of primary documents, historians generally shy away from the deductive method favored in the social sciences as well as the case studies favored in business disciplines. Just as importantly, historical research is generally done in busy, reflective solitude. Culling meaning from historical texts demands unusually protracted stretches of attention, as well as sustained exercises of imagination – in other words, long periods alone with data and words. Extensive collaboration on projects is one of the great benefits of undergraduate business education. But there are diminishing marginal returns. Those returns may be further diminished by the fact that, as Richard Arum and Josipa Roksa note, teamwork encourages students to continually serve in the same capacity (as the writer, the accountant, the marketing guru, etc.) (Arum and Roksa, 2011). By contrast, the student working alone is usually forced to deploy a wider range of skills, as well as having to imaginatively conjure other minds and other perspectives.

Given that the time most business students spend in history classes will be limited, course content matters more than it might otherwise. A possibility entertained at seemingly every professional college and university is to teach the history of the dominant subject matter. Some business universities offer courses on the history of business, labor, and technology that promote serious reflection on the entwining of commercial enterprises and the societies in which they are embedded. At other institutions, students can take more focused courses on the history of advertising and international finance. And no doubt one could design parallel courses on the history of corporate accounting, interface design, or business law. However, narrowing historical study to that degree surely runs the danger of reducing university education to self-study, turning history's deepening purpose against its broadening function.

If the predominant concerns of historical researchers and the predominant concern of undergraduate business majors sometimes seem hopelessly divergent, historians can take comfort in the fact that their subject is preeminently accessible and can be approached at many levels of analysis. With work, it can be made as compelling to the business student enrolled in an introductory history course as it is to the business professional lugging the latest David McCullough tome onto an airplane. Alongside the narrative accounts of war, escape, and natural disaster and epic, celebrity-like biographies are the historical books that purport to explain 'how' something came into being – *How the Irish Saved Civilization; How the Daughters of Genghis Khan Rescued His Empire; How Climate Made History, 1300–1850*, for example. The search for the sources of our modern world is clearly a line of inquiry that grabs non-specialized readers and can be lashed to still more edifying enterprises within the university.

There are ideological gaps between right-leaning students and left-leaning historians at business universities that could also benefit from some conscious bridging. The emphasis on stakeholders in elite business programs occasionally obscures the fact that stockholders also have legitimate interests and that concerns about the security of property, the sanctity of family, and communal dignity cannot be written off as the bigoted expression of the privileged. Honestly and actively engaging with students at a business university means finding common ground. One has to take the *Wall Street Journal* and Milton Friedman seriously as intellectual sources if a useful conversation about the past is to take place with free market-leaning students. And while the history graduate should be as well trained as any graduate in the identification of fools and the exposure of idiocy, she should also be aware of the many instances when the fool has been on the right side of history and orthodoxy has been unceremoniously turned on its head.

*   *   *

The challenge of teaching history to business students is hardly a singular one. The rigorous study of the past is not something that every person, let alone every 18-year-old, takes to without encouragement. It may ultimately represent, what Sam Wineburg (2001) terms, 'an unnatural act'. In general, humans possess a strong inclination to compress the distance between themselves and earlier generations by rendering earlier subjects in familiar hues or by simply focusing on recent events. But this presentist tendency does seem particularly acute among business students. That is understandable. After all, the corporate earnings that matter are those earned in 2012, not 1912. Historians at business colleges and universities thus have a special obligation to counter the tendency that events have to recede from view. It is their job to bring earlier developments into focus, qualifying the seeming novelty of the present (as well as the alluring prospect of the future), and offering the expansive perspective that builds through the empirical study of other people and times.

By diving deeply into the origins of beliefs, practices, and institutions that are ordinarily taken for granted, historical training renders the current situation less mysterious and the distant implications of actions less remote. It better equips students to do good in their work and on behalf of the larger world by instilling their education with the perspective that comes with a chronologically expansive social, political, and economic context, one attentive to both the wisdom offered by the past and to the judgments that will be rendered the future.

References

Anthony P. Carnevale, Jeff Strohl, and Michelle Melton (2011), 'What's It Worth? The Economic Value of College Majors,' Georgetown University Center for Education and the Workforce, http://www.agu.org/education/pdf/whatsitworth-complete.pdf (Accessed: May 8, 2012).

Arum, Richard and Roksa, Josipa (2011), *Academically Adrift: Limited Learning on College Campuses* (Chicago: University of Chicago Press).

Curti, Merle (1959) *The Social Ideas of American Educators* (Paterson, NJ: Pageant Books), p. 516.

The Daily Beast 'The 13 Most Useless Majors, From Philosophy to Journalism' *The Daily Beast* http://www.thedailybeast.com/galleries/2012/04/23/the-13-most-useless-majors-from-philosophy-to-journalism.html (Accessed: April 28, 2012).

'Major Decisions,' Inside Higher Ed (May 24, 2011), http://www.insidehighered.com/news/2011/05/24/georgetown_study_of_salaries_for_different_majors_finds_big_discrepancy_women_and_minorities_in_low_paying_fields (Accessed on May 24, 2011).

Schultz, Eric B. (2009) 'Why Historians Make Superb Strategists (and Other Self-Serving Notions)' (November 21): http://theoccasionalceo.blogspot.com/2009/11/why-historians-make-superb-strategists.html, accessed: May 8, 2012.

Wineburg, Samuel (2001). *Historical Thinking and Other Unnatural Acts: Charting the Future of Teaching the Past* (Philadelphia: Temple University Press).

Wright, Robert (2009) *The Evolution of God* (New York: Little, Brown and Company), p. 26 and ff. See also Yerxa, Don (ed.) (2012), *British Abolitionism and the Question of Moral Progress in History* (Columbia: University of South Carolina Press).

10
The Need to Read

Joan L. Atlas

Traditionally, business education has had a narrow focus. Students learn a specific set of skills that enables them to enter the corporate world and help their employers function effectively, i.e., help them make money. In turn, they will be rewarded – with money. But today's world is fraught with complexity and constant, rapid change – environmental, economic, technological, and social – and businesses are looking for more from their employees.

In addition, many students realize that there is more to life than financial security. Events such as the 9/11/2001 terrorist attacks and Hurricane Katrina, for example, have impelled hundreds of thousands of students to contribute their time, energy, and talents to trying to solve some of the countless problems they see around them.

In the classroom, however, many business students are still focused on acquiring expertise in their field of study. They have little curiosity and little appreciation for the broad range of subjects included in the arts and sciences. They tend to be 'A to Z' students who have no interest in veering from the straight path, and thus little interest in questioning who they are and what their place in the world should be. Thus, even when business students are required to take arts and sciences classes, and even when they enjoy those classes, their reading often does not go beyond what is required – and it perhaps does not even include that, as many students find ways to avoid required reading.

This issue is not unique to business students; across the board, a high percentage of young people are not reading for pleasure.

In November 2007, the National Endowment for the Arts issued a research report entitled *To Read or Not to Read: A Question of National Consequence*. The findings were striking. For instance, the report stated that '[n]early half of all Americans ages 18 to 24 read no books for pleasure.' The report also stated that while the amount that 17-year-olds 'read for school or homework...has stayed the same' over the past 20 years, '[t]he percentage of 17-year-olds who read nothing at all for pleasure has doubled' during this same period, And '15- to 24-year-olds spend only 7 to 10 minutes per day on voluntary reading – about 60 percent less time than the average American.' Moreover, the report stated that when young people do read, they often do so while using other media, sharing their reading time with 'TV-watching, video/ computer game-playing, instant messaging, e-mailing or Web surfing,' all of which suggests 'less focused engagement with a text.' Since this report was written before texting, Facebook, and Twitter came into the lives of young people, the sharing of reading time with other media could only have increased. Another significant finding is that while '[r] eading test scores for 9-year-olds – who show no declines in voluntary reading – are at an all-time high,' reading scores of 17-year-olds 'began a slow downward trend in 1992.'

A more recent (2009) National Endowment for the Arts report, 'Reading on the Rise: A New Chapter in American Literacy,' sounds a more promising note. Claiming improvements due to the efforts of educators, librarians, civic leaders, and parents, the report stated that the downward trend has been reversed, with the result that in the 2008 Survey of Public Participation in the Arts, there was a 'decisive and unambiguous increase [in literary reading] among virtually every group.' But when we take a closer look at the NEA's enthusiastic pronouncement, we see that close to half of all adults in the United States are not reading. For 18- to 24-year-olds, the percentage of readers in 2008 was 51.7 percent; in contrast, in 1982 this percentage was 59.8 percent. To be sure, 2008 marked a significant increase from 42.8 percent of 18- to 24-year-olds reading in 2002, but a significant problem obviously still exists.

Why does this matter? *To Read or Not to Read* makes it clear that reading for pleasure is related to better reading and writing skills, and that this translates to higher grades and academic achievement. This in turn relates to personal, professional, and social outcomes: 'deficient readers run higher risks of failure in all three areas' (p. 14). These findings are not new, as other studies have noted the connection between reading and 'degrees earned, adult income and occupational status' (Richardson and Eccles, 2007, p. 341). Therefore, even considering only the more narrow goals of degree attainment, economic security, and professional success, reading is essential, and must be promoted and expected as part of any college education, including one focused on business.

But the value of reading extends far beyond practical life skills. As philosopher Allan Bloom put it, 'The failure to read good books both enfeebles the vision and strengthens our most fatal tendency – the belief that the here and now is all there is' (1987, p. 64). Bloom aptly describes what is occurring among young Americans, who are focused only on getting a high grade point average, getting their degree, and getting ahead. But the opposite inference is the key: reading good books – whether fiction or nonfiction – widens our perspective on ourselves and others, helps us to learn and grow, and enriches our lives.

As my son's second-grade teacher explained it so succinctly, literature – and this is equally true of nonfiction – is about making connections: text to text, text to self, and text to world. When we read a book, assuming we are focused on it, we are drawn into the text and engage with it, and we start to think: this book reminds me of another book, or movie, or play, that also took place in Afghanistan, that also dealt with the Civil Rights Movement, that also involved a character who was treated unfairly by the justice system. This book is better than the movie, which is condensed and does not let us into the main character's mind, though the movie does a good job of bringing the setting to life. This book reminds me of myself at age 10, when I also felt innocent and protected in a suburban neighborhood; this book makes me think of how lucky I am to have grown up in a middle class American family instead of in poverty in Appalachia; the woman in this book is similar to me because we are both frustrated by the glass ceiling that professional women continue to bang their heads against. And this book makes me see what the 'Lost Boys of Sudan' went through and how awful it was; this book shows me what it was like to be herded into a ghetto and then taken away on a train to Auschwitz; this book helps me to understand what it is like to suffer from Alzheimer's disease. Because of these connections, we see more than we can possibly see in our own little corners of the world.

When we take off our blinders, we learn about other times and places, but this is only the beginning of the story. With good literature and nonfiction, the connections resonate on an emotional level. We gain an understanding of the motivations of others, which helps us to understand other points of view. And when this occurs, we are able to develop compassion and empathy. Consider *To Kill a Mockingbird*; through the eyes of an eight-year-old child, the reader experiences the harsh injustices and prejudices of a small Southern town. In reading this story, we see what life was like in the South in the 1940s, but more importantly, we learn along with Scout to empathize with the reclusive character of Boo Radley, and with the black residents of Maycomb. When we are able to do this, we become more open-minded, and we grow as human beings.

In addition to teaching us empathy and compassion, good books teach us how to interpret and handle internal and external conflicts. In *To Kill A Mockingbird*, the reader is drawn into the conflict between Atticus Finch and the prejudiced white community of Maycomb. We see Atticus steadfastly and calmly proceed to do what is right regardless of what those around him think and regardless of the pressure placed on him by the town's powerful political forces. And we see Scout struggle internally in an attempt to comprehend what is going on around her, ultimately coming to an understanding of good and evil. By immersing ourselves in conflicts like these in good literature, we gain insight on how to handle conflicts in our own lives, and we come away with a new understanding of issues that we ourselves confront.

All of these aspects of immersive reading lead to an additional significant benefit: reading teaches you to think critically. The term 'critical thinking' is of course used widely, but it is worth examining what it is and considering why it is so important. One way to understand the concept is through the model based on the following quote by Oliver Wendell Holmes: 'There are one-story intellects, two-story intellects, and three-story intellects with skylights. All fact collectors with no aim beyond their facts are one-story men. Two-story men compare, reason and generalize, using labors of the fact collectors. Three-story men idealize, imagine, predict – their best illumination comes from above the skylight' (1872, p. 43). The three-story intellect begins on the bottom level, the input or fact-collecting level, moves up to the second, process level, where labor begins to occur with the facts that have been collected, and culminates in the third, output level, where true critical thinking occurs though speculation, hypothesis, and imagination, and where the presence of the skylight means that there is no limit to thought. Thus critical thinking is the ability to think at a higher level, to pose and answer questions by taking different perspectives into account. This is an essential skill in any profession, including business. In fact, with the multiple levels on which businesspeople must operate – within the company, locally, nationally, globally, and with employees, shareholders, customers, and the public at large – it may be that critical thinking is more important in this arena than in other professions.

In the twenty-first century, moreover, businesses need workers who are able to do more than simply put their noses to the grindstone and produce; instead, they need creative, critical thinkers who will help them to innovate and solve problems. As described in the American Management Association (AMA) 2010 Critical Skills Survey, twenty-first-century businesses need workers with 'the ability to see what's *not* there and make something happen' (p. 2). When asked to rate their employees in critical thinking and creativity, 48.1 percent of executives said that their employees were average or below in critical thinking ability, and 62.5 percent of executives said that their employees were average or below in creativity and innovation (p. 5). For anyone who may be inclined to think that these figures are not concerning – after all, more than half of executives stated that their employees were above average in critical thinking, and almost 40 percent stated that their employees were creative and innovative – consider how alarming it would be if 48 percent of employers said their workers were only 'OK' in performing the basic 'Three R's' skills of reading, writing and arithmetic. Similarly, in an article entitled 'Building the 21st-Century Curriculum,' author Phillip Phan (2011) stated that research conducted before launching the new Carey Business School at Johns Hopkins University revealed that 'companies want graduates who know how to manage highly ambiguous projects and how to innovate internally, ... students who know what it means to be resilient – in the face of failure, ambiguity, and resistance to change ... [and] students who can start working on a messy problem without having to overanalyze it or without being certain they'll end up where they expect' (2011, p. 39). True engagement with literature forces readers to confront ambiguity, to realize that there are no easy answers, to stretch their minds beyond the 'input level,' and to think creatively.

Reading literature should be an essential part of changing the equation so that business students are more broadly trained and ready to engage in higher level thinking. And ultimately, the purpose of any type of college education, including business education, must be to develop the entire human being, not simply to churn out degree recipients who know how to put tab A into slot B. In other words, higher level thinking is not a goal in and of itself – it is part and parcel of human growth. Moreover, the objective is not to stamp students as 'developed' upon graduation; instead, colleges recognize that students who have truly benefited from their higher education will set out on a path of continuous development and lifelong learning. Reading good fiction and nonfiction must be seen as an integral part of this ongoing process of personal growth.

The issue cannot be addressed simply by requiring business students to take a course in literature during their four years of college. Instead, business schools should expect students to read works of fiction and nonfiction over the course of their college career. The options for implementing such a plan may well include the 'freshman class book' concept that has been popular recently, where incoming freshmen are assigned a particular book to read during the summer which is the subject of discussion during the days before classes formally begin. It might also include assigning a book for all freshmen to read and discuss during the first year seminar classes that most colleges require to orient freshmen to the college experience. But colleges must go further – for instance, students may be required to read at least one book during winter break and three books during the summer, with the expectation that they will maintain an online reading portfolio throughout the four years of college. An important component of this approach would be the incorporation of group sharing of reading experiences: what did you read; what did you get out of it; do you recommend it to others? There is perhaps no more powerful way to encourage young people to read than by the enthusiastic recommendations of their peers.

We must also expect, and even train, students to read without sharing their time with other media. Today's young people believe that multitasking is the answer to success, and that they are failures if they cannot do at least two things at the same time. I ask my students how they can think – let alone think critically – in such circumstances; the question is not whether they can do two, three or four things at once, but rather whether they can do one thing at once. Multitasking does not merely discourage critical thinking – it destroys it, and the result will be businesspeople that perform their work without adequate care and without creativity. Expecting business students to focus their attention on the reading of fiction and nonfiction will help them focus throughout their lives and will improve their ability to become 'three-story,' output thinkers.

It is an unfortunate reality that a great number of young people are not making time for reading, and it should be obvious from the foregoing that this is likely to have serious consequences for tomorrow's business leaders. However, with a deliberate and concerted effort, the situation can change so that we will produce businesspeople that are not simply ready to juggle multiple tasks as quickly as possible and churn their way to the top, but are ready to embark on a lifelong exploration of the possibilities that life can offer them, and that they can offer to our society.

References

American Management Association (AMA) (2010) Critical Skills Survey, April 15 (http://www.amanet.org/news/AMA-2010-critcal-skills-survey.aspx), accessed August 17, 2011.

Bloom, Allan (1987) 'The Closing of the American Mind: How Higher Education Has Failed Democracy and Impoverished the Souls of Today's Students' (New York).

Holmes, Oliver Wendell (1872) 'The Poet at the Breakfast-Table' (Boston: James R. Osgood and Company).

National Endowment for the Arts (2007), 'To Read or Not To Read: A Question of National Consequence,' November.

National Endowment for the Arts (2009), 'Reading on the Rise: A New Chapter in American Literacy,' January.

Phan, Phillip (2011) 'Building the 21st Century Curriculum,' *Biz Ed*, AACSB (Association to Advance Collegiate Schools of Business) International, September/October, 10(5), pp. 38–39.

Richardson, Paul W. and Jacquelynne S. Eccles (2007) 'Rewards of Reading: Toward the Development of Possible Selves and Identities,' *International Journal of Educational Research*, 46, pp. 341–356.

11
The Role of Law in Business Education

Elizabeth A. Brown

One of the first things we teach first-year students in their introductory law and ethics course at Bentley University is that they will use business law throughout their careers, even if they never go to law school or interact with an actual lawyer. Business law courses help students develop critical thinking skills in three equally important ways. These courses focus firstly on teaching students the substantive legal basics of law that inform every aspect and stage of industry. By understanding the legal principles that determine, for example, whether a company can stop others from copying its products, whether its contracts are enforceable, and whether it can hire only male executives, business students learn how to identify and head off potential legal problems. In doing so, these students get a competitive edge over students who have only a vague idea of how law works. As a result, they are more valuable to and valued by their employers.

More importantly, law courses teach students how to think in ways that are essential to a successful business career. Law courses require students to sharpen their analytical skills and evaluate their own thought processes more carefully. In most law courses, students read case summaries that illustrate the plaintiff's arguments and defendant's counter-arguments, as well as the court's ruling on the issue at hand. By analyzing why one side or the other prevailed, students improve their own ability to develop arguments and to anticipate what the counter-arguments might be. Learning how to think critically and argue persuasively should form part of any business education. Business leaders who have studied law – even a single semester of business law – use that training almost every day.

Finally, law courses enhance the value of a business education by grounding executives in the ethical consequences of the decisions they make as well as their legal consequences. Laws such as the Sarbanes–Oxley Act and the Foreign Corrupt Practices Act address, in part, the ethical behavior of senior executives. Violating them can result in serious penalties for individuals as well as corporate entities. Employers benefit from hiring people whose knowledge of ethics extends beyond the simplistic. In exploring the ethical frameworks that guide business decisions, business law courses ground students in both the short-term and longer-term benefits of ethical action as well as the principles behind corporate social responsibility.

Learning to think analytically

Beyond the substance of any course – for example, what federal and state law actually state – law improves students' ability to reason and analyze. These skills emerge in several distinct and equally important ways. They include appreciating how consequences flow from actions, honing interpretive skills, and improving logic by identifying and overcoming biases in reasoning.

Law courses often use real cases, condensed and simplified, to help students learn how to evaluate actions on the basis of their likely consequences. In business law classes, students learn how certain decisions made in the workplace might give rise to various legal claims. By studying cases, they come to understand how executives have resolved various factual situations and the legal consequences of their choices. Good law professors help students put themselves in the shoes of the parties – plaintiff and defendant. Through case studies, students consider what alternatives were available to the parties and how their decisions affected both the individuals and the companies involved.

For example, one of the first cases Bentley University first-year students read is 1964's *Heart of Atlanta Motel*, in which a small business owner challenged the federal government's right to tell him – via the passage of the Civil Rights Act – whom he could and could not allow in his motel. We teach this case not only because it makes the important historical point that racial discrimination was legal only 50 years ago. It also helps students grasp the larger point that even small businesses are almost always subject to federal as well as state regulation. They can put themselves in the shoes of the motel owner who simply wants to make his own call about what kind of guests he will rent to (although it's doubtful any of them would want to run a racially restrictive business of their own). By studying the reasoning of the United States Supreme Court, they learn to appreciate why the Commerce Clause enables a sweeping federal law like the Civil Rights Act to touch even a relatively small operation like the Heart of Atlanta Motel. Cases like *Heart of Atlanta Motel* help make legal principles real and relevant. Like any good analogy, they make it easier for students to learn an otherwise abstract principle and to understand more clearly the interplay between law and business.

An important benefit of legal studies is the understanding that few legal issues are black and white, but that there are infinite shadings of gray. Law also teaches students the importance of language and perspective in evaluating positions. By debating legal principles in any situation, whether we are discussing a real case or a hypothetical I have given them, students learn from each other that every issue has at least two sides. They are encouraged to explain the bases for their positions in enough detail for their classmates to understand the way they have applied the basic legal principles we learn to the specific facts at issue and, in doing so, what conclusion they reach. In taking sides against their classmates for the duration of our exercise, they learn that for every argument there is almost always a valid counter-argument. In the process, we hope they learn that each side in a given debate can have a rational basis.

By discussing their own perspectives on law as applied to business, they also learn how individual experiences and perceptions can shape our views on legal issues. For example, when I teach first-year students about gender discrimination as part of a larger discussion of employment law, we usually discuss Hooters. Most students appreciate fairly easily that it is illegal to deny someone a job because of her gender. Most students, however, are also familiar with Hooters' business model, which relies on hiring only female servers – and only those female servers with certain physical characteristics. I ask students to argue for and against this practice. Many students initially believe that Hooters should be able to hire anyone they want to, even if that means potentially discriminating against otherwise qualified male applicants. Others argue to the contrary, applying not only the antidiscrimination laws but the categorical imperative (an ethical framework we discuss early in the semester) to argue against Hooters' employment practices. Invariably, some students will argue that hiring only young, attractive female waitresses is essential to Hooters' business model and that Hooters should be free to operate in this profitable niche. In this context, we discuss *Diaz v. Pan American Airlines*, a 1972 case in which a man claimed that Pan Am's refusal to hire him as a flight attendant constituted gender discrimination in violation of the Civil Rights Act. In that case, the trial court accepted Pan Am's arguments that being female was a 'bona fide occupational qualification' for stewardesses because, among other things, the airline's male passengers were more comfortable with the maternal attentions of women. A higher court reversed, however, and held that Pan Am's practice violated the law. Students discuss the ways in which arguments in Hooters' favor are similar to the ultimately unsuccessful arguments Pan Am made in a similar situation. Conversations like these help students appreciate the real-world impact of legal principles on business operations, and often help them re-evaluate their reactions to common business scenarios.

Mock trials, in which students form teams to present each side of a legal argument in some depth, provide an excellent way to develop these critical skills further. In a basic mock trial course, students are divided into two camps and presented with similar sets of facts. The facts describe a complex business situation that gives rise to discrete legal issues, to be decided by a panel of mock trial judges (and/or the professor). The teams compete against each other, much as a plaintiff and defendant would in court. The students prepare legal briefs that lay out their arguments with reference to specific 'evidence' from their set of facts. They also present their oral arguments before the panel of judges.

In writing their briefs, students learn to clarify their thinking as well as their writing skills. The competitive nature of the exercise increases their incentive to make a stronger case than their opponents. In order to do so, of course, they have to become proficient at the kind of persuasive reasoning that makes a case stronger. The oral arguments teach students how to prepare and present their arguments in an entirely different format, adding another layer of complexity and effectiveness to the class.

Mock trials do more than sharpen students' persuasive writing and speaking skills. They train students to be stronger, more effective advocates for themselves and their companies. They help students learn to identify the gaps and weaknesses in other people's arguments. We expect that they will use these skills to negotiate better contracts in the workplace and, perhaps, better working conditions for themselves. Given the exponential rise of mandatory arbitration provisions in business contracts, they will also develop skills they are increasingly likely to need as they resolve business disputes out of court. Perhaps most importantly, mock trials train our business students to be more articulate, logical, and thoughtful business leaders.

Learning how to manage ethically

Another critical component of a sound business law education is business ethics. Ethics can, of course, perfuse many aspects of a business education. Students learn about the ethical violation reporting requirements of the Sarbanes–Oxley Act, for example, in their accounting classes as well as their law classes. Legal studies, however, provide a unique context in which future business leaders can and should study the ethical framework of business.

At Bentley, first year students learn fundamental law and ethics of the business world in a single course. This early introduction to the importance of ethical business behavior, and its interplay with law, establishes what we believe is a vitally important framework for the rest of their business education. Our students learn why ethics matter for long-term business success and how acting ethically differs from, but relates to, acting legally. Their coursework encompasses much more than the lessons learned from unethical and illegal behavior, illustrated vividly by studying the fall of Enron and other well-known corporate implosions. We also teach students in some detail why ethics is actually good for business. They learn, for example, how ethical management increases the level of trust with customers and business partners. They learn the principles of 'conscious capitalism' which posit that acting ethically toward multiple stakeholders, including employees, customers, suppliers, the larger community and shareholders, tends to increase overall profitability over time. While law sets a moral minimum as to what employers may do, business ethics help shape students' views of what the maximum could be: the potential social benefits that businesses can generate beyond mere product and job creation.

Without this synthesis of legal and ethical training, business students risk developing the belief that acting ethically is optional, impractical, or inconsistent with long-term profits. Students need to hear this not only from professors but from business leaders. For that reason, we ask Fortune 100 executives to speak directly to them about how their companies establish ethical guidelines and ensure compliance with those guidelines. Their approaches can be as different as the businesses themselves, but the importance they attribute to ethical decision making is common to all of them.

The interplay between law and ethics is particularly important in the context of international business operations. U.S. companies doing business abroad face not only a more complex regulatory situation, but a more complex ethical framework in which to make decisions.

For example, students in Bentley's business law classes might discuss whether U.S. businesses operating in a foreign country should adopt local practices even if they conflict with U.S. practices. Some common foreign practices may be illegal under U.S. law, for example; while making additional payments to local leaders may be how business gets done in some countries, those payments may well violate the Foreign Corrupt Practices Act. But in other cases, the lines are not as clear. Issues of racial (or tribal) and gender discrimination, or intellectual property protection, may get blurry when the host country's laws and practices differ radically from our own. As most businesses develop at least an online presence, if not the actual practice of doing business abroad, these issues become more important in business education.

Learning to spot the issues

In addition to learning how to think, a clear understanding of the substantive legal issues every business faces is critical to a sound business education. In order to train responsible business leaders, we have to provide them with a working vocabulary of the legal issues affecting all companies, regardless of size, so they can learn to identify and mitigate potential legal problems. Heading off these potential problems before they mature into lawsuits – and before they risk investor confidence – is an integral part of business leadership.

While most larger companies have either access to outside counsel or at least one in-house lawyer, executives themselves must also be able to spot potential legal issues as (and ideally before) they arise. Key business decisions are usually made well before and separate from consultations with lawyers. Executives must understand how law affects the consequences of these decisions.

It would be unreasonable, of course, to expect business leaders to know how to solve every kind of complex legal problem that comes up in business every day. That should not be the goal of the legal component of business education. Instead, we can and should expect business leaders to develop the ability to identify potential legal problems, much as first year law students do. In the first year of law school, the exams are generally designed to test whether students can 'spot the issue' – that is, whether the students can identify potential legal issues given a set of hypothetical facts. They are not expected to provide a definitive solution to the problem; indeed, they should know that the complexities of discovery and precedent make it risky to predict how a court might rule on any high-level set of facts. Just 'spotting the issue' is enough at that level. Similarly, if a manager can 'spot the issue' within his company before it develops into a serious legal matter, that company gains a significant advantage over its competitors. This kind of basic issue-spotting ability also makes graduates stronger candidates in the job market.

This is increasingly true as businesses change the way they choose and work with lawyers. Fifteen years ago, even large companies had a relatively small number of in-house counsel. These companies routinely farmed out legal issues to elite law firms, which would handle their complaints for several hundred dollars an hour. Companies are increasingly, and understandably, reluctant to incur the expense of these large law firms and are turning to a range of other options. These include smaller and more flexible firms, such as those that have no bricks-and-mortar expenses, and the growth of in-house counsel ranks. Companies increasingly value the ability to manage legal issues in-house, and that ability depends in part on whether its executives can spot potential legal issues before they develop into genuine, and genuinely expensive, problems for the lawyers to solve. If a company is going to consult a lawyer, it makes the most sense to do so early – so that the lawyer can help resolve issues before they escalate – and not often, because ideally the company will be able to manage and mitigate legal risks before they arise. That's where the value of a basic legal education comes into play for business students.

Using law to grow businesses

Understanding how law affects every element of a business is essential to managing any business well. Consider, for example, how law affects every stage of a start-up company:

- As the company begins its operations, the founders have to decide on a business form. They may choose to form any one of a number of different kinds of partnerships, or they may choose to incorporate the company. The form they choose will depend in part on their need for flexibility, their desire to control ownership, the potential need to share equity with funders, and the need to protect their personal assets from any debts that the company might incur. If they incorporate or form a partnership, their choice of where to do so will be influenced by state law.
- The company's name, logo, products, website, and literature all raise questions of intellectual property law. The founders' choice of a

name and logo for the company depend in part on what trademark protection is available for each option. The choice of domain name also raises legal issues, especially if the company encounters cyber-squatters. The company will also need to understand copyright law in order to know how to protect against the unauthorized copying of any new software it creates.

- If the company has been formed to sell particular devices, each device will probably need to be patented or licensed. In designing and evaluating new products, the company will need to understand how to secure patent protection and enforce its patents if another company infringes them. Selling certain products that are subject to government regulation and approval (e.g., medical devices or cosmetics) also requires an understanding of how administrative agencies create and enforce regulations.

- The company's decisions as to who they hire, how they hire, and whether they use employees or independent contractors for various roles will be informed by employment law. A company's hiring and advancement processes are, of course, subject to federal and state laws. Every employee the company hires can create potential liability, based on the legal principles of agency. Whether a particular hire is an independent contractor or an employee is also determined by law rather than intent.

- The company's acquisition or rental of office space and any manufacturing facilities may raise issues of real estate law. What the company does on its premises, whether they are owned or leased, is likely to be subject to regulation. Understanding administrative law will be key to determining which regulations might apply, and how.

- Whether the company sells to other businesses or directly to consumers, issues of contract law come up frequently in almost every business. Supply chains also depend on valid and enforceable contracts. These contractual issues may be complicated by jurisdictional questions if the company's business partners are in another state or another country.

- Any company selling goods to consumers must also understand its potential exposure to product liability and/or strict liability claims. By understanding the various forms of product liability claims, the company can minimize its potential exposure during the design, testing, and marketing of its products.

Standard business law courses like the ones taught at Bentley University teach students at least the basics of every one of these legal issues. In doing so, they help future executives learn to make the best decisions in every phase of business operations.

Consulting a lawyer with the appropriate expertise at every one of these stages of company development might be ideal, but it's neither practical nor realistic. Few companies have the resources to hire attorneys who review all potential legal issues stemming from their operations. Instead, senior management and corporate counsel rely on executives to manage legal risk. In order to minimize the risk of future legal problems, however, the ideal manager – whether at a C-level or a much lower level – needs to know enough about business law to 'spot the issue' and consult a lawyer when it makes sense to do so.

Another example of how legal studies help future business leaders become more competent is in the study of consumer law. The students in Bentley's consumer law course learn about the obligations that companies owe to consumers under state and federal law and across a variety of sectors. Many of these students plan to become marketing executives, and the knowledge they gain from studying the laws of deceptive advertising, for example, will make them more valuable assets to their future employers. At the same time, of course, studying consumer law makes them more educated consumers and improves their ability to know and assert their rights in the marketplace.

The special vulnerability of small businesses

Small businesses, which make up two-thirds of American employers, can benefit from a basic legal education even more than larger businesses can. Even the smallest company operates in a regulated environment, and is affected by administrative law (that is, law created by regulatory agencies) as well as federal, state, and local laws. Its leaders must understand the sources and content of that regulation in order to compete effectively, but small business owners are often at a disadvantage in this regard.

Yet small business owners are often unable to mitigate legal risk because they simply don't have the bandwidth. These owners are usually managing not only the operational details of their business but also the marketing, management, human resources, and accounting functions. In juggling all of these roles, which would each be handled by a separate department at a larger company, the small business owner may have little time and/or ability to manage legal issues. Yet small businesses are just as likely to face prosecution or litigation for their failure to comply with the laws that affect them as larger businesses.

While some regulatory agencies may focus their enforcement actions on larger entities, other government agencies, including the state attorneys in general, are just as likely to investigate smaller businesses as larger ones for potential violation of state laws. Customers, of course, can file lawsuits against any company regardless of its size to allege, for example, an unfair or deceptive business practice. Small businesses, operating on a smaller margin, may be less able to absorb the impact of any penalties they may face on the losing end.

Unlike larger companies, which may have at least one lawyer on staff as general counsel, the smaller businesses rarely have easy access to legal counsel for basic questions. The leaders of these companies must be sufficiently well versed in the basics of business law that they can operate successfully without incurring the expense and hassle of consulting a lawyer at every step. More importantly, these leaders also need to know enough law to spot the issues and to know when they absolutely do need to consult a lawyer in order to minimize cost and frustration down the road. Small business owners who are conversant in business law basics are simply better positioned to succeed.

A basic legal education can help a small business from the moment of its inception. Entrepreneurs starting a company need to understand the pros and cons of various corporate forms, as well as the sources of law that affect their businesses, including regulatory law. At Bentley, entrepreneurs enrolled in Business Law 201 learn enough business law to not only decide which legal form their companies should take and why, but how to incorporate a company themselves. These legal basics not only empower young entrepreneurs but save their businesses money by helping them avoid unnecessary legal fees.

Conclusion

The role of law in a business education is at least as great as the need for business leaders who can think critically, who can lead ethically, who can spot potential legal issues before they develop into problems, and who can use law strategically to help their businesses grow. As the global economy becomes more competitive, this role and the skills business law courses help hone will become increasingly valuable. As a greater percentage of new jobs come from young companies, which have not yet accumulated the institutionalized legal knowledge of their older competitors, it will be particularly important for the people who fill those jobs to spot potential legal issues before they become 'bet the company' lawsuits. Providing students with the opportunity to study business law helps them develop new ways of thinking which help them throughout their careers and in all aspects of their employers' operations.

References

2010–2011 Undergraduate Fellows Report, 'Business, Values and Law: Forging a New Dialogue, Berkley Center for Religion, Peace and World Affairs,' accessed July 17, 2012 at http://repository.berkleycenter.georgetown.edu/BusinessValuesLawUGReport.pdf.

Atkinson, Rob (2004) 'Connecting Business Ethics and Legal Ethics for the Common Good: Come, Let Us Reason Together,' *Journal of Corporation Law*, 29(3), pp. 469–533.

Bagley, C. E. (2005) *Winning Legally: How to Use the Law to Create Value, Marshal Resources, and Manage Risk* (Boston: Harvard Business Review Press).

Bagley C. E. (2006), 'What's Law Got to Do with It: A Systems Approach to Management,' Harvard Business School Working Paper Number: 06–038.

Collins, J. W. (1977), 'Law in the Business Curriculum,' *American Business Law Journal*, 15, pp. 46–52.

Freeman, Seth (2008) 'Bridging the Gaps: How Cross-Disciplinary Training with MBAs Can Improve Transactional Education, Prepare Students for Private Practice, and Enhance University Life,' *Fordham Journal of Corporate & Financial Law*, 13(1), pp. 89–137.

Gabel, Joan T. A. (2005) 'Editor's Corner: Law and Ethics in the Business School,' *American Business Law Journal*, 42, pp. 1–6.

Hasnas, John, Robert Prentice, and Alan Strudler (2010) 'New Directions in Legal Scholarship: Implications for Business Ethics Research, Theory, and Practice,' *Business Ethics Quarterly* 20(3), p. 503.

Kocakülåh, Mehmet, C., A. D. Austill, and Brett J. Long (2008) 'The Business Law Education of Accounting Students in the USA: The Accounting Chairperson's Perspective,' *Accounting Education* 17, S17.

Mytton, Elizabeth, and Chris Gale (2012) 'Prevailing Issues in Legal Education within Management and Business Environments,' *International Journal of Law and Management*, 54(4), pp. 311–321.

12
Psychology in Business Education: A Response to Rapid Economic and Technological Change

Gregory J. Hall

For many decades, psychological theory in business education was largely limited to understanding organizational behavior, consumer behavior, and human resource management. Today, all that has changed. The emergence of e-commerce, informatics, healthcare management, environmental business policy, and wealth management as critical twenty-first-century issues requires that contemporary business curricula apply and integrate psychological theory to these domains. Two particular areas of curriculum development – financial psychology and cyber psychology – serve as examples of the crucial need to integrate psychology with business in today's education.

Financial psychology

Financial psychology studies the ways in which the human mind, and particularly the irrational side of human behavior, work upon financial behavior. Traditionally, professors of economics and finance present a rational model of economics, meaning that the markets behave efficiently and objectively. Real-life economic and financial decisions by individuals, however, are neither totally rational nor totally irrational. A psychological perspective focuses on the irrationality of human behavior in markets under certain conditions.

While applying psychology to economics and finance is not new (Keynes, 1936; Kahneman & Tversky, 1984; Thaler, 1992), only in the past 15 years has it gained a foothold in mainstream thought. Daniel Kahneman, the psychologist who won the 2002 Nobel Prize in Economic Sciences, represents perhaps the most significant symbolic acknowledgement of financial psychology's relevance, and the need to integrate psychology into economics and finance. Kahneman and another cognitive psychologist, Amos Tversky, collaborated on research that led to their work on prospect theory, which analyzes the behavioral process of decision making (Kahneman and Tversky, 1984, pp. 341–350). In addition to Kahneman and Tversky, Herbert Simon, Richard Thaler, George Lowenstein, and Hersh Shefrin are among the psychologists and economists who have made major contributions to the field of behavioral economics.

Retirement planning offers an excellent example of the need for psychology in financial decision-making. The gradual elimination of defined pension plans in business and industry over the past 30 years, coupled with the steady increase in life expectancy, means that a significant percentage of people must take responsibility for their own retirement planning. As a result (and because the level of financial literacy is low, even among the most educated segment of society), the field of financial planning and wealth management has grown rapidly since 1990. With that growth has come an increase in finance programs and courses at both the graduate and undergraduate level.

Psychological theory offers part of the solution to the task of retirement planning. Richard Thaler introduced Nudge theory to explain the role of 'choice architecture' in one's ability to influence or manipulate the decision making of human beings. A few simple changes through the application of behavioral decision making can make a significant difference in financial choice.

Applying that theory to our retirement example, policy makers have been routinely frustrated with the low percentages of employees who choose not to opt into retirement 401k plans even when employer-matched dollars are left on the table. Psychologists know that immediate gratification (more money in their take home pay) will, more often than not, trump delayed gratification (more money in their retirement years). Policy makers recognize that as the majority of the population has transitioned from defined pension plans to individual responsibility for retirement planning, failure to opt for delayed gratification amongst significant percentages of the population presents a looming future crisis. One simple and effective solution to increasing participation in employee-sponsored 401k plans is to tweak the choice architecture. When employers move from an 'opt in' to an 'opt out' choice for participation in a 401k plan, participation increases significantly. This is but one example of applying behavioral psychology to addressing a significant policy concern.

The global economic boom and bust of the 2000 to 2008 period and the subsequent Great Recession demonstrated the importance in understanding the difference between rational economic theory and the counter intuitive irrational behavior exhibited by humans. In 2000 Robert Shiller correctly predicted the looming financial crisis by applying behavioral concepts to the speculative decision making of financial experts and lay people alike. Borrowing from social psychology concepts such as herd behavior, heuristics, group dynamics, and recency effect, Shiller determined the predominant decision-making process of the general populace to be irrational. His warnings were generally viewed as unfounded and simply the result of a fundamental misunderstanding of the 'new economy.' Unfortunately, it took the painful lessons of the Great Recession for many to realize the importance of balancing the knowledge of rational market theory with a concurrent understanding of human cognitive and emotional behavior is necessary to fully appreciate economic policy.

In the academy, financial psychology courses seek to add the irrational perspective to the critical thinking of both undergraduate and graduate students. Graduate and undergraduate programs have been developing courses over the past 15 years that address the emotional and cognitive behavioral processes of human beings in their financial decision interactions. Bentley University, for example, offers a Master of Science degree in Financial Planning which includes a course, Psychology in Financial Planning. An undergraduate course in financial psychology is popular with both economics and finance majors at Bentley. Courses in the interdisciplinary field alternately referred to as behavioral economics or financial psychology are offered in most business schools including Stanford, Harvard, London School of Economics, Yale, Carnegie-Mellon, and the University of Chicago.

With increased life expectancy and increased requirements for personal responsibility in financial planning, the need for continual interdisciplinary curriculum development integrating rational economic theory, finance, and human behavior will be necessary to meet the future needs of financial professionals, economic policy makers, and the general public.

Cyber-psychology

Cyber-psychology focuses on the influence of computer technology on human behavior. Nowhere is this influence more keenly felt as in the change the internet has brought to society. Tim Berners-Lee, the inventor of the world wide web, envisioned the web as first and foremost an agent of social change. Indeed, the web has changed the way we conduct commerce, gather information, develop social communities, communicate, entertainment, politics, and initiate social movements. Our behavior in all aspects of life is now significantly influenced by the web, which, at just 20 years old, is still in its developmental infancy.

At the same time, there is only a nascent understanding of how human beings interact with current technology. Researchers attempt to close the knowledge gap, yet technology advances exponentially, always seemingly one step ahead of the research. Given this, continual curriculum development at the intersection of human behavior and technology will be necessary for many years to come. Psychology faculty must be prepared to play an important role in this process, focusing on topics such as consumer behavior, ecommerce, social interaction, information design, identity theft, corporate espionage, property rights, and workplace productivity.

The advent of the web has created many new professional career paths in business. Take, for example, just one segment of the technology sector: 'app jobs.' These positions focus on computer and mobile device application development that did not exist 10 years ago. They require knowledge of the human interface with technology. Fully 500,000 positions are available today, with many more likely in the future.

To stay relevant, business education needs to keep pace with this change in the job market. Psychology faculty in institutions with business programs must develop innovative curricula that apply social psychology and behavioral theory to themes such as information management, e-commerce, informatics, and e-finance.

Such future endeavors will require cross-disciplinary research and curriculum development. What follows are several current examples of business/liberal arts interdisciplinary degree programs designed to meet the needs of the emerging economy.

Cyber-psychology and health care

The health care field is projected to be one of the most significant growth industries in the coming decades. Factors such as the aging baby boomer population, advances in biotechnology, health care economics, and politics, informatics, and increased competition are projected to accelerate this sector of the global economy. This future growth requires universities to rethink their approach to training its graduates.

Bentley University has developed innovative liberal studies programs to address contemporary societal needs. These programs can be elected by students majoring in business programs. Students graduate with both their primary business major and a second liberal studies major (LSM). One such LSM is in Health and Industry. The Health and Industry program is designed for business graduates who wish to pursue careers in health care administration, pharmaceuticals, or the biotechnology industry, all rapidly growing fields. Thus, graduates entering the workforce have preparation in human biology, psychology, health, and disease in addition to their business education. A structural innovation at Bentley combines psychology, biology, and health sciences in the same department of Natural and Applied Sciences. This arrangement facilitates a synergy in research, curriculum development, and program design. These innovative LSM degree programs at the intersection of business and the liberal arts are attracting significant interest among undergraduates. Well over 500 Bentley University undergraduates enroll in the LSM programs in addition to their business major.

Graduate schools of business are also developing programs that reach across the divide. The Wharton School at the University of Pennsylvania offers a MBA degree in Health Management drawing from several disciplines. The Kellogg School of Management has a similar program in Health Industry Management.

The American Psychological Association (APA) has recognized the importance of an interdisciplinary approach to addressing the future needs of society. In June 2009 the APA issued a report, 'Psychology as a Core Science, Technology, Engineering, and Mathematics (STEM) Discipline,' that argues for a more consistent inclusion of psychology in STEM education. The report notes that although the National Science Foundation includes the discipline of psychology in its STEM definition, in practice, psychology is often excluded in funding opportunities and in the consideration of curriculum. This exclusion ignores the role of psychological factors in health:

> The costs of healthcare are steadily rising, burdening governments and businesses and thereby reducing economic competitiveness. Human behavior is a major contributor to these rising costs: Diet, exercise, smoking and substance use contribute significantly to preventable chronic disease and acute trauma, including major killers such as cardiovascular disease, cancer, and physical trauma (e.g., gun violence and traffic fatalities). According to the American Medical

Association, at least 25 cents of every health care dollar are spent on the treatment of diseases or disabilities that result from changeable behaviors. (APA, 2009)

The field of psychology must be proactive in anticipating the emerging needs of the health care industry. Curriculum in cognitive, social, and emotional theory should be applied to the best practices of patient care and health care delivery. The interdisciplinary relationship between technology, biology, health sciences, and psychology will be of increasing importance to meet the challenges of the future.

Informatics

One particular emergent interdisciplinary field heavily dependent on the knowledge of human behavior is informatics. 'Informatics' refers to information processing and is usually applied to complex organizations and internet commerce, where considerations of human cognitive and social behaviors are important factors in determining efficient processes. The rapid technological advances of the past decade have made the study and application of informatics critical, and academic programs at both the undergraduate level and in particular, at the graduate level, have been developed in recent years to answer this need.

Health informatics, for example, seeks to analyze the user interface with technology to improve the efficiency and quality of health care delivery systems. Simmons College in Boston offers an undergraduate interdisciplinary major in Health Informatics that draws from the disciplines of computer science, mathematical science, biology, public health, and philosophy. The University of Illinois at Chicago has a Master of Science degree in Health Informatics and Health Information Management. The program includes courses in information science, computer science, and health care. Organizational behavior and consumer behavior in addition to health science are part of the curriculum. The University of California at Davis offers a master's degree in Health Informatics.

These graduate majors as well as similar programs at other universities have a common interdisciplinary approach to addressing the needs of the health care business. Large health care organizations, health care insurance companies, managed care businesses, and pharmaceutical businesses all require professionals with multi-disciplinary training that includes psychology.

The field of informatics is not limited to health care applications. Bentley University offers a Master of Science degree in Human Factors in Information Design. The degree program includes a focus on human behavior as it applies to product design and usability. Degree students work with actual clients through the Design and Usability Center (DUC) a state-of-the-art facility that monitors and records the user experience, including emotional communication. California State University, Long Beach developed a Master of Science degree in Human Factors in 2005. The program includes experimental psychology, computer applications, and human factors in interface design. The City University London houses the Center for Human Computer Interaction Design with a focus on human behavior and innovative technology. Stanford University, Columbia, Indiana University, Georgia Tech, and Michigan State University are among the growing number of schools who have developed similar programs.

Informatics will grow in importance as advances in technological innovation continue more rapidly over the coming decades. The interdisciplinary nature of the field will require business schools to develop processes and structures that facilitate opportunities for knowledge leaders from varied disciplines including the social sciences to collaborate on research and curriculum.

Business and the environment

In addition to healthcare and informatics, environmental business and sustainability are rapidly developing as central concerns. The evolving global economy will be significantly influenced by continued innovation and advances in sustainability and environmental policy. Environmental psychology explores the relationship between human behavior and natural environments and natural resources. Researchers in behavior modification, behavioral modeling, and choice architecture have much to contribute to the field of environmental business. Interdisciplinary programs in environmental studies have been increasingly developed over the past decade. The School of Natural Resources and Environment, University of Michigan includes an Environmental Psychology Lab with thought leaders from the disciplines of psychology, sociology, anthropology, political science as well as the natural sciences. The University of Colorado at Boulder has a dual-degree program, Master of Science in Environmental Studies and Master of Business Administration, preparing graduates for a future in environmental business. These types of collaborations across disciplines present models that could be adopted by business schools who envision the future of environmental business.

Future challenges and opportunities

Interdisciplinary study still faces significant headwinds in today's colleges and universities. The organizational structure of the academic disciplines has remained largely unchanged over the past 150 years (longer, some would argue). The arrangement of discipline-specific academic departments, their corresponding research journals, and the associated values and reward structure within the academy serve as impediments to integrative research and curriculum design.

At the same time, business leaders and policy experts are calling loudly for reform, in order to produce a sufficient supply of effective professionals in tomorrow's economy. According to the President's Council of Economic Advisors, 'Employers noted that professionalism/ work ethic, teamwork/collaboration, oral communication, and critical thinking/problem solving are among the most important skills labor market entrants need' (2009, p. 10). These are among the skills associated with the arts and sciences.

Our contemporary economy would be better served by a curriculum that did not reflect the historical organizational silos of our academic disciplines. A radical restructuring of the academy, however, is unlikely over the near future. Thus, we must recognize and capitalize on opportunities to incrementally overcome the obstacles to valued research and curriculum design at the intersection of business and arts and sciences.

The social sciences have an opportunity to contribute to the preparation of tomorrow's professionals. However, the thought leaders in the social sciences, psychology in particular, must develop a research agenda and curricula with a vision of the future rather than a reliance on the traditional disciplinary silo.

The emerging role of psychology in business education is moving well beyond the traditional scope of organizational behavior, consumer behavior, and resources management to include the disciplines of accounting, economics, finance, information technology, health care business, and environmental business. The economic landscape has changed significantly over the past 20 years and is projected to continue to evolve. The traditional approaches to research and curriculum development that have served society well for most of the twentieth century are not likely to do so in the twenty-first century. Psychology faculty will need to develop the ability and motivation to apply psychological principles, concepts, and theories to the changing nature of how people work, recreate, socialize, and identify. Business students of the new millennium will respond with enthusiasm knowing that the knowledge of human behavior has utility not only in their personal lives but also in their professional endeavors.

References

Berners-Lee, T. (1999) *Weaving the WEB* (San Francisco: Harper).

Kahneman, D. and A. Tversky (1984) 'Choices, Values, and Frames,' *American Psychologist*, 39(4), pp. 341–350.

Keynes, J. M. (1936) *The General Theory of Employment, Interest and Money* (New York: Harcourt, Brace).

Shiller, R. (2000) *Irrational Exuberance*, (Princeton, NJ: Princeton University Press).

Thaler, R. (1992) *The Winner's Curse: Paradoxes and Anomalies of Economic Life* (New York: Free Press).

Report of the American Psychological Association 2009 Presidential Task Force on the Future of Psychology as a STEM Discipline President's Council of Economic Advisors, 2009.

13
Business Education in an Age of Science and Technology

Fred D. Ledley and Eric A. Oches

In a 1994 interview, Carl Sagan described the relationship between science and society thus: 'We live in a society absolutely dependent on science and technology and yet have cleverly arranged things so that almost no one understands science and technology. That's a clear prescription for disaster' (Kalosh, 1994). This view of a world dependent on, yet largely ignorant of, science and technology is an apt description of the situation facing business today. The global economy is increasingly dependent on science and technology. Joseph McCann, Dean of the Sykes College of Business at the University of Tampa in Florida, has written in BizEd that the 'Next Economy' is a 'science and knowledge economy' in which 'industries revolve around the convergence of technologies such as computing, communications, and engineering, and the growing importance of life sciences such as physics, biology, and chemistry.' (2006, pp. 40–41). In part, this transition reflects the commercial opportunities afforded by the persistent, exponential progress of scientific and technical innovation in fields such as computers, communications, genomics, genetic engineering, and nanotechnology. In part, it is also necessitated by circumstance, as our societies and economies confront the multifaceted challenges of stagnant economic growth, globalization, global climate change, and feeding and meeting the resource demands of a world population expected to reach 9 billion individuals by mid-century.

Already, one-third of the companies in the Fortune 100 are in R&D-intensive industries such as information technology, computing technology, biopharmaceuticals, energy, and agriculture; another third are in industries where competitive advantage requires continuous implementation of new scientific and technological capabilities in healthcare, communications, logistics, or automobiles. These fractions do not even include industries such as financial services or retailing, whose business models have been radically transformed, and continue to be transformed, by new technologies and their enabling impact on commerce and globalization. Rapid growth in sustainability planning, which emphasizes efficiency enhancements through reductions in energy, water, natural resource consumption, pollution, emissions, and waste generation, and mitigating risks related to climate change, is evident in a wide range of companies, requiring significant investments in science and technology to accommodate growing regulatory and natural resource constraints (McKinsey, 2011).

Furthermore, industry has not begun to grapple with the challenges of a burgeoning global population in which almost 1.5 billion people live on less than \$1.25/day and 1 billion people do not have enough food, a world where 40 percent of infant mortality is due to treatable causes, and more than one-sixth of the global population lacks adequate, safe drinking water and basic sanitation (UN, 2010). Increasing resource scarcity, energy demands, environmental degradation, intensifying competition for ecosystem services, and the threat of global climate change represent challenges that that will require even more effective applications of science and technology to advance 'sustainable well-being' for a growing global population in the future (Holdren, 2008). Economic growth driven by technological advances can help address many of these global challenges, but only with a scientifically literate population of citizens, policy makers, and business leaders.

Even as our national and global economies and our industries have become increasingly dependent on science and technology, the population at large remains largely scientifically illiterate. The 2008 *Digest of Education Statistics* reported that only 18 percent of 12th grade U.S. students achieved Science Scale Scores of 'at or above proficient' (Snyder et al., 2009) and that only 17 percent of American adults achieved 'minimal' measures of literacy (Miller and Pardo, 2000; Miller 2004). Many studies indicate that American students rank below their peers in Europe and Asia (Baldi et al., 2007; NSF, 2008; Schmidt et al., 1997).

As Carl Sagan noted, 'this is a prescription for disaster.' Employer surveys by the AAC&U (2007) have shown that 82 percent of employers believe that colleges and universities need to place more emphasis on 'concepts and new development in science and technology' to meet the needs of business. Numerous expert reports from industry, academia, and government agree, most notably the 2007 report from the National Academies, *Rising Above the Gathering Storm: Energizing and Employing America for a Brighter Economic Future* (Council on Competitiveness,

2005; NAS, 2007; PKAL, 2006; US Chamber of Commerce, 2005; President's Council, 2012). These reports warn that global competitiveness is critically dependent on continued innovation in STEM fields, and that the number of individuals who are being trained in STEM disciplines is inadequate to meet the needs of the workforce. While the educational initiatives that have resulted from these reports have focused primarily on improving the number, quality, and diversity of STEM professionals entering the workforce, a report from the National Academy of Engineering and National Research Council also noted that 'Technological literacy is especially important for leaders in business, government, and the media, who make or influence decisions that affect many others, sometimes the entire nation' (NAE, 2002).

Why science and technology matter for business professionals

The effective implementation of science and technology in industry requires more than a workforce of qualified STEM professionals. It requires that science and technology be integrated with corporate missions, business strategy, and management. Benchmarking studies on the management of technology within organizations demonstrates that this is happening, and that R&D and technology are increasingly integrated with business, often under the direction of senior managers, including the chief executive officer and business-unit general managers (Maglitta, 1994; Lichtenthaler, 2003; Elder et al., 2002). As a result, it is business professionals who are often responsible for deciding the direction for research and development and formulating the goals, strategy, content, and budget for technical functions. Moreover, technology-based companies also depend on business professionals to establish finance, accounting, marketing, and human resource functions that effectively promote technological innovation and product development.

To function effectively in such corporate roles, business leaders need to have a pluralistic, integrative, and interdisciplinary knowledge of science and technology, what has been described as 'a sophisticated appreciation of their nature, as well as of their economic, social, and ethical consequences' (McCann, 2006) and the ability to 'understand the technical issues facing their organizations and the portfolio of ideas and projects that are in the pipeline at any time' (Harvard Business Essentials, 2003).

These perspectives do not suppose that business professionals require extensive knowledge of disciplinary science or the ability to participate in scientific or technical work. Rather, what business professionals need is an interdisciplinary knowledge of science as it is applied in a business context (Mallick and Chaudhury, 2000; IAMOT, 2007; NRC, 2008). Management research suggests that this requires 'technology-centered knowledge' in addition to business skills, specifically, an understanding of the nature of science and technology, the strategic role of technology in business, the implementation of technology, and the process of technological innovation (IAMOT, 2007; Mallick and Chaudhury, 2000).

Business professionals also play an important role in the process of science itself (Ledley, 2012). Businesses not only invest in the development and distribution of the products of science, but also fund more scientific research than government, non-government, and non-profit organizations combined. Moreover, many business professionals serve as leaders of non-profit and philanthropic organizations that are at the forefront of basic science and positioned to exert significant influence on the direction of science itself. John Holdren, then President of the American Association for the Advancement of Science (AAAS) has written that science and technology have a fundamental responsibility to promote the sustainable well-being of society by improving economic conditions, sociopolitical conditions, and environmental conditions. (Holdren, 2008). As partners in the scientific enterprise, business professionals have a critical role to play in achieving these goals.

The role of the undergraduate science curriculum

Given the demonstrated inadequacy of secondary science and technology education, and increasing demands for interdisciplinary competencies in business, there have been calls for business schools to see science and technology as essential elements of management education. Laprise et al. (2008) have proposed that a working knowledge of science should be considered a core element of an undergraduate management curriculum. McCann similarly argues, 'The entire undergraduate and graduate cores in the b-school curriculum must be examined to assure a multidisciplinary understanding of these new challenges and opportunities. Freshmen and sophomores should be given a solid grounding in math and science' (2006 p. 42). We have argued that there should be a 'concerted focus on developing undergraduate science curricula that prepare business graduates to be effective partners in advancing science and technology in a competitive global economy' (Ledley, 2012, p. 171).

There is evidence that the undergraduate science curriculum can be an effective venue for promoting scientific literacy. Most colleges and universities in the United States require students to take two science courses as part of a general education or distribution requirement (Miller, 2007), and the number of science courses taken in college has been shown to be the best predictor of civic scientific literacy independent of age, level of educational attainment, or informal scientific learning (Miller, 2004). Research also shows that students who complete general education science courses have an enhanced ability to understand articles in the lay press about science and technology and make sense of scientific research, which are skills similar to those required by business professionals (Hobson, 2008; Miller, 2004; Miller, 2007).

Imagining an undergraduate science curriculum for business students

In several recent studies, we have begun to define the landscape of undergraduate science education for business students. Specifically, we asked whether undergraduate business programs require students to take courses in science and technology, and what scientific content, learning objectives, and applications would be most appropriate for students focused on business careers.

We conducted a survey of the graduation requirements at 59 business schools listed in *BusinessWeek*'s 'top business programs,' asking how many science courses were required for an undergraduate business degree (Ledley, 2012). At 57 schools, there was a stated requirement for science as part of the general education requirement. At 19 of these schools, however, this requirement could be fulfilled, at least in part, by taking courses outside of traditional science, technology, or engineering disciplines. In all cases, the requirement was stated in terms of taking courses in one or more disciplinary departments identified by department name or course code. Only one school offered interdisciplinary courses in 'scientific inquiry' and 'science and its significance,' and only two stand-alone business schools offered science courses that were designed explicitly for students majoring in business disciplines (Ledley, 2012).

A questionnaire sent to deans of these schools indicated that at the majority of schools, business faculties or administration had at least some role in determining the composition of the general education requirement for business students including the number of courses, disciplines of courses, or listing of specific courses required to fulfill the requirement. Few reported any involvement in developing the goals, learning objectives, or content of these courses. Interestingly, career services and corporate partners were also reported to have little or no involvement in construction of the science requirement, despite the active voice of employers and industry organizations in calling a greater focus on undergraduate STEM skills (Ledley, 2012).

The inclusion of science courses in the general education requirement at most leading business schools suggests that there is a pre-existing platform that could be used for a curriculum that specifically addresses the need for interdisciplinary knowledge of science and technology together with business. The creation of such courses within science departments might not only better prepare business students for careers in which such interdisciplinary facility will be required, but might also improve the outcomes of science education itself.

Contemporary scholarship of teaching and learning in science revolves around the concepts of 'scientific teaching' (Handelsman et al., 2004; Miller et al.,2008) and 'evidence-based' curriculum development (NRC, 2002; ED, 2003). These approaches posit that student outcomes may be improved by introducing content in a context that is meaningful to students and adopting pedagogical methods that complement their learning strengths. This is exemplified by the 'Mathematics for Business Decisions' curriculum developed for business students by the Mathematics Association of America (MAA). This calculus and statistics curriculum focuses on context-based learning in which mathematical principles and their applications are taught with reference to business problems (Lamoureux, 2004; Thompson et al., 2005). Preliminary evidence suggests that this curriculum improves grades and retention rates in math courses as well as attitudes toward the use of mathematics among business students (Albers, 2002; Thompson, 2004).

To assess how principles of evidence-based curriculum design might be applied in developing science courses for business students, we conducted a study of science educators as well as educators in arts and sciences and educators in business, asking what learning objectives, content goals, and applications in science might best meet the needs of business students (Ledley and Holt, 2012). A sizable majority of respondents in all three groups indicated that the primary purposes of science education were to provide a broad overview of scientific principles; teach critical thinking; provide a foundation for understanding scientific research, technical innovation, and novel products; and provide a foundation for understanding the ethical and social implications of scientific research. A majority of all three groups ranked the application of inductive reasoning and understanding scientific principles in everyday observations among the major learning objectives. The ability to design controlled experiments and carry out laboratory experiments or data mining experiments ranked low in importance (Ledley and Holt, 2012).

These observations are largely consistent with the nature of the 'technology-centered knowledge' identified by management studies as being useful for business professionals involved in managing technology (Mallick and Chaudhury, 2000; IAMOT, 2007). These perspectives also parallel emerging concepts of scientific literacy that emphasize the process and nature of science over fact-based disciplinary knowledge (Hodson, 2008) as well as the concepts embodied in curriculum on Science, Technology, and Society (STS) (Kumar and Chubin, 2000), which similarly favor instruction in the context rather than the content of science.

Importantly, all of these observations emphasize the need for a science curriculum that is distinctly different from the curriculum designed for STEM majors or most 'non-major' curricula, which commonly parallel the major curriculum with less detail. Specifically, these results teach away from requiring courses focused on specific disciplines, experimental methods, or the methods of scientific investigation in favor of courses that would span multiple scientific disciplines, provide scientific and technical content in the context of management practices, and focus on skills in inductive- and evidence-based reasoning, rather than retention of scientific theories or facts. The dissidence expressed towards inquiry-based laboratory exercises points specifically to the need for new pedagogical approaches distinct from the inquiry-based learning in laboratory and field exercises that are the mainstay of education for science majors (Hofstein and Lunetta, 2004).

Implementation of a science curriculum for business students: the Bentley model

Bentley University is an atypical environment for STEM education. While Bentley emphasizes the integration of business with liberal arts and sciences in the undergraduate curriculum, more than 90 percent of Bentley students major in business degree programs. Without STEM majors, our challenge as science faculty is to contextualize core science concepts and educate business students whose STEM educational experience may be limited to two general education electives, including one introductory lab science and one intermediate science or math elective. Bentley faculty, however, have a tradition of effectively integrating liberal learning principles across the business-dominated curriculum, recognizing that Arts & Sciences and Business educational goals at the university are complementary, rather than competitive (Arenella et al., 2009). This approach is embodied in the opportunity for students to complete a major in Liberal Studies in conjunction with their business majors.

Over the past decade, the Natural & Applied Sciences Department has moved away from a traditional disciplinary structure to focus on scholarship and curriculum in two domains of particular importance to business and society: Earth, Environment and Global Sustainability, and Health and Industry. The laboratory-based science courses, which were formerly discipline-based, have been gradually revised so that they provide complementary perspectives on one or both of the two domains. The department also offers a broad portfolio of more than 30 elective courses, most of which focus on topics related to the two domains. Some provide advanced instruction in such disciplinary topics as atmospheric science, oceanography, climate change, genetics, nutrition, and health. Some focus explicitly on the integration of science with business in such areas as biotechnology, sustainability, space exploration, health systems, futurism, and management of technology. Students have the opportunity to complete a liberal studies major with concentrations in either Earth, Environment and Global Sustainability or Health and Industry, by taking additional elective courses in Natural and Applied Science with thematically related courses in other departments.

Most importantly, the department has developed a novel approach to science instruction, which focuses the scientific content on a limited number of basic scientific concepts, and emphasizes the critical thinking, evidence-based reasoning, methodological inquiry, and problem-solving skills required to extrapolate these concepts to higher-order phenomenon and real-world issues beyond the classroom. For example:

- A core course in human biology focuses on the mechanisms of genomics, biological pathways, and electricity at a nanomolecular level, and challenges students to apply those principles to explain aspects of physiology, health, disease, and biopharmaceutical products.
- A core course in geology focuses on basic concepts underlying the origin and distribution of economic mineral and energy resources, the supply and protection of water resources, and natural hazards,

allowing students to contextualize observations in Earth science and issues of environmental risk, resource management, sustainability, and green technology.

- A core course in environmental chemistry frames environmental problems in terms of the movement and change of matter and the flow of energy in natural and human-modified systems, allowing students to identify the relationships among air pollution, water pollution, greenhouse gas emissions, climate change, and energy production and consumption.
- A core course in astronomy focuses on the evolution of the solar system and challenges students to understand parallels to environmental and sustainability issues on our planet.

Recently, with funding from an NSF Course, Curriculum, and Laboratory Improvement (CCLI) grant, Bentley science and business faculty have been working cooperatively to develop a series of interdisciplinary course modules that more effectively integrate principles of Earth and environmental sciences into the broader undergraduate business curriculum. For example, faculty teaching the courses Environmental Chemistry, Principles of Geology, Ecology, Macroeconomics, Public Policy, and Economic Geography collaborated in a summer workshop to develop an interdisciplinary exploration of corn ethanol. A common module was developed to introduce students in participating courses to the complex problem comprising technological, environmental, societal, economic, and public policy considerations associated with the development of a renewable energy source. Next, students explore the issue from a disciplinary perspective, learning to do in-depth analysis of one aspect of the ethanol topic as a basis for learning fundamental principles in their enrolled course. Finally, a closing activity relates the students' new disciplinary expertise back to the original trans-disciplinary problem. The expectation, currently being tested through assessment activities, is that students will be more scientifically literate, more effective problem solvers, and better able to link their scientific foundations to real-world problems representing complex, integrative societal, business, natural resource, and environmental challenges.

Another distinctive feature of the Bentley curriculum is the focus on immersion in scientific data including the hands-on use of a state-of-the-art analytical chemistry laboratory, mining of genomic databases, and exercises with GIS-linked Earth science data. Bentley also offers opportunities for experiential scientific learning through participation in undergraduate research, field experiences involving research or global travel, service-learning, and supervised internships in technology-based companies.

While Bentley is a business-focused institution, a similar science curriculum contextualized within the framework of business could have broad appeal at other universities. Business students currently represent the largest cohort of undergraduate majors, accounting for more than 20 percent of all bachelor degrees (Snyder et al., 2009) and more than 25 percent of those majoring outside the STEM disciplines. It is likely that science courses tailored to the needs of business students would also appeal to students majoring in other liberal arts or professional disciplines that lead to careers in business. Such a curriculum would, thus, not only improve the ability of business professionals to manage in technology rich environments, but more broadly contribute to promoting scientific literacy in general.

The combustible mix

Carl Sagan's comment that the 'combustible mixture of ignorance and power is going to blow up in our faces' seems eminently prescient in the context of such high-profile calamities including the Deepwater Horizon failure, the Fukushima Daiichi nuclear disaster, growing concern about drug toxicities, environmental degradation, and global climate change, and the social disruptions caused by globalization. These events, however, are not the inevitable consequence of technological progress, but rather the failure to appropriately manage scientific knowledge and technologies for the benefit of either corporate enterprise or society. There are myriad opportunities for applying science and technology in ways that might meaningfully improve health, prevent famine, preserve our environment, mitigate climate change, and ensure both economic growth and equity of economic opportunity that are missed because of the failure to effectively integrate the potentials of science with effective, complementary business practices.

While ignorance and power may comprise a 'combustible mix,' the equally combustible mix of knowledge and power remains the engine for our industries, our economy, our personal and environmental health, and our future. Harnessing that power requires that business professionals be empowered with sufficient knowledge of science and technology, both to avoid lessons from past disasters, and to fairly and efficiently exploit the opportunities that will continue to arise from the progress of scientific discovery and advancing technology.

*We wish to acknowledge the many insights and ideas of our colleagues in the Department of Natural and Applied Sciences and throughout Bentley that are represented in this chapter. This chapter was supported, in part, by NSF (DUE 0941131), the National Biomedical Research Foundation, the ACTA Foundation, and grants from Bentley University.

References

AAC&U (2007) *College Learning for the New Global Century.* Association of American Colleges and Universities, Washington, DC, ISBN 978-0-9779210-4-1. Retrieved from http://www.aacu.org/leap/documents/GlobalCentury_final.pdf

Albers, D. (2002) 'a Genuine Interdisciplinary Partnership: MAA unveils "Mathematics for Business Decisions"'. *FOCUS*, 22, pp. 14–16.

Arenella, L. S., Davi, A. M., Veeser, C.R., and Wiggins, R. A. (2009) 'The Best of Both Worlds: Infusing Liberal Learning into a Business Curriculum,' *Liberal Education*, 95, pp. 50–55.

Baldi, S., Jin, Y., Skemer, M., Green, P.J., and Herget, D. (2007) *Highlights from PISA 2006: Performance of U.S. 15-year-old Students in Science and Mathematics Literacy in an International Context.* National Center for Education Statistics, NCES 2008–016. Retrieved from http://nces.ed.gov/pubs2008/2008016.pdf

Council on Competitiveness (2005) *National Innovation Initiative Summit and Report: Thriving in a World of Challenge and Change.* Retrieved from http://www.compete.org/publications/detail/202/innovate-america/

ED (2003) *Identifying and Implementing Educational Practices Supported by Rigorous Evidence.* U.S. Department of Education Institute of Education Sciences National Center for Education Evaluation and Regional Assistance. Retrieved from http://www2.ed.gov/rschstat/research/pubs/rigorousevid/rigorousevid.pdf

Elder, J., Meyer-Krahmer, F., and Reger, G. (2002) 'Changes in the Strategic Management of Technology: Results of a Global Benchmarking Study,' *R&D Management*, 32, pp. 149–164.

Handelsman, J., Miller S., and Pfund, C. (2006) *Scientific Teaching* (New York: W. H. Freeman).

Handelsman, J., Ebert-May, D., Beichner, R., Bruns, P., Chang, A., DeHaan, R., Gentile J., Lauffer, S., Stewart, J., Tilghman, S.M., and Wood, W.B. (2004) 'Scientific Teaching,' *Science*, 304, pp. 521–522.

Harvard Business Essentials (2003) *Managing Creativity and Innovation, Practical Strategies to Encourage Creativity* (Boston, MA: Harvard Business Press).

Hobson, A. (2008) 'The Surprising Effectiveness of College Scientific Literacy Courses,' *Physics Teacher*, 46, pp. 404–406.

Hodson, D. (2008) *Towards Scientific Literacy. A Teachers' Guide to the History, Philosophy, and Sociology of Science* (Rotterdam: Sense Publishers).

Hofstein A. and Lunetta V.N. (2004) 'The Laboratory in Science Education: Foundations for the Twenty-First Century,' *Science Education* 88, pp. 28–54.

Holdren, John P. (2008) 'Science and Technology for Sustainable Well-Being,' *Science*, 319, pp. 424–434.

IAMOT (2007) 'Program Guidelines for Management of Technology (MOT) Graduate Level Academic Institution Certification.' The International

Association for Management of Technology. Retrieved from http://www.iamot.org/

Kalosh, Anne (2006), 'Bringing Science Down to Earth,' in T. Head (ed.), *Conversations with Carl Sagan*, (Jackson: University Press of Mississippi), pp. 99–106.

Kumar D.D. and Chubin, D.E. (2000) *Science, Technology, and Society Education A Sourcebook on Research and Practice* (Springer: New York).

Lamoureux, C. (ed.) (2004) 'Business and Management' (chapter 3), in *CRAFTY/CUPM Curriculum Foundations Project: Voices of the Partner Disciplines*, Susan Gantner and William Barker (eds). Mathematical Association of America, pp. 19–25. Retrieved from http://www.maa.org/cupm/crafty/welcome.html

Laprise, S.L., Winrich, C., and Sharpe, N.R. (2008) 'Business Students Should Learn More about Science,' *Chronicle of Higher Education*, 54, A35.

Ledley, F.D. (2012) 'Bridging the Boundary between Science and Business,' *International Journal of Science in Society*.

Ledley, F.D. and Holt, S.E. (2012) 'Goals and Objectives of a Science Curriculum in Undergraduate Management Education,' *Journal of Management Education*, November. Retrieved from http://jme.sagepub.com/citmgr?gca=spjme;105256 2912462137v1

Lichtenthaler, E. (2003) 'Third Generation Management of Technology Intelligence Processes,' *R&D Management*, 33, pp. 361–375.

Maglitta, J. (1994) 'Meet the New Boss: A New Tradition,' *Computerworld*, 28(11), pp. 80–82.

Mallick, D.N. and Chaudhury, A. (2000) 'Technology Management Education in mba Programs: a Comparative Study of Knowledge and Skill Requirements,' *Journal of Engineering and Technology Management*, 17, pp. 153–173.

McCann, J. (2006) 'The Next Economy,' *BizEd*, 5(3), pp. 40–44.

McKinsey & Company (2011) 'The Business of Sustainability: McKinsey Global Survey Results,' *McKinsey Quarterly*, October. http://www.mckinseyquarterly.com/The_business_of_sustainability_McKinsey_Global_Survey_results_2867, accessed March 20, 2012.

Miller, J. D. (2004) 'Public Understanding of, and Attitudes toward, Scientific Research: What We Know and What We Need to Know,' *Public Understanding of Science*, 13, pp. 273–294.

Miller, J. D. (2007) 'The Public Understanding of Science in Europe and the United States,' paper presented at the 173rd Annual Meeting of the American Association for the Advancement of Science, San Francisco, CA, February 17. Retrieved from http://ucll.msu.edu/files ucll.msu.edu/docs/miller-science-europe.doc

Miller, J. D. and Pardo, R. (2000) 'Civic Scientific Literacy and Attitude to Science and Technology: a Comparative Analysis of the European Union, the United States, Japan, and Canada,' in M. Dierkes and C. von Grote (eds) *Between Understanding and Trust: the Public, Science, and Technology*, pp. 81–129 (Amsterdam: Harwood Academic Publishers).

Miller, S., Pfund, C., Pribbenow, C. M., and Handelsman, J. (2008) 'Scientific Teaching in Practice,' *Science*, 322, pp. 1329–1330.

NAE (2002) *Technically Speaking: Why All Americans Need to Know More about Technology*. Pearson, G. and Young, A.T. (eds). National Academy of Engineering, National Research Council, Report of the Committee on Technological

Literacy. Washington, DC: The National Academies Press. Retrieved from http://www.nap.edu/openbook.php?isbn=0309082625.

NAS (2007) *Rising Above the Gathering Storm: Energizing and Employing America for a Brighter Economic Future.* Committee on Prospering in the Global Economy of the 21st Century: An Agenda for American Science and Technology. National Academy of Sciences, National Academy of Engineering, and Institute of Medicine. Washington, DC: The National Academies Press.

NRC (2002) *Scientific Research in Education.* Committee on Scientific Principles for Education Research, National Research Council. Retrieved from http://www.nap.edu/catalog/10236.html

NRC (2008) *Science Professionals: Master's Education for a Competitive World.* Committee on Enhancing the Master's Degree in the Natural Sciences, National Research Council. Washington, DC: The National Academies Press. Retrieved from http://www.nap.edu/catalog.php?record_id=12064

NSF (2008) *Science and Engineering Indicators: 2008.* National Science Board, vol. 1 NSB 08–01, vol. 2, NSB08–01A. Retrieved from http://www.nsf.gov/statistics/seind08/pdfstart.htm

PKAL (2006) 'Report on Reports II: Recommendations for Urgent Action 2006.' Project Kaleidoscope. Washington, DC Retrieved from http://www.pkal.org/documents/ReportOnReportsII.cfm

President's Council (2012) 'Engage to Excel: Producing One Million Additional Graduates with Degrees in Science, Technology, and Mathematics,' President's Council of Advisors on Science and Technology. Retrieved from http://www.whitehouse.gov/sites/default/files/microsites/ostp/pcast-engage-to-excel-final_feb.pdf

Schmidt, W.H., McKnight, C.C., and Raizen, S.A. (1997) *A Splintered Vision: An Investigation of U.S. Science and Mathematics Education* (Norwell, MA: Kluwer).

Snyder, T.D., Dillow, S.A., and Hoffman, C.M. (2009) *Digest of Education Statistics 2008.* National Center for Education Statistics, NCES 2009–020. Retrieved from http://nces.ed.gov/pubs2009/2009020.pdf

Thompson, R. (2004) 'Business College Support of Mathematics for Business Decisions Motivates Students,' *FOCUS*, 24, pp. 16–17.

Thompson, R., Lamoureux, C., and Slaten, P. (2005) 'Mathematics for Business Decisions With Interdisciplinary Multimedia Projects, Parts 1 and 2,' Washington, DC: Mathematical Association of America. Retrieved from http://business.math.arizona.edu/MBD/mbd.html.

UN (2010) The Millennium Development Goals Report (New York: United Nations), p. 80.

US Chamber of Commerce (2005) *Tapping America's Potential: The Education for Innovation Initiative.* Retrieved from http://www.uschamber.com/reports/tapping-americas-potential-education-innovation-initiative.

14

Starving for Knowledge: The Need for Business Education in the Arts

Gregory L. Farber

In business schools across the country, the question arises of how to integrate the liberal arts into the business curriculum. Every business school has general education requirements that mandate that undergraduate students receive some exposure to things like literature, science, psychology, or history. The question of how to integrate liberal arts into business studies is an important one, especially as employers continually look to hire and promote intelligent and creative employees. Business leaders regularly point out that their new business school hires are missing essential knowledge and abilities, such as communication and critical thinking skills, skills that are often the focus of a liberal arts degree.

Even if business universities often struggle to decide how best to incorporate the liberal arts into a business education, they generally agree on the importance of doing so. But can business education reciprocate? While business schools offer literature and sociology classes, liberal arts schools don't necessarily offer business courses. What then, if anything, can business education offer those in the liberal arts classroom? A lot.

Students graduating with liberal arts degrees ultimately need to enter the workforce. Even students who pursue post-graduate degrees and ultimately continue working in academia are part of a larger industry. The question is, 'how prepared are those students to enter their industries?' The answer, 'less than they could be.'

This is especially true in the fine arts. Arts students, whether in the visual or performing arts, are often consumed by their craft. They just want to dance, paint, or write. But they need guidance in the business world if they want to succeed, and not just succeeding financially. If they want to reach larger audiences, more effectively communicate their messages, and effect social change, they need to get grants, sell more tickets or artwork, and keep their businesses afloat. They need what a business education offers.

One problem is that many arts students see business people as enemies. Artists criticize corporate America and complain that anyone who makes money is a sell-out. What they fail to realize is that to be able to fund their work, to be able to make a living creating art, to have the supplies, facilities, collaborators, and audiences necessary for art to be meaningful, having money is essential.

This often overlooked (or willfully ignored) financial component of the fine arts means that business and arts are not as antithetical as they may appear to some. Looking at how these disciplines can be mutually beneficial allows us to then apply those lessons to liberal arts education as a whole. Theatre is a good example of a field that often eschews good business practices in the name of 'art.' Looking at studies of organizations and at what practitioners have to say after gaining experience in their fields provides some useful insight into where their education might have failed them.

A 2008 report, 'Vital Signs,' by the Boston Foundation, an organization dedicated to developing and sustaining the local community, including arts and culture, commented on the current state of arts and culture organizations: 'An increasing number of organizations seem to be competing for resources that may not be expanding to match increasing needs. Organizations may not be calibrating their investments in facilities and staff in response to these market forces' (Nelson and McQueen, 2008, p. 7). While it may come as no shock that arts organizations are suffering, what may be surprising is why this should be so. The Boston Foundation's report suggests that in the greater Boston area, at least, it is not simply a diminished interest in the arts that is responsible for a declining attendance. Organizations' lack of business acumen and inability to understand and respond to the market around them has been their biggest problem.

And which organizations are the most vulnerable or least prepared? Size seems to be a major indicator of success. 'The smallest organizations,' according to the Boston Foundation's report, 'experienced weakening health' (Nelson and McQueen, 2008, p. 7). While on the other hand, 'the largest organizations ... seem to be the healthiest' (p. 8). On the surface, this may seem obvious – larger organizations tend to have larger payrolls and profits and are therefore better able to absorb fluctuations in the market. Their brand recognition keeps audiences returning, and economies of scale allow them to be more efficient overall.

Yet these organizations were once fledgling companies themselves. What qualities allowed them to grow and succeed? Those same qualities that are so often derided by artistic types, the skills and knowledge that students learn at a quality business university: knowledge of the marketplace, the skills to address the finances of a company, and the ability to market and promote the services of the organization. Most arts organizations succeed in part because of their business acumen or their recognition of the importance of the skills and abilities taught in a business school setting.

In the arts world, small organizations collapse all the time. Between 1999 and 2004 in Boston alone, 76 organizations 'ceased operations' (Nelson and McQueen, 2008, p. 21). The ones that stuck around, the ones that have been consistently most successful over a long period of time tend to have something in common: they appreciate business knowledge. While many are large, plenty of these are also small organizations with fewer than ten full-time employees and modest operating budgets. Regardless of size, most successful organizations have staff with a range of traditional business-oriented positions, including finance, marketing, and human resource professionals. In addition to the usual suspects of BFAs or MFAs, staff biographies reveal business degrees along with theatre or non-profit management degrees. Conversely, many of the smaller, struggling (or now defunct) organizations consist primarily of artists with arts education or degrees.

Though many are starting to realize that such formal business training is beneficial, the percentage of arts administrators who have such degrees is still low (Rhine, 2007). As of 2006, nationally, there are only around 40 academic programs, both undergraduate and graduate combined, that offer a focus in the business of theatre (Blakemore, 2006). As Jeffery Hermann, managing director for the Albany Berkshire Ballet, says, 'I was always haunted by the idea that my lack of formal training in arts administration was somehow preventing even greater achievement' (Blakemore, 2006). This isn't to say that people with traditional arts degrees in acting, designing, or directing can't or shouldn't immerse themselves in producing live theatre. It does suggest, however, that a good business sense or background – whether it's through formal education or practical experience – is extremely important.

Interviews with professionals in the field further illustrate this point. While a small sampling of interviews is by no means a scientific study of the industry, some specific examples can provide a snapshot of the situation many organizations find themselves in.

One such example is the Arizona-based Word of Mouth Tour Company. Founded in 2008 by Louis Farber (no relation) and Jeremiah Neal, Word of Mouth has produced a few shows, but is currently struggling for its survival. Farber, the artistic director, has a BA in theatre while Neal, the production manager, holds an MFA in Theatre for Youth. When talking about the artistic side of things, both became very animated and excited. They discuss the productions they've been involved with and the success they've had artistically. They've had work produced in several states. They recently had a work commissioned by Pennsylvania Youth Theatre, and their recent play *The Line* was a semifinalist at the prestigious Bonderman Festival in 2011.

Neal praised his collaboration with Farber saying, 'Louis and I work really well artistically together' (Neal, 2011). However, as a business, Word of Mouth leaves something to be desired. Neal said that he doesn't have a good business sense, and even if he did focus more of his energies on that part of the company, he doesn't know whether he could ever be good at it. He admitted, 'Louis and I are not the greatest with finances, so that's given us some problems' (Neal, 2011). They had problems such as fewer productions as well as financial troubles.

Word of Mouth has yet to make any money, and they haven't received any of the grants they've applied for. According to Farber, 'Things aren't happening as quickly or as grandly as we would like,' in part because as a company they don't have anyone to manage the business end of things (Farber 2011). When asked how much focus there was on the business of starting a theatre company, Farber replied, 'There was none.' They have since realized this problem, but it may be too late. Farber said they're currently looking for someone to help with the marketing for Word of Mouth and that they need someone more business-minded who is 'a good counterpoint to Jeremiah and me, who are less business-heady' (Farber, 2011).

Their problem is not an uncommon one. Both Farber and Neal are good at what they do – performing, writing, and directing. But their problem is the same as many other theatre companies started without the business portion of the company in mind. Neal put it best when he said, 'We just want to create the product; we don't really know how to sell it' (Neal, 2011).

Another company in difficult financial straits is Theatre in My Basement (TIMB), created in 1999 and run by Chris Danowski. TIMB has regularly produced new experimental work and hosted a variety of performance festivals despite starting without a clear business plan. However, Danowski acknowledged the importance of business acumen in running his company: 'It's terribly important' (Danowski, 2011). Danowski has been forced to become that business presence in the company, taking part in Creative Capital's program to help develop business skills, and participating in a workshop by the Arizona Commission (Danowski, 2011). While Danowski's own drive and constant desire to expand his own business knowledge seems to keep the company afloat, even he admits:

> Looking at how the last 2 years have gone, fiscally speaking, the company is really done. There's no money at all, the local grants have dried up, and it's impossible to get support. But we still keep doing new work in spite of all that. I don't know how that happens, I guess I learned enough to figure out how to put things together for next to nothing. (Danowski, 2011)

That doesn't necessarily mean that having a better business plan going in or having a more knowledgeable or experienced person to deal with the business would have put TIMB in a more stable financial position. However, looking at theatres that have been more successful, their ability to manage the business along with the artistry is hard to deny.

Opening in 2000, Stray Cat Theatre, run by artistic director Ron May completed its ninth full season in 2012. While still a small company, more than ten years since its founding, Stray Cat is financially stable and looks to be well into the future. While Stray Cat was also comprised of only theatre majors at its inception, May credits his success to a class he took in theatre organization and management. 'That was probably the best class I took [in college]. (No offense to any of my other classes.) But that's the class that Stray Cat kind of came out of. The idea anyway. And the blueprint. Once the class was one, it was seriously like, 'wow ... I think we know what we need to know to go try and do this' (May, 2011).

Additionally, May said that he thinks 'theater majors are done a huge disservice by not having to take business courses. Hell, even if you're an actor' it's essential to know how the company functions' (May, 2011). He feels that he has been helped by taking additional workshops on improving business skills and that the inclusion of several successful business people on their board 'is a godsend' (May, 2011).

A similar success story is Boston-based Company One. Founded in the summer of 1998, it has made quite a reputation for itself in that short time. Co-founder and current artistic director Shawn LaCount, who also owns a bed and breakfast, understood the importance of having that business knowledge from the start. In addition to his personal experience, several others who helped found the company had business experience. One had a masters in communications, one a masters in non-profit management, and another an MFA in theatre administration. Since then, their managing director has earned another degree, this one in non-profit management, and they have made it a point to include many 'financial-minded folks' on their board (LaCount, 2011). LaCount acknowledged that when they started, they 'struggled with the staff being the board being the artists,' but they were able to figure it out. He continued, 'Knowledge of business is almost more important than creating good art ... almost' (LaCount, 2011).

Then there is Amy Beck. Beck is currently the theatre arts department chair at Arizona School for the Arts, but has also worked as the director of a non-profit social service agency, a job she got immediately after earning her MFA. She attributes her hiring at both institutions in part to the focus she put on incorporating business into her theatre training. In addition to her MFA, she completed a masters' certificate program in nonprofit leadership and management. She said that the 'certificate program filled in the huge gaps that my classmates and colleagues have still not been able to fill in their training' (Beck, 2011). She elaborated on the program:

> This certificate program threw me into several local non-profits and allowed me to analyze their own structures to learn about different sizes of organizations, best practices, worst practices, growth opportunities, collaboration opportunities, funding opportunities, all those things you really need to know to do any of those jobs that my [classmates and I] wanted to pursue. ... I think I got a great edge by adding this certificate program and I wonder why my graduate program did not require at least a few of the courses as part of our program of study. (Beck, 2011)

Beck said that she even feels more knowledgeable and capable than some of her colleagues with more experience: 'I felt comfortable stepping into my nonprofit management positions because I received a comprehensive and practical education ... while many in management positions in nonprofit learn by trial and error' (Beck, 2011). And while trial and error can be an extremely useful way to learn and gain experience, sometimes the time it takes and the errors made can be too costly. And while many people learn a great deal on the job, especially in established companies that have other people to instruct or serve as mentors, young theatre companies can ill-afford to waste their limited time and resources making costly mistakes.

Beck reiterated her conviction that business education is one easy way to avoid those kinds of mistakes:

> If you want an advanced degree then you should be exploring *all* aspects of understanding for your field, not just a piece of the pie ... How can you be an expert in your field without knowing how to really work in the field? ... I think depending on what you are studying, there are particular courses that should be *required* as part of the scope of study and all courses should be included as possible electives. (Beck, 2011)

If we believe that business education is an essential component of an arts education, what does that mean for business educators? It means we need to offer more business education in traditionally non-business programs, institutions, and classes, and it means that business schools may be able to open themselves up to new markets.

Some schools, both those with a liberal arts focus and those with a business focus, have begun to better prepare their liberal arts students for the world after the academy. The strategy is deceptively simple, especially for someone who has practiced in the field: approach the teaching as one would approach the practice, which sufficiently and constantly blends the creative, critical, theoretical, and the practical. This emerging idea is favored by many, according to Paula Wasley in 'Entrepreneurship 101: Not Just for Business School Anymore.' In her article, she says that several schools are looking at, and struggling with, how to combine business and the liberal arts. While some people may be 'troubled by the idea of inserting entrepreneurship across the undergraduate experience,' others, such as Philip R. Regier, executive dean of Arizona State University's W. P. Carey School of Business, say the aim 'is not to have students run businesses out of their dorm rooms'; it's about understanding the practicalities of the world around them and making the most of the opportunities that present themselves (Wasley, 2008).

Ramon Ricker, senior associate dean for professional students at the University of Rochester's Eastman School of Music, says that 'indeed, entrepreneurship is a natural fit for performing artists.... We're trying to give our students tools that they will use to make the road to success in music a little smoother.... To be successful, you can't just be a good player. You have to have some entrepreneurial savvy' (Wasley, 2008). This is reiterated by Andrea Kalyn, associate dean for academic affairs at Oberlin's

Conservatory of Music. She talks about arts students' general disregard for business classes. But she says, 'if you know you have this idea to start a theatre company and you don't know how to balance a checkbook, but you have an opportunity where somebody is going to give you $1,500, then the accounting class is suddenly meaningful' (Wasley, 2008).

Often business and liberal arts institutions feel as though they have no students in common. Liberal arts schools pull from one set of students while business schools pull from another. Arts institutions need to offer business classes for their students, while business schools can open their doors to more arts students.

Personally, my background as an undergraduate at a business school, with a business minor and a significant portion of my classes in business, has been invaluable in my own work in the theatre industry. More often than not, I have been the one writing grants and devising a marketing plan. Most recently, as director of development for a local Boston-area theatre company, I helped organize our first formal fundraiser, got our first grant, and developed community contacts. All of these were possible not because of my MFA in playwriting, but because of what I learned as an undergraduate at a business school.

Arts and entertainment is a $350 billion-per year industry; some of our business students are going to work with artists at some point, either personally or professionally (US Bureau of Labor Statistics, 2010). Knowing how they can best work together – not only knowing where they're coming from, but how they can offer business knowledge to these people or companies – is important.

Steps to the future

The easiest and most obvious first step is to offer more business classes for arts students, both at business and liberal arts schools. Liberal arts institutions need to offer major-specific business courses. Arts students need to be convinced that knowing the business of their field is important. Requiring classes is one way for programs to signal their commitment to helping arts students prepare for the world after college. Additionally, programs need to make sure their institutional and program-specific documents, such as their website and mission statement, stress understanding the business of a field. Faculty should also be more aware that students don't necessarily enter the classroom or program knowing just how important such an understanding is. Mentors, advisers, and teachers need to encourage students to take business classes, and to take those classes seriously.

Sculptors should be required to take classes in entrepreneurship or gallery management, as screenwriters should have to take production classes. Doing so would allow students more career options after college. But even if those students never worked in a gallery, it would allow them to become more knowledgeable about their field as a whole. In the same way that acting majors are often required to take directing or writing classes because it helps them understand theatre – not just acting – as their craft, so too would taking related business classes allows them to gain a more comprehensive view of their field. Seeing art as something that involves not only inspiration and creativity, but marketing and salesmanship, will allow students to create better artistic products, sell their creations more effectively, and make a livable wage from their chosen venture.

But even as requiring business classes signals its importance to art students, if that is the only reinforcement, it simultaneously undermines that importance. Our goal should not simply be to have students take such classes concurrently with their major classes. As Byron Chew and Cecilia McInnis-Bowers explain in their article 'Blending Liberal Arts and Business Education,' there is a 'traditional, artificial distinction between liberal and practical education' (Chew and McInnis-Bowers, 2004, p. 56). They continue by explaining that this results in 'students [who] do not perceive a cohesive learning experience' because of the 'curricular disconnect between the domains' of liberal arts and business (Chew and McInnis-Bowers, 2004, p. 59). Such a distinction is false, and even adding classes or programs may ultimately reinforce this division.

In part this results from our current approaches. We talk about combining the two as either 'bridging' or 'embedding,' according to Chew and McInnis-Bowers. These suggest that the two are fundamentally distinct. The 'bridge' language suggests two different entities that are naturally separate and between which an artificial construct must connect the two. Even embedding, which suggests a closer relationship, signals one distinct entity within another. The 'embedded' material is still a single unit within a larger whole, like hiding a pet's pill in a more desirable treat. Chew and McInnis-Bowers prefer the term 'blending,' which suggests a much more inseparable combination (Chew and McInnis-Bowers, 2004).

Such blending means making business part of the creative classroom. Primarily, arts classes need to be taught by successful practitioners. Those artists understand that the creation and business of art are not distinct. Teachers who have been in the field should discuss the realities of creating and distributing an artistic product. Continual discussion of the realities of the world that creative artists are entering is essential to their success in that world. When those discussions become a regular part of the classroom, they do not take away from the creativity and artistry that must be the focus of any such class. Those discussions, in fact, do the opposite, heightening students' focus on potential audiences, encouraging them to take more pride in their work, and thinking about their craft beyond the narrow confines of the classroom walls. Those teachers also need to integrate practical exercises into their classes. In my own playwriting classes, for example, we constantly talk about how plays get performed. Students read their plays and stage them. Students also write synopses with which to sell their plays, and they write query letters to contact interested producers. When I teach screenwriting, we discuss the structure of a Hollywood film studio. Students do mock pitches to learn how to present their initial ideas or finished products. When students complete my writing courses, they have not only practiced and improved their writing skills, but they have thought about how to put those skills to use. They leave with a sense of what can happen to their writing in a professional context and how a writer for theatre or film fits into the larger mechanisms of that industry.

Ultimately we need to break down the barriers between arts and business, from both sides. That's not to say that there shouldn't be any differences; specialization allows for mastery and dedication in a specific field. There is a significant danger of trying too hard to turn the liberal arts into something 'useful.' As Sacred Heart University professor John Jalbert cautions, colleges should teach liberal arts 'disciplines as ends-in-themselves, rather than as a means to external ends,' lest they risk turning students into '"slaves" who exist for the sake of others' (Jalbert, 2009, p. 224). Stanford professor David Labaree complains that we are already at a point where 'liberal education has succeeded in colonizing professional education, but credentialism has turned this liberal education back toward vocational goals. The content is liberal, but credentialism means that the content does not really matter' (Labaree, 2006, p. 15). In other words, by focusing too much on the practical applications of arts or education, schools may rob students of their abilities to appreciate their real purpose: 'it disrupts, it challenges, it undermines, in a word, it questions' (Jalbert, 2009, p. 223).

But as important as it is to encourage students – through classes, curricula, and institutions – to enjoy learning and thinking, where are they left if they do not learn how to put that thinking into practice? Artists call this desire for practicality 'selling out.' yet they worry about how their ideas, innovations, or art will get disseminated. They often forget that distributing their work takes money. They need to understand that when spreading their ideas through organizations such as performing arts companies, media outlets, or art galleries, those organizations with solid financial foundations are the ones that will allow artists to have the greatest impact. Without an understanding of how to put themselves in the best positions to succeed in the workplace after college, regardless of discipline, students will not be able to take advantage of whatever liberal education they receive.

All universities require general education courses because they realize the importance of a well-rounded foundational education. Maybe it's time we started including business education as part of that essential base.

References

Beck, Amy (2011), message to the author, June 28, email.

Blakemore, Erin (2006) 'Taking the Academic Route Into Theatre Administration,' *Dramabiz.com*, July/August.

Chew, E. Byron and Cecilia McInnis-Bowers (2004) 'Blending Liberal Arts & Business Education,' *Liberal Education*, Winter.

Danowski, Chris (2011), message to the author, June 27, Facebook.

Farber, Louis (2011), telephone interview, June 8.

Jalbert, John (2009) 'Leisure and Liberal Education: A Plea for Uselessness,' *Philosophical Studies in Education*, 40, pp. 223–233.

Labaree, David (2006) 'Mutual Subversion: A Short History of the Liberal and the Professional in American Higher Education,' *History of Education Quarterly*, 6(1), pp. 1–15.

LaCount, Shawn (2011), message to the author, June 13, email.

May, Ron (2011), message to the author, June 29, Facebook.

Neal, Jeremiah (2011), telephone interview, June 9.

Nelson, Susan, and Ann McQueen (2008) *Vital Signs: Metro Boston's Arts and Cultural Nonprofits, 1999 and 2004* (Boston: The Boston Foundation).

Rhine, Anthony S. (2007) 'The mfa in Theater Management and the mba: An Examination of Perspectives of Decision Makes at Theaters in the United States,' *Journal of Arts Management, Law and Society*, 37(2), 113.

United States, Bureau of Labor Statistics. Department of Labor (2010), 'Consumer Expenditures 2009,' Bureau of Labor Statistics. Department of Labor, October 5, (http://bls.gov/news.release/cesan.nr0.htm)

Wasley, Paula (2008) 'Entrepreneurship 101: Not Just for Business School Anymore,' *Chronicle of Higher Education*, 54, p. 41.

Part IV

Current and Future Educational Trends at the Heart of the Crucial Fusion

15
Technology in Business Education
William T. Schiano

A wealth of technologies is becoming viable in the mainstream of business education, as complements to and substitutes for the traditional classroom. This wave of new technologies comes at a time of great economic pressure on higher education in general and business education in particular. The sustainability of the traditional economic model of higher education in the United States is being actively questioned. The responses of colleges and universities, instituting often drastic cutbacks during the recent economic downturn, highlight the tenuousness of the traditional classroom-centric business model. Many are advocating technology as the solution to higher education's woes. The novelty of a new technology can be appealing and creates an opportunity to overcome prior resistance.

Hanging on to old ideas to the exclusion of new ones is hardly the exclusive purview of academics, but academia has been slower to adapt than many industries. Christensen and Eyring (2011) note that higher education has been largely immune to major competitive disruptions due to a persistent role for prestige (in an industry where quality is difficult to measure), an incestuous accreditation process, and a lack of disruptive technology. While it is easy to criticize slow-moving academics, the zealots of newer technologies tend to be cavalier about their shortcomings. The challenge lies in determining the likely impact of technology over time.

The change, however, is already upon us. Accrediting bodies now routinely approve non-traditional delivery models for courses and programs, and technology is now capable of disrupting and is already showing signs of doing so. Major initiatives such as the May 2012 $60 million joint distance-learning enterprise between Harvard University and the Massachusetts Institute of Technology reflect that top universities are committed to technology-based learning for the future.

Compounding the challenge for business education, companies are already quite comfortable with online learning within their organizations, and business students are more comfortable measuring quality by outcomes, particularly placement statistics, including salaries. While all areas of education are vulnerable, business is likely to be among those facing the earliest and greatest disruptions.

The corporate challenge

Corporate educational programs have been moving aggressively toward online classes. Much of the leading-edge work on online learning is being done in corporate training environments. While corporate applications are often more narrowly focused on skills development than are higher education courses, many programs cover material quite similar to what can be found in the core of business programs. Figure 15.1 shows the adoption rate of online classes in corporate training and higher education over the past decade.

Part of the reason online training resonates among corporate participants is that work is increasingly being conducted among people

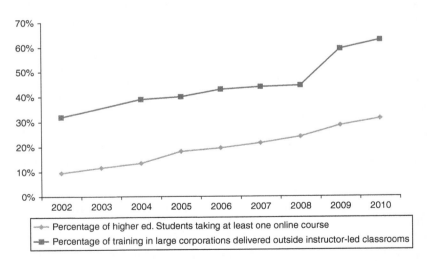

Figure 15.1 Use of online classes in higher education and corporate training
Source: Allen, 2011 and *Training Magazine* Annual Industry Reports, 2002–2010.

working in different places at different times. Employees in most large organizations are accustomed to working with others through technology mediation, so using the same technology for training is a logical extension.

This corporate move to online is having a particularly strong impact on business education. First, employers value online training and are increasingly open to hiring students who have studied in online courses or programs. Second, and possibly more importantly, students graduating from business programs are expected to be able to function well in computer-mediated, geographically distributed environments. It will be difficult for students to develop these skills unless schools incorporate elements of online learning into traditional programs.

e-Learning

PowerPoint's impact on pedagogy has been widely discussed and often bemoaned, in part due to its impact on cognitive style (Tufte, 2006). PowerPoint has achieved an astounding market share in classrooms (Williamson et al., 2011), and has homogenized presentations and stifled creative expression. Online technology has the potential to make at least as major a shift. Whether the overall impact will be positive has not yet been determined, and will be driven by how the technology is implemented and used in courses and programs.

The ingrained arguments framing e-learning as a less effective, marginal modality have been falling quickly. Forrester Research (Schooley, 2009) acknowledges that in-person may be the preference of most people, but notes that economic realities are such that corporations are turning to online for most training. The remaining robust exceptions are for the development of soft skills and personal and team trust. Socialization is a major component of business education, and socialization and in-person presentation skills are much harder to develop remotely.

While determining the effectiveness of e-learning is beyond the scope of this chapter, it has been the subject of exhaustive analysis. Widely cited meta-analyses (Bernard et al. 2004, cited in Clark and Mayer, 2011; Means et al., 2010) have found online learning to be as good or better than in person for the vast majority of effects studied. A 2011 survey by the Pew Research Center and the *Chronicle of Higher Education* found that 51 percent of college presidents believed that an online course offered at least the same value as one taught in a traditional classroom (*Chronicle of Higher Education*, 2011). One major ongoing annual study

(Allen and Seaman, 2011) shows that 65 percent of chief academic officers believe that online learning is a major part of their strategy, but less than one-third of those same officers believe their faculty 'accept the value and legitimacy of online education,' reflecting the perceived resistance of faculty (Allen and Seaman, 2011, p. 9).

Adoption of e-learning is driven by a desire to increase access for students unwilling or unable to come to campus, and to reduce necessary campus infrastructure per student. The market is growing rapidly, with 31 percent of higher education students taking at least one online course (Allen and Seaman, 2011, p. 4), Similarly, Seaman (2009) found that 34 percent of faculty have taught an online course and 24 percent were teaching an online course at the time of the survey.

Providing lecture content outside of class via prerecorded video, and using class time for discussion, is becoming increasingly popular. While this seems novel and has generated excitement, it has been feasible for years, allowing students to watch videotapes of lectures or, of course, to read the lecture material in preparation for a class discussion. Just as distance learning has existed for centuries, distributing video has been feasible for decades. So what is different now? Video production and distribution are cheaper and easier today, but it is not clear those were the impediments to past implementations.

Bentley University's McCallum Graduate School has moved aggressively to blend traditional and online courses, implementing hybrid synchronous courses that allow students to participate in class or remotely. Video and audio of the faculty and students in the traditional classroom are streamed along with an electronic whiteboard and any presentation materials to remote students, who participate in class discussions via audio and, whenever possible, video. An average of 39 percent of students in hybrid classes participate remotely, and 37 percent of all students take at least one hybrid course. Students have valued hybrid courses as highly as traditional courses: student evaluations and attrition rates are the same for both formats, and all remote hybrid participants wanted more hybrid courses. The approach has enabled Bentley to increase profit by reaching remote students while maintaining quality without the need for dramatic changes in curriculum development.

Clark and Mayer (2011) distinguish psychological engagement, based on the cognitive efforts involved and behavioral engagement, the actions students take during a class. E-learning can facilitate both, employing multimedia technologies as well as interaction between and among students and faculty. The immersiveness of online education can be high for intellectual intensity even if the quality of the presentation of the material may be below that of traditional in-person classes. Such immersive experiences can facilitate social learning: small group interactions among students have been shown to be a powerful determinant of learning (Brown and Adler, 2008).

Some attempts have been made at using virtual worlds such as Second Life in higher education and simulations are becoming more sophisticated by employing technologies originally used in videogames. Such 'gamification' is growing increasingly popular in commercial applications and we can expect that credible three-dimensional renderings will become cost effective and common within the decade.

Program quality is heavily studied, with an ongoing battle over metrics (Mariasingam and Hanna, 2006). Online tools can gather assessment data during usage, capturing inputs and providing feedback to students and instructors (U.S. Department of Education, 2010). Comparing online and traditional classroom courses is difficult because the benchmarks for in-person courses vary widely. In schools where the de facto standard for teaching is maintaining a low level of students' complaints and keeping the school's accreditation, student engagement, challenge, and learning are not explicit concerns for many faculty. Other schools seek a variety of facets of quality in the classroom. In many schools, students in face-to-face classes have little contact with senior faculty teaching classes outside of large lectures and often little interaction with faculty giving the lectures, making it unsurprising that research would find online classes at least as effective.

While broader access to students has been a primary driver of e-learning adoption, Doyle (2009) found that the demographics of online students are remarkably similar to those in traditional classrooms. Doyle found a median distance of 15 miles from the school providing the online course. According to Doyle (2009), most students take online course as a complement to traditional classroom courses.

Profit has been a powerful motivator for schools to move courses online. A 2009 study of 96 schools found 65 percent reported their online operations were profitable (Parry, 2009). Fully equipping a traditional classroom with modern technology to support e-learning is now within the reach of most schools and will become an expectation for students. As telepresence technology gets inevitably cheaper, it will become feasible to see video of all participants and their body language nearly as well as in person. Such technology is currently prohibitively expensive for individual remote students, but is already practical for point-to-point setups where students attend classes in groups from dedicated remote locations. The school's entire infrastructure can be run in the cloud, dramatically lowering cost and reducing the need for in-house expertise.

e-Books

The shift toward e-books has been slow in coming due to factors including lack of standards, threat to the established business model of publishers, and difficulty among customers in finding the material (Epps, 2011), but finally appears to be taking hold, with sales of e-books accounting for 27 percent of book sales in 2011, up from 10 percent in 2010 (http://ebookcomments.blogspot.com/2012_03_01_archive.html). Initially most of the products have been simply electronic versions of existing traditional texts. As the nature of the texts changes, with more interactive and immersive elements, more course content could potentially be delivered through the media rather than in the classroom. As the quality of those products improves, how much of class preparation, assuming students can be convinced to prepare, will need to be taken up by individual-teacher-generated original video material? We must consider whether the use of this technology is fundamentally better.

Developing such e-books is much more expensive than traditional course material, but tools to support development are becoming more powerful and easy to use. Apple, Inc., among other companies, has developed tools that educators can use to render their coursework more interactive, attractive, and complete for a generation of students raised on computers and in the online environment. This trend, along with adoption of such tools by major textbook publishers, can only increase as demand increases for immersive, interactive learning content.

But open educational resources, notably MIT's OpenCourseWare, provide free electronic materials and the base of content available is expanding rapidly (Smith, 2009). As students adopt the electronic texts, it will be harder to forbid the use of computers in the classroom.

Technology's impact on the traditional classroom

Control of student technology in the classroom has always been difficult. An increasing number of students prefer to take notes on a computer, but they are also tempted to use the computer for tasks unrelated to the class. Faculty can forbid the use of any technology, but that eliminates the opportunity for students to make appropriate use of it. As students become accustomed to typing notes and papers, they may not be capable of doing anything approaching their best work when hand-writing.

Some schools enable faculty to disable network connectivity in the classroom, but in many cases WiFi connectivity bleeds in from adjacent rooms. And with the increasing prevalence of high-speed mobile data networks, which are illegal to jam in the United States, turning off the school-provided connectivity may not be sufficient to disconnect student machines. The problem can be addressed, with varying degrees of success, by managing norms about appropriate use, improving sight lines to student screens, having the instructor moving around the classroom, and even providing instructors with remote access to student screens.

Study groups of students, ongoing asynchronous student interaction, analysis, and discussions via microblogs, blogs, wikis, and other venues can engage students and sustain intellectual energy from class, increasing student willingness to devote time to the course. The extent of use of such tools remains governed by concerns about how best to use the finite amount of time students will devote to a course outside of class.

Academic integrity and rigor

It is striking that rigor and academic integrity are not primary foci of the vast majority of studies of online learning. One widely cited study found the majority of MBA students admitted to cheating in the previous year (McCabe et al., 2006). Giving exams remotely introduces the obvious issues of not being able to proctor them. While many traditional courses offer unproctored exams, often these are given in the presence of other students, and on a campus where norms about academic integrity are developed. Developing such norms in a purely electronic community will be more difficult. While there may be arguments for allowing some classes without proctored exams, running an entire program with exclusively independent work used for evaluation creates grave risks for the credibility of the grades.

Many instructors use open book exams as the solution to this problem. However, that does not address the possibility of work being done by others. Some schools use proctoring networks in remote locations where identification can be verified. Others evaluate intermediate deliverables, raising the cost and complexity for students buying assignments. Tools for detecting plagiarism such as Turnitin can identify collusion among students in the course and copying from other documents. But these are not useful against original work created by someone other than the student(s) responsible for the assignment. The market for outsourcing assigned work, referred to as contract cheating (Lancaster and Clarke, 2008), has grown more liquid over the years, with websites supporting transactions.

One way out of the problem is grading class participation, assuming there is some way to authenticate the identity of participants. As video of students becomes a routine part of synchronous classes, this will be viable. For asynchronous courses, there are not currently successful measures to prevent motivated, dishonest students from cheating throughout programs.

What it means for faculty

For the adoption of technology to succeed, faculty will need to agree to circulate curricular content in ways they resisted in the past. In many cases, exams and other content from class, including the contents of what would have been on the blackboard in a traditional classroom, will be distributed in electronic form. Technology can make the copying of material more difficult through various digital rights management techniques, but would not impede motivated students from circulating material meant to be kept confidential to those participating in a specific section of a course.

Technology increases the complexity of teaching, and requires more adaptation by faculty than in a traditional classroom, which for most faculty, with the exception of a computer projector in the room, still looks as it did a century ago. Seaman (2009) found that over 63 percent of faculty estimate that online courses take more effort to deliver, and 85 percent of faculty who have developed them found that it takes more effort than creating traditional courses. Software interfaces and functionality change regularly. The effort necessary to manage the changes may vary in scope, but add to burden of teaching the course. In most modes of online delivery, course material needs to be developed more robustly to make it digestible online.

Outsourcing becomes far more feasible for online education. Technology relaxes geographic restrictions on staffing, although remote instructors and course developers could still be employees of the school. Most schools have little expertise in hiring and managing remote employees, and having a third party handle the remote operations is appealing. Online programs can be modularized, separating development and delivery and creating components of courses as independent modules that can be outsourced to third party vendors (Parry, 2010).

Case teaching is a powerful methodology widely used in business schools in person, but very different online, at least for now. Case teachers strive to facilitate discussion among students. When done asynchronously, the momentum and energy of the traditional class is lost, as well as the need for students to learn to think on their feet. In the vast majority of current synchronous online classes, discussion among students is impeded by lack of high quality video of students, lags in audio and video, and often poor sound quality from students. Holding the attention of participants in synchronous online classes, already difficult in faculty-driven courses, can be more difficult when the production quality drops.

What the future holds

Email, learning management systems, and in-classroom projection have moved into the mainstream. The wealth of web 2.0 technologies including blogs, wikis, and interactive websites that Diaz (2010) describes as emerging based on the usage rates by students have posed little threat to the traditional classroom and many of the tools are now integrated in learning management systems. Podcasts and webcasts are often used as a compliment to traditional courses.

We are in an awkward transition point in the technology. Many online programs were built on technical assumptions that are no longer valid. Most business students in the first world have access to high speed connections and reasonably powerful computers. Students are routinely using far more advanced technologies for personal use than in the official portions of their online courses and emerging technologies are likely to dramatically change what is feasible. Johnson et al. (2011) see augmented reality and game-based technology coming to education within two to three years, with gesture-based technology a year or two later. These technologies will enable more immersive e-learning environments, with richer simulations and enhanced analytic tools.

Existing technology makes the replacement of non-interactive lecture courses viable and, if we are to believe the bulk of the research to date, preferable for students at lower costs for schools. Except for undergraduate institutions where the residential component and *in loco parentis* is sufficiently appealing to justify the cost, it is not likely that such teaching can survive. And even in schools with resident students, if some classes are taught electronically, the need for expensive classroom space is reduced. If instructors do not take advantage of the physical presence of students in the classroom, they will be replaced by online delivery.

But even for great, interactive courses, the gap between the in-person and online experience will continue to close. The coming decade will go a long way toward closing that gap with inexpensive telepresence quality technology available to many first world students. And in subsequent decades, three-dimensional renderings will become routine, making the experience even more immersive and lowering the value of being physically co-located.

References

Allen, E. and Seaman, J. (2011) *Going the Distance: Online Education in the United States, 2011*. Babson Survey Research Group, November. Retrieved from http://babson.qualtrics.com/SE/?SID=SV_6Xpu84FGPyTh6CM

Bernard, R.M., Abrami, P.C., Lou, Y., Borokhovski, E., Wade, A., Wozney, L., Wallet, P.A., Fixet, M., and Huant, B. (2004) 'How Does Distance Education Compare with Classroom Instruction? a Meta-Analysis of the Empirical Literature,' *Review of Educational Research*, 74, pp. 379–439.

Brown, J. S., and Adler, R. P. (2008) 'Minds on Fire: Open Education, the Long Tail, and Learning 2.0,' *Educause Review*, 43(1), pp. 16–32.

Christensen, C. and Eyring, H. (2011) *The Innovative University* (San Francisco: John Wiley & Sons).

Chronicle of Higher Education (2011) '6 Online Learning Trends,' *Chronicle of Higher Education*, B20–B21.

Clark, R. C. and Mayer, R. E. (2011) 'e-Learning: Promise and Pitfalls,' in *e-Learning and the Science of Instruction: Proven Guidelines for Consumers and Designers of Multimedia Learning, Third Edition* (San Francisco: John Wiley & Sons).

Diaz, V. (2010) 'Web 2.0 and Emerging Technologies in Online Learning. New Directions for Community Colleges,' pp. 57–66. doi: 10.1002/cc.405.

Doyle, W. (2009) 'Online Education: The Revolution That Wasn't,' *Change*, May/June, pp. 56–58.

Johnson, L., Smith, R., Willis, H., Levine, A., and Haywood, K. (2011) *The 2011 Horizon Report* (Austin, TX: The New Media Consortium).

Lancaster, T. and Clarke, R. (2007) *The Phenomena of Contract Cheating in Student Plagiarism in an Online World: Problems and Solutions*, Roberts, T. S. (ed.) (Hershey, PA: Idea Group Inc.)

Mariasingam, M. and Hanna, D. (2006) 'Benchmarking Quality in Online Degree Programs: Status and Prospects,' *Online Journal of Distance Learning Administration*, 9(3).

Massachusetts Institute of Technology and Harvard University (2012) 'MIT and Harvard announce edX.' Retrieved from http://web.mit.edu/newsoffice/2012/mit-harvard-edx-announcement-050212.html.

McCabe, D., Butterfield, K., and Trevino, L. (2006) 'Academic Dishonesty in Graduate Business Programs: Prevalence, Causes, and Proposed Action,' *Academy of Management Learning and Education Archive*, 5(3), September.

Means, B., Toyama, Y., Murphy, R. Bakia, M., and Jones, K. (2010) *Evaluation of Evidence-Based Practices in Online Learning: A Meta-Analysis and Review of Online Learning Studies* (US Department of Education).

Parry, M. (2009) 'Online Education is Still Mired in Old Technology,' *Chronicle of Higher Education*, October 30, A12.

Parry, M. (2010) 'Outsourced Ed: Colleges Hire Companies to Build Their Online Courses,' *Chronicle of Higher Education*, July 18.

Rottman Epps, S. (2011). 'E-Textbooks Are a Transitional Product,' Forrester, November 2.

Schooley, C. (2009) 'The ROI Of eLearning.' April 13, Forrester.

Seaman, J. (2009) *Online Learning as a Strategic Asset, Volume II: The Paradox of Faculty Voices: Views and Experiences with Online Learning.* Association of Public and Land Grant Universities, August.

Smith, M. S. (2009) 'Opening Education.' *Science*, 323(89), pp. 89–93.

Tufte, E. (Cheshire, CT: 2006) *The Cognitive Style of PowerPoint: Pitching Out Corrupts from Within.* (Graphics Press).

Transforming American Education Powered by Technology, National Education Technology Plan 2010. US Department of Education, Office of Educational Technology, 2010. Retrieved from www2.ed.gov/about/offices/list/os/technology/netp.pdf

Williamson, S., Clow, K., and Stevens, R. (2011) 'To the Point: How Management Faculty Use: Powerpoint Slides And Quizzes,' *Administrative Issues Journal*, 1(2), pp. 144–154.

16
Cases and Emotions
Robert E. Frederick

It is characteristic of business ethics pedagogy (but not only business ethics) that it frequently uses specific and concrete ethics cases for which there are plausible competing responses. These 'difficult ethical cases,' as I so inventively call them, resist neat and easy solutions. All too often the more one knows or is told about them the more intractable they seem. In my experience these cases sometimes cause considerable distress for students, who, when asked to analyze or discuss the problems the case presents, exhibit responses ranging from helplessness and despair ('What can we do when the "experts" disagree?') to restlessness and irritation ('Let's forget all this philosophical nonsense and get on with it').

Naturally such responses cause a certain amount of difficulty when one is trying to teach business ethics. Part of the difficulty seems to originate in the different ways students approach ethics cases. One group (future CEOs) wants only the answer, never mind the intricacies of the ethical problems in the case. Another much smaller group (future philosophers) is interested only in the ethical problem, never mind the answer. A third group has reinforced what they suspected all along – that searching for answers in ethics is a quest for fools and simpletons – and so stick with the easy subjectivity of 'what's right for me may not be right for you.' But a fourth group sees that there is something significant here, that finding a defensible and practical solution to ethical problems really does matter. Can anything be done for these students, and, with more luck, the others as well?

One thing I have tried is the 'traditional strategy.' It goes something like this. Pick an ethical theory that large numbers of philosophers have championed over the years. Apply the theory to the case and try to figure out what it tells you to do. Resolve to do it. End of problem.

Well, yes, that's one way to teach the case. But it suffers from certain defects. For instance, picking the theory turns out to be tricky. One doesn't want to be accused of making an arbitrary choice, or even worse, a choice that is no more than a personal preference or bias, so the choice must be justified. Yet is it really possible for the instructor, much less the students, to justify a choice between, e.g., Kantianism and utilitarianism? Could the choice be justified to those who deny that these theories are applicable in non-Western cultures, or reject them because they perpetuate unacceptable assumptions about race, class, or gender? No doubt opinions will differ. But, of course, that's just the point.

A second defect is that the theories usually taught in applied ethics classes seldom or never tell one precisely what to do. They just don't give clear and exact instructions. Further, it's of little help to be told to 'maximize the good' or 'act on universalizable maxims' when what counts as maximizing the good or acting on a universalizable maxim is itself a matter of intense theoretical dispute. So when it comes to really trying to apply the theories, whether singly or in some Rube Goldberg combination, about the best that can be said to students is 'you should keep these sorts of things in mind when you make your decision.' From an instructor's point of view, this is less than ideal.

As if these difficulties were not enough, there is another that will be the main focus of the remainder of this chapter – and that is the case method itself. We all use cases – myself included – and we all think they are, for the most part, effective teaching tools. And they do have their virtues. For example, they seem to try to bring the reality of practice into the classroom, they at least expose students to the big picture, they allegedly develop decision-making skills, they encourage critical thinking, and they are participative. But they have limitations as well. In no particular order, some of them are:

1. limited information, sometimes very limited;
2. emphasis on rapid analysis and decision-making;
3. danger of the fundamental attribution error;
4. force students to make decisions about totally unfamiliar matters;
5. little or no historical perspective or cultural context;
6. limit the amount of time an instructor has to teach ethical concepts and analytical techniques in ethics.

All of these problems are familiar, and no doubt many instructors have devised methods for dealing with them in one way or another. But the one I want to discuss can't be handled so easily by clever pedagogical devices. It is that in business ethics cases, as taught in business ethics classes, nothing is at stake. No matter what members of the class propose to do about the problem, no one will die or be seriously harmed, no money will be lost, no one will be fired, no reputations destroyed, no careers ruined, no lives turned upside down. And when the discussion is over, the students can leave class with a clear conscience, with no trace of the worry, guilt, or regret that so often accompany real ethical decisions.

Okay, but so what, you might say. True, since nothing is at stake (except a grade) in the classroom, it's about as unlike a real ethics problem as anything could be, but neither is anything at stake when law students learn about law cases or medical students learn about medical cases. What we as instructors are doing in all these circumstances is teaching a process of analysis and decision making. That's what really matters since it is this process that we want our students to internalize and put to good use when the occasion arises. The fact that nothing is at stake doesn't interfere with this at all.

I concede the point – partially, anyway. We are trying to teach a process of analysis and decision making and sometimes cases are a useful tool for doing that. But I am not yet persuaded that we can leave it there and go on about our business. Let me explain.

Think for a moment about real ethics problems as they are experienced in private life, or in the practice of business, engineering, or medicine. I'm going to make several assumptions about these problems, assumptions I won't try to defend in this chapter. The first is that in real ethics problems we are free to choose from among genuine alternatives. Thus the reasons we may have for making one choice rather than another, no matter how compelling they may be, never *cause* us to make the decision. The agent may act on reasons but is never caused to act by those reasons. As some philosophers say, there is always a 'gap' between the reasons we have for making a decision, and the decision itself (Searle, 2007, p. 58). In that gap is free choice. It's always possible, even if rare, that an agent freely chooses not to do what he or she has most reason to do.

The second assumption is that real ethics problems are frequently dilemmas in the sense that for any choice one might make there are always countervailing considerations, always apparently good reasons to make a different choice. Thus when the decision is made it is, to borrow from law, frequently, perhaps even typically, made on what we take to be the preponderance of the reasons. However, and this is a point I want to stress, what counts as the preponderance of reasons is a highly subjective matter. There is no objective measure, no rational standard agreed to by all, of how to weigh one reason against another, or how to tie them tidily into a neat package stamped with an official measure of epistemic weight (Raz, 1975; Phillips, 1987; Kagan, 1988; Broome, 2003). To an extent that perhaps many of us would be uncomfortable admitting, each individual is on his or her own here.

The third assumption is that real ethics decisions are often made in the face of indeterminacy both about the ethical status of the decision itself, and about the consequences of the decision for the agent and those affected by the decision. It almost always makes sense to ask ourselves: is this the ethically right decision? Can I be so sure? Moreover, given our limited abilities, before things play themselves out the consequences of the decision will in important respects be unknown to us. Real ethics decisions are almost always risky decisions.

Granted all this there is one more point I would like to make. It is that real ethics decisions are normally made from a first person point of view, from the perspective of the agent who makes the decision. It is a person who makes the decision, who operates in the gap, and, we hope, from that person's perspective the decision makes sense, or at least as much sense as any complex decision with uncertain outcomes can. However, there is no guarantee that what makes sense from a first person perspective will also make sense from an outside, third person perspective. Recall Sartre's famous example of the young man in Second World War who could either care for his ailing mother or leave and join the resistance (2002, p. 445). Sartre claims that there are reasons for the young man to go, and reasons for him to stay, but no compelling reasons for him to do one or the other. There is no correct answer, nothing that is clearly right or wrong. In the end, the young man has to make a decision, but his decision will not be based on reasons that compel him to do one thing rather than another. It will be based, Sartre says, on what *feels* like the right decision. Thus, as my colleague Axel Seemann says, 'in order to completely understand why an agent makes this decision rather than another in the face of compelling evidence for both decisions, you have to be that man.'

If Seemann is right, and I think he is, at this point we have abandoned the public realm of reasons, analysis, and argument, and entered the private domain of emotion and intuition. In ethics, reason only goes so far (Haidt, 2008). It will not carry us through all the way to the individual's final decision. The person making the decision can tell us for what reasons the decision was made, but ultimately cannot tell us why it was just those reasons, and not others, that the person found persuasive in the end. Since there is no objective standard of epistemic weight, no common measure either of why one reason is more important than another or of how much more important one reason is than another, the final judgment about which reasons prevail is necessarily a private matter. We can argue about the 'weight' of reasons, and discuss their 'force' or 'significance,' but when all is said and done, the tools of persuasion are all we have. We have stepped beyond the requirements of rationality, and into the world of emotional attachment.

Now, to recap briefly, I claim that real ethical decisions are free choices, made on the basis of, but not caused by, what the individual takes to be the preponderance of reasons, that they are often indeterminate in both the ethical status of the decision and its consequences, and that they are first person decisions that ineliminably involve a first person feeling or intuition somewhere in the neighborhood of 'all things considered, this feels like the right choice to make.'

Let's turn now to what happens in the typical business ethics case as presented in the classroom. Almost without exception these are what I called 'difficult ethical cases': they are specifically designed to present a range of possible decisions for which there are good or seemingly good reasons. And they are presented as scenarios in which an individual has to make a decision. What we do, as instructors, is ask the students to analyze the situation and then 'decide' what to do. But what do the students take themselves to be doing here? There are two possibilities, I think. The first is that the students put themselves in a kind of third person position and make a judgment about what *that* person should do in this situation. The second, and probably much more common, is that students insert themselves in the case and make a judgment about what 'I' would do were I in that situation. (In this respect ethical decisions are somewhat different from offering legal or medical advice, which is typically about what some other person should do.) Thus, in the classroom students are asked to decide about unfamiliar matters given limited information and little or no historical context – a tough enough job by itself. But even more crucial, I believe, they are asked to decide when they have nothing at stake – not their career, not their money, not their reputation, not the welfare of their family or fellows, nothing. What all this amounts to, I suggest, is a complete lack of the essential elements of the emotional context of the decision. The students are making counterfactual judgments – this is what I would do – that are barren of the kinds of emotion they would feel were they really in the situation depicted. They don't know how they would actually feel, how they would experience the emotional weight of the reasons they have or the options they face. Thus, they don't know, they can't know, what they would take to be the preponderance of reasons, or what they eventually would decide, because crucial elements of the decision – e.g., what it feels right to do – are absent. So in effect what we are asking them to do is to imagine that they are Sartre's young man, but make a decision in an emotional vacuum that deprives that decision of the emotional weight that accompanies it, and is an absolutely essential first person component of it.

I don't deny that on occasion the classroom is an emotionally charged place. Sometimes the students get quite passionate about their decisions, and the discussion can get heated. But it seems to me that the emotions involved are of the wrong kind, and occur at the wrong time. They are the wrong kind because they occur in the context of nothing to lose, and they occur at the wrong time because, in my experience, they occur after a decision is made and some student challenges the decision maker. Then positions and attitudes begin to harden. But it's too late by then. The emotions needed occur prior to and during the decision, not after it.

Further, I acknowledge that empirical research shows that research subjects have areas of their brain associated with emotion activated when they consider how they would respond to certain kinds of ethical problems, e.g., the famous trolley problem (Cushman and Greene, 2012). And I suspect that researchers would find something similar if they used the kind of difficult ethical problems mentioned earlier. But it is worth recalling that in none of these scenarios is anything *really* at stake. The trolley isn't going to run over anybody, and in none of the business ethics cases presented in class will any actual person suffer a smidgen of harm. Nothing is at stake for the subjects of these experiments, so it seems unlikely to me that the experiments show much if anything about the kind, intensity, or duration of emotion that would actually occur if the subjects were actually in the circumstances described. Perhaps future research will be more helpful, but for now we shouldn't assume that imaginary trolleys or imaginary business dilemmas give us reliable insight into the real emotions experienced in real decisions.

Where does this leave us? Well, what we teach in the business ethics classroom is a version of a rational decision-making process: recognize the ethical problem, gather the ethically relevant facts, creatively assess the alternatives from some ethical point of view, and make the best ethical choice given the constraints of the circumstances. But we all know that, in the real world outside the class, at each stage of this process emotion plays a significant role. The problems we see, the facts we gather and the epistemic weight we give to them, the alternatives we consider and the preference order we attach to them, and the eventual choice we make, all carry a heavy emotional content, especially when something is at stake. It is here, in the arena of real decisions, that anger, fear, jealousy, guilt, shame, pity, lust, compassion, love, devotion to ideology, and all the rest, come to the forefront, and come to stay.

I'm not saying that emotions are 'bad' and ought to be avoided. Far from it. Emotions are inextricably bound to ethical decisions and can't be eliminated (Haidt, 2012). Moreover, it is certainly true that emotion sometimes leads us to make the right decision, not the wrong one. And I'm not saying that emotion is uncontrollable, that we can do nothing or learn nothing about how to make better decisions in an emotional context. No doubt there are insights to be gained from the extensive, though fairly recent, research about how emotions affect ethical decisions, and perhaps from the literature on emotional intelligence (Goleman, 1995). But I am saying that as teachers who use ethics cases we are in a tight spot, pedagogically speaking. We teach only part of what happens when ethical decisions are made, and, I suspect, not the most important part.

Let me emphasize that I'm not suggesting that we abandon cases. I plan to continue using them and I'm sure others do too. What I am suggesting, however, is that we be rather modest about their effectiveness as tools for teaching the process of ethical decision making, and even more modest about thinking, or hinting to the students, that decisions made in class are reliable predictors of how decisions will be made in the world of actual practice. When something is at stake, things feel very different to decision makers. That feeling cannot be duplicated in the classroom.

References

Ariely, D. (2008) *Predictably Irrational: The Hidden Factors that Shape Our Decisions* (New York: Harper-Collins).

Broome, J. (2003) 'Reasons,' in Wallace, R., Smith, M., Scheffler, S., Pettit, P. (eds) *Reasons and Value: Essays on the Moral Philosophy of Joseph Raz* (New York: Oxford University Press), pp. 29–55.

Cushman, F. and Greene, J. (2012) 'Finding Faults: How Moral Dilemmas Illuminate Cognitive Structure,' *Social Neuroscience*, 7(3), pp. 269–279.

Goleman, D. (1995) *Emotional Intelligence* (New York: Bantam Books).

Haidt, J. (2008), 'Social Intuitionists Answer Six Questions about Moral Psychology,' in Sinnott-Armstrong, W. (ed.), *Moral Psychology*, vol. 2 (Cambridge, MA: MIT Press).

Haidt, J. (2012) *The Righteous Mind: Why Good People Are divided by Politics and Religion* (New York: Random House).

Kagan, S. (1988) 'The Additive Fallacy,' *Ethics*, 99(1), pp. 5–31.

Phillips, M. (1987) 'Weighing Moral Reasons,' *Mind*, 96(383), pp. 367–375.

Raz, J. (1975) 'Reasons for Action,' *Mind*, 84(336), pp. 481–499.

Sartre, Jean-Paul (2002) 'Existentialism Is a Humanism,' in S. Cahn and P. Markie (eds) *Ethics: History, Theory, and Contemporary Issues* (New York: Oxford University Press), pp. 443–450.

Searle, J. (2007) *Freedom and Neurobiology: Reflections on Free Will, Language, and Political Power* (New York: Columbia University Press).

17
Creativity and Fusion: Moving the Circles

Andrew B. Aylesworth

Creativity is widely recognized as an important, even essential, driver for society in general, and for the economy specifically. In its 2010 report, *The Creative Economy*, the United Nations stated that 'adequately nurtured, creativity fuels culture, infuses a human centered development and constitutes the key ingredient for job creation, innovation and trade while contributing to social inclusion, cultural diversity and environmental sustainability'(2010, xix). In his 2008 book *Who's Your City*, Richard Florida claims that the economic transformation we are undergoing today,

> is bigger in scale than the shift from farms to factories a century or two ago. As a consequence (advanced economies) are shedding manufacturing jobs and generating jobs in two other economic sectors – low-paid service work in everything from retail sales to personal service, and high-paid professional, innovative and design work in what I call the *creative* sector of the economy. (p. 102; emphasis added)

If business school graduates are to positively affect society in general and the economy specifically, one of the primary goals of business schools *must* be to develop and nurture the creative skills of their students.

But what is creativity? Legendary Apple Inc., founder and CEO Steve Jobs, in a 1993 interview with G. Wolf in *Wired* magazine, said:

> Creativity is just connecting things. When you ask a creative person how they did something, they may feel a little guilty because they didn't really do it, they just saw something. It seemed obvious to them after a while. That's because they were able to connect

experiences they've had and synthesize new things. And the reason they were able to do that was that they've had more experiences or have thought more about their experiences than other people have. Unfortunately, that's too rare a commodity. A lot of people in our industry haven't had very diverse experiences. They don't have enough dots to connect, and they end up with very linear solutions, without a broad perspective on the problem. The broader one's understanding of the human experience, the better designs we will have. (Wolf, 1996)

Creativity as connections is not just true in information technology; it applies to all areas of human endeavor, including business. One way to develop and nurture students' creativity, then, is to provide more dots to connect and more chances to connect those dots, more experiences and knowledge, and therefore a 'broader understanding of the human experience.'

In its essence, university education provides two broad types of knowledge: generalized knowledge and disciplinary knowledge. Generalized knowledge focuses on understanding the basic human experience, and provides the foundation upon which more specific disciplinary knowledge can be built. Disciplinary knowledge, on the other hand, comprises preparation to enter and be successful in a specific field, whether that field is architecture, medicine, business, or any other profession. Very broadly speaking, generalized knowledge has typically been seen as the domain of the arts and sciences. Disciplinary knowledge *can* be provided by disciplines from the arts and sciences (such as linguistics, history, or biology) or by disciplines within the business domain (accounting, marketing, management).

Thriving creativity

It is where these two broad knowledge domains intersect that creativity *thrives*, and where universities can actively develop and nurture creativity. Figure 17.1 represents this relationship as well as some of the influences upon it.

Disciplinary knowledge, or what Amabile calls domain knowledge or expertise in her classic 'Three Component Model of Creativity' (1997, pp. 39–58) is clearly a necessary component of creativity. You must know the area in which you are trying to create something new. Van Gogh had to have some knowledge of color and brushstrokes, Edison some knowledge of electricity, and Jobs some knowledge of circuit

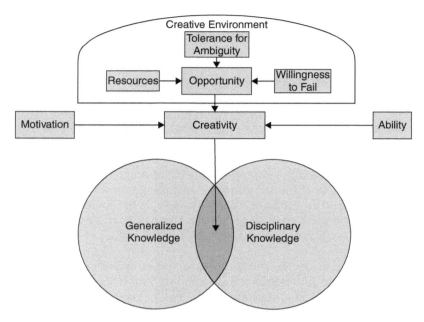

Figure 17.1 Creativity at the intersection of generalized and disciplinary knowledge

boards and business, before they could make their marks on the world. It is, of course, possible for creativity to exist solely within the disciplinary knowledge circle or solely within the generalized knowledge circle. There are plenty of 'dots' to connect within each of these domains.

However, when a person can draw from *both* domains, there are not only more dots to connect, but the dots are more disparate, and connecting them leads to more novel conceptual combinations – more creativity.

Another of Amabile's components is 'creativity relevant processes.' These skills 'include a cognitive style favorable to taking new perspectives on problems, an application of techniques (or "heuristics") for the exploration of new cognitive pathways' (Amabile, 1997, p. 43). This ability to look at problems from new perspectives, or cognitive flexibility, is enhanced by exposure to more, and more different, domains of knowledge. In fact, over-focusing on one discipline or knowledge domain can lead to a kind of tunnel vision known as functional fixedness, and such inflexibility limits our ability to develop creative connections.

Sternberg et al. (2002, pp. 11–13) identify seven types of creativity:

1. conceptual replication (the known is transferred to a new setting);
2. redefinition (the known is seen in a new way);
3. forward incrementation (the known is extended in an existing direction);
4. advance forward incrementation (the known is extended in an existing direction, but goes beyond what is currently tolerable);
5. redirection (the known is extended in a new direction);
6. reconstruction and redirection (new life is breathed into an approach previously abandoned);
7. reinitiation (thinking begins at a radically different point from the current one and takes off in a new direction).

At the intersection of general and disciplinary knowledge, because there are more dots to connect and because those dots are so different from one another, each of these types of creativity becomes more likely. The cognitive flexibility gained by studying the different domains allows the student to know more, and to see how what he or she knows might be extended.

As noted earlier, disciplinary knowledge can come from either the arts and sciences or the business domain. For example, disciplinary knowledge in graphic design might come in the form of knowledge of composition and color, and when combined with generalized knowledge of the human experience might result in the creation of fine art. Or, disciplinary knowledge in marketing might come in the form of an understanding of a target market and product positioning, and when combined with generalized knowledge of human experience might result in the creation of a new and useful product.

This crucial fusion of knowledge bases, the intersection of disciplinary and generalized knowledge, can be expanded by enlarging the circles and/or by moving the circles closer together.

Enlarging the circles

One way to increase the size of the intersection is to increase the size of the circles. That is, instill more generalized and/or disciplinary knowledge into university students, providing them with more 'dots' and therefore more opportunities to connect those dots.

Generally speaking, one credit hour is awarded to college students for each hour they spend in class per week, and most college courses consist of three credit hours. In addition, the rule of thumb is that students are expected to spend two to three hours per week working outside of class for every credit hour awarded.

The amount of work this entails, however, can quickly get problematic. A 'typical' full time student completes 15 credit hours of study per semester, earning a degree in eight semesters of study, or a total of 120 credit hours over four years. Indeed, the New England Association of Schools and Colleges, an organization that accredits university programs, states that 120 credit hours is the minimum required for awarding an undergraduate degree (New England, Standard 4.30). Thus, applying the rule of thumb above, typical students are expected to be in class or studying between 45 and 60 hours per week.

But is it possible to require *more than* 120 credit hours to earn a degree? Requiring more than 120 hours has obvious costs to students and to institutions in terms of time, tuition, and resources. Some state legislatures *forbid* requiring more than 120 credit hours in order to graduate. For example, the Texas legislature enacted a statute that states:

> To earn a baccalaureate degree, a student may not be required by a general academic teaching institution to complete more than the minimum number of semester credit hours required for the degree by the Southern Association of Colleges and Schools or its successor unless the institution determines that there is a compelling academic reason for requiring completion of additional semester credit hours for the degree (Texas, Section 61.0515) (the minimum number of semester credit hours required for the degree by the Southern Association of Colleges and Schools is 120, and has been for many years).

To be sure, some colleges and some degree programs do require more than this minimum. Private institutions are not covered by such rules, and some degree programs do offer 'compelling academic reasons' for requiring additional credit hours. For example, the Mechanical Engineering degree offered by the University of Texas requires completion of 131 credit hours. By and large, however, institutions consider 120 to be the maximum requirement for an undergraduate degree.

Enlarging the circles, then, becomes a zero-sum game. There may be compelling reasons for, and students and faculty may desire, requiring more focus on generalized knowledge. But when that circle grows, the disciplinary knowledge circle must, of necessity, shrink. Similarly, there may be compelling reasons for, and students and faculty may desire, requiring more focus on disciplinary knowledge. But when that circle grows, the generalized knowledge circle must, of necessity, shrink. This zero-sum game is the source of the tension often seen between students and faculty advocating for a more liberal education and students and faculty advocating for a more vocational education.

In terms of creativity, however, the relative size of each circle does not matter. If we cannot grow the total area of the circles (beyond, for example, 120 credit hours), when one grows, the other necessarily shrinks. The size of the intersection between the two, where creativity is born, remains the same. Thus, in order to enhance the creativity of students, it is necessary to move the circles.

Moving the circles

Moving the circles closer together, and increasing the area of their intersection, involves demonstrating to students and faculty the relevance of each domain to the other. When they can see the relevance of one domain to the other, they are more likely to make the crucial connections that are central to creativity. Demonstrating relevance and moving the circles can be accomplished by affecting student motivation, ability and/or opportunity.

- By *motivating* students, who, in business and professional schools, are often focused on attaining the disciplinary knowledge that they believe is the key to success in the workplace, to see that generalized knowledge is *also key to* that success – that they build upon each other.
- By giving students the *ability* to see how the knowledge domains are connected – and how to connect the dots.
- By allowing students the *opportunity* to make the connections themselves, in an environment that supports the students and values their creativity.

Motivation to see connections

Students, particularly business students, are often focused on what they perceive to be the 'bottom line.' 'What is going to make me as successful as possible?' they ask themselves. And in answering that question they often focus on the short term and come to the conclusion that good grades, professor recommendations, and deep understanding of disciplinary knowledge is the shortest, most sure path to success. How, then, can we make a finance major, for example, understand the benefits of a semester studying Shakespeare?

One method is to develop generalized knowledge coursework that is explicitly tied to disciplinary knowledge. For this method to truly result in increased motivation to 'connect the dots,' however, we have to be careful to not simply turn the generalized knowledge class into another avenue for delivery of *disciplinary knowledge*. If a generalized knowledge class becomes another path to delivering disciplinary knowledge rather than teaching the topic of the field, all that results is the enlarging of one circle at the expense of the other – and no more dots to connect. The coursework must retain its focus on generalized knowledge.

For example, the philosophy department at Bentley University offers a course titled 'Corporate Social Responsibility.' The course description follows:

> Examines the various meanings of corporate social responsibility by looking at the nature of the corporation and the character structure of its managers, both historically and in the present. After investigating several philosophical theories concerning the ideal use of power, the emphasis is on the application of principled moral thinking concerning corporate responsibility to such topics as employees, consumers, local communities, government, environmental issues, advertising, payoffs and bribes, the role and structure of corporate whistleblowing, privacy rights, poverty and equal rights, and other ethical issues that relate to corporate technology and the individual. Some attention is given to the moral evaluation of entire economic systems. (www.bentley.edu)

A class on corporate social responsibility could easily devolve into a management course. But in this class the focus remains on teaching philosophy, but in the context of business. In this way students are better able to see the relevance of the generalized knowledge topic of philosophy to their future success in the business world, and are therefore motivated to connect those dots – drawing the circles closer together.

Developing such classes should be an explicit goal, not simply a happy accident. The Jeanne and Dan Valente Center for Arts and Sciences at Bentley encourages this development. The Center's mission is 'to help make the arts and sciences a vital, integral and challenging aspect of undergraduate and graduate education at Bentley. The center promotes research and teaching in the disciplines and at the intersection of arts, sciences and business. The center, through its programs, promotes individual scholarship while encouraging cross-disciplinary discussion and research' (www.bentley.edu). Two Bentley faculty members, working with the Valente Center, were awarded a grant from the National Science Foundation for a project titled 'Integrating Earth and Environmental Science Education into a Business Curriculum Using Technology Enhanced Learning' (NSF, Abstract 0941131). The program focuses on 'improving the scientific literacy of future business and civic leaders by further integrating Earth, Environment and Global Sustainability courses into the business curriculum'. Note that the focus of this course is *science*, but the context in which the science is discussed is *business*. Again, such courses that focus on a generalized knowledge domain, using a disciplinary context, motivate students to see the relevance of each domain to the other.

Another method of motivating students to move the circles is to show them it works. Students sit up and pay attention to success stories. So, we can show them people who have succeeded while applying one domain to the other. One of the Valente Center's activities is to bring in outside speakers. Some of these speakers are solely discussing arts and sciences topics, but some are at the 'intersection' of arts and sciences and business. It is these speakers that have the most potential to move the circles for the students, to motivate them to connect more dots. For example, an event called 'Confessions of a Lapsed Historian' on April 1, 2011, featured a presentation by Dr. Eric Schultz, a distinguished historian and successful entrepreneur. Attendees learned how Dr. Schultz's background in history contributed to his success in the business world. (Schultz)

Ability to see connections

Students focused on attaining knowledge from either domain, whether in an individual class or in a degree program, cannot be counted on to make the connections between the domains on their own. They are too worried about studying for their biology midterm, completing their accounting balance sheet, or finishing the requirements for their bachelor of science degree to think about how these disparate things might be connected. They do not have the bandwidth to step back and see the bigger picture, and thereby connect the dots from the different domains.

If we value creativity, it is our responsibility to enhance their ability to see those connections. One way is to structure programs in either or both knowledge domains such that seeing the connections is required, giving students practice in developing the ability.

As discussed above, individual classes that cross the domains, courses with names like Managing Diversity in the Workplace and the Sociology of Organizations and Work, not only motivate students to see the connections, but can also provide the opportunity for students to actually make the connections and put them to use. Even teaching methods within a specific class can do so. For example, in a marketing class, cases that revolve around understanding different cultures can give students practice at applying the knowledge they learn in one domain to the other. This fosters the *ability* to connect the dots.

Bentley University has developed a liberal studies major (LSM) that structures connections and develops the ability to see them. In this program students earn a double major: one major in one of the business disciplines (e.g., accounting, marketing) and a second in Liberal Studies. Students choose one of several concentrations for the LSM (e.g., Ethics and Social Responsibility, Global Perspectives) and structure their generalized knowledge courses around that theme. An additional requirement to earn the second major, however, is an annual paper and a capstone project that illustrates how LSM classes connect with each other *and with other classes* the student is taking, including the business core classes and the major specific classes. Thus, the student majoring in accounting with an LSM concentrating on Ethics and Social Responsibility would not only take the Environmental Ethics course as part of the LSM, but would also consider how the topics covered in that course might impact the topics covered in his or her Managerial Accounting class. And when this student successfully makes a connection between these two seemingly different courses, creativity is born.

The LSM program requires students to make these connections, which is of course very *motivating* to them. However, in obliging them to practice this skill, we are also developing the *ability* to make the connections, and it is this ability that will continue to stimulate their creativity after graduation.

Opportunity to see connections

Perhaps the most important aspect of moving the circles involves creating an environment that affords the students the opportunity to make the connections themselves. An environment that supports the students and values their creativity will enhance their motivation *and* their ability to move the circles.

An environment that supports creative development should provide three things: sufficient resources, tolerance for ambiguity, and acceptance of the inevitability of occasional failure.

Perhaps the most important resource to provide a student is time: time to explore, time to try new ideas, time to connect the dots. (This further argues against the 'enlarging the circles' strategy discussed above.) Another resource would be physical space: comfortable areas for students to work, together and separately, to explore the new knowledge they are gaining from each domain and the connections between the domains.

One of the most common characteristics of creative people is their tolerance for ambiguity, their willingness to attack a problem with no clear parameters and possibly no single answer. Unfortunately, much of our education system does not build such a tolerance. From an early age children are taught to look for the one right answer, to discover the facts of the case, and then use those facts to answer the questions. For creativity to bloom at the intersection of generalized and disciplinary knowledge, however, students must be able to avoid prematurely jumping to conclusions. They have to be willing to let those connections build. Part of providing this environment, then, is giving students ambiguous situations, where there may not be clear solutions or even clear parameters to the problem, and letting them struggle. Giving students experience with struggling with such ambiguous problems, and failing at some (see below) will allow them to see the value of *ambiguity*, and will build their comfort level with it.

For example, corporate immersion classes at Bentley put students in the position of consulting with 'real world' organizations, with all of those organizations' unpredictable situations, changing personnel, and moving strategic targets. The problem to be worked on is often ill-defined, and the parameters of the problem may change over the course of the semester, just as they would in the corporate world. These are not classes in which students can look forward to memorizing formulae and reproducing them on a final exam in order to pass. Students are not judged on whether they find the 'right' answer for the organization; often that right answer does not exist. Rather, students are graded on how well they struggle with the problem, how well they identify the changing parameters, and the creativity of their proposed solution(s).

Finally, in order to build the creative environment, students must be willing to occasionally fail, and faculty must be willing to let that happen. Thomas Edison famously said, 'I have not failed 10,000 times. I have successfully found 10,000 ways that will not work.' The student who is asked to get 'the right answer' every time will not even try to be creative. There are, of course, some topics where there *is* a right answer, a right way of doing things, and students do need to learn them. But if we want to build creativity, we must also allow students to explore different 'right' answers and occasionally be wrong. This means that we should not grade the students on whether they found the single right answer, but, in some cases, on what they learned when they found a wrong answer. Students in the Corporate Immersion classes often propose solutions that might be untenable due to constraints they were unaware of, and therefore might be deemed 'wrong.' But grades do not suffer in these cases, as long as students demonstrate that they learned something in the process. Thus, students are more willing to think creatively and, hopefully, connect the dots from the different knowledge domains in new and interesting ways.

Conclusion

Marketing is often seen as the most 'creative' of the business disciplines, though it must be said, of course, that *each* business discipline benefits from the creativity of its adherents. Marketers use their disciplinary knowledge (e.g., understanding consumers, environmental scanning, the value of branding) to develop new products and services, create new methods of communicating the benefits of their goods to the population, and foster innovative methods of creating value for customers. The more students of marketing recognize the value of the overlap between the circles, the more dots they have to connect, the more valuable they will be in the marketplace and to society.

One of the most famous marketing success stories involves an advertisement widely regarded by academics and practitioners alike as the 'Citizen Kane' of advertising, the best ad ever created: Apple's '1984' (Adweek, 2011). The ad introducing Apple's revolutionary Mac computer features a young heroine (representing Apple, of course) destroying a screen featuring an evil, Big Brother character (representing IBM, of course), and ends with the tag line 'Why 1984, won't be like "1984"'. The ad utilized marketing disciplinary knowledge (understanding consumer perceptions, knowing the competition, and so on) to develop a marketing strategy. And that marketing strategy combined with knowledge from the generalized domain, in this case, Orwell's classic novel, resulting in an ad that drew attention *and* got the message across. Clearly, the marketers at Chiat/Day, Apple's advertising agency, had many 'dots' to draw from when they created this message.

Virginia Postrel, author of *The Substance of Style* and *The Future and Its Enemies*, wrote in a 2012 article for Bloomberg.com:

> ... a tremendous amount of economic value arises from pleasure and meaning – the stuff of art, literature, psychology and anthropology. These qualities, built into goods and services, increasingly provide the work for all those computer programmers. And there are many categories of jobs, from public relations to interaction design to retailing, where insights and skills from these supposedly frivolous fields can be quite valuable.

By moving the circles closer together, we provide students with a larger tool box from which to develop new and useful solutions to problems. Indeed, we provide them with a larger area from which to recognize the problems themselves. The fusion of arts and sciences and business, the intersection of generalized knowledge and disciplinary knowledge, is thus fertile ground for creativity, and creativity is crucial.

References

Amabile, T. (1997) 'Motivating Creativity in Organizations: On Doing What You Love and Loving What You Do,' *California Management Review*, 40(1), pp. 39–58.

Bentley University Philosophy Department, *Business Ethics: Corporate Social Responsibility*, www.bentley.edu/offices/registrar/undergraduate-courses

Florida, R. (2008) *Who's Your City?* (New York: Basic Books), p. 102.

Hayden, S. (2011) '"1984": As Good As It Gets,' Adweek, January 30.

National Science Foundation, 'Award Abstract #0941131: Integrating Earth and Environmental Science Education into a Business Curriculum Using Technology Enhanced Learning'

New England Association of Schools and Colleges, Standard 4.30.

Postrel, V. (2012) 'How Art History Majors Power the U.S. Economy,' Bloomberg. com, January 5.

Schultz, William (2011), 'Confessions of a Lapsed Historian,' April 1.

Sternberg, R. J., Kaufman, J. C., and Pretz, J. E. (2002) *The Creativity Conundrum: A Propulsion Model of Kinds of Creative Contributions* (New York: Psychology Press).

Texas Education Code, Section 61.0515. 'Semester Credit Hours Required For Baccalaureate Degree'

United Nations (2010) United Nations Creative Economy Report (www.unctad.org/creative-economy), p. xix.

Wolf, G. (1996) 'The Next Insanely Great Thing,' *Wired*, February.

18
Rethinking the End(s) of Education: An Aesthetics for Renewal in American Higher Education

Samir Dayal

Talk about renewal in education is at least as old as educational institutions themselves, and contemporary debates often seem like variations on past debates (Robinson, 1923; Vesey, 1973; Donaldson and Freeman, 2005; Klein, 2005; Bok, 2006). Still, we seem again to be witnessing an acute crisis in American higher education, with a widening gulf between the humanities and 'practical' disciplines such as the hard sciences and business. One symptom is the New York State Commission on Higher Education's recent report, giving short shrift to the arts and humanities, while gesturing vaguely to 'the world of ideas' (NY State Commission, 12, 55). But, especially in contemporary America, there are many other signs of anxiety about higher education's purpose and success. On the one hand, there is an urge to assert its relevance or utility. On the other, there is a hunger for meaning and purpose, for an intellectually, spiritually, and aesthetically fulfilling reinvention of education. This essay briefly traces some important antecedents and identifies salient contours of the current crisis and proposes a route to the renewal of American higher education along three vectors: aesthetic, structural, and philosophical.

Aesthetic renewal

The first vector, aesthetic renewal, is crucial if we wish to maintain the relevance and sustain the quality of national higher education. Yet even aesthetic renewal must be routed through the pragmatic defiles of business and submit to perennial critical vigilance about its intellectual seriousness and commitment to rigor. Among the most 'deeply ingrained American values' is a utilitarian conception of education, as Jennifer Washburn reminds us,' as a means to *other* ends' (2005, p. 26). This can be linked to the anti-intellectualism Richard Hofstadter famously showed to be characteristic of American life, 'older than our national identity, and [with] a long historical background' (1963 [1962], p. 6). Admittedly, it may be intellectuals who are most acutely sensitive to this trait. Derek Bok, former Harvard president, writes that while academics and intellectuals have heaped criticism on contemporary American universities for their failures, most of their alumni themselves report being quite content with their perceived progress and learning at college (Bok, 2006, p. 6) Why the discrepancy?

A historical perspective is illuminating. The first American colleges, writes Washburn, were 'training grounds of a sort – not for industry but for the clergy' (Washburn, 2005, pp. 27). Before the American Revolution, there were only nine colleges in the country. Only in the last half-century have universities become established at the heart of American life. As the Civil War drew to a close, higher education entered what Bok calls 'a period of unprecedented reform.' At Harvard under President Charles W. Eliot, students were free to study whatever subjects interested them; until the end of his 40-year tenure in 1909, only one English composition course and one on the study of a foreign language ever came to be required. This was an extreme example of the commitment to the pursuit of knowledge *not* beholden to commercial interests or extraneous ends. Yet the model held general sway for decades, Bok notes, 'In 1890, 80 percent of the curriculum was required in the average college.' Requirements grew less stringent during the first half of the twentieth century: by 1901, curricula in more than one-third of American colleges were 70 percent elective. By 1940, the share of mandatory courses in the typical college curriculum had settled at 40 percent (Bok, 2006, p. 16). However, under A. Lawrence Lowell, Eliot's successor at Harvard, students had to choose a major or concentration and not just a string of introductory courses.

These changes reflected broader historical transformations. Starting around 1787, sectarian controversies forced the religious denominations to cede control of universities to the forces of advancing secularism. The states stopped providing tax assistance and in 1804 the federal government began granting land to states west of the Appalachians to endow new universities. This inaugurated a period of greater emphasis on 'the pragmatic uses of higher education.' In 1862, Congress passed the Morrill Act, expanding land-grant funding, especially to promote education in 'agriculture and mechanic arts,' in the interest of 'liberal and practical education of the industrial classes' (Bok, 2006, p. 26; Washburn, 2005, p. 29). Presidents of prestigious institutions of higher education such as Eliot (Harvard), Andrew D. White (Cornell), and Francis Wayland (Brown) began to advocate for a more relevant, modern, practical mission for universities, distancing from the elitist commitments of their earlier, European-style arrangement.

The Cold War proved a boom time for federally funded university science research, feeding what Senator J. William Fulbright called the 'military-industrial-academic complex.' But by the 1970s, that funding began to dry up. Universities shifted their emphasis to emerging fields like biotechnology and the knowledge economy, which made close allies of industry and academia. A crucial catalyst for this alliance was the University Small Business Patent Procedures Act of 1980, later called the Bayh–Dole Act after its main sponsors, Senators Birch Bayh (Democrat) and Bob Dole (Republican). It purged from the discourse of higher education any remaining stigma against the patenting of academic knowledge. The Bayh–Dole act permitted universities to patent and license federally supported research on a large scale. Under a new, uniform policy, taxpayer-funded research could now be moved from universities and developed under exclusive patent by universities, nonprofits, and small businesses. Effectively, public funds (taxpayers' money channeled by the federal government to university research initiatives) would now be laundered of all the earmarks of publicness, and transferred into closed holdings and ultimately private coffers. The Act not only contradicted studies on public funding of science but also went against the traditional function of the government to preserve the scientific commons.

This business or practical reorientation of higher education carries a legacy for contemporary education. Many contemporary institutional organizations are even redefining themselves as businesses. And the 'for-profit' model has paid off for some: Christopher R. Beha, associate editor of *Harper's Magazine*, reports that since 2000, 'enrollment at America's roughly 3,000 for-profit colleges and universities has risen from 365,000 to 1.8 million' (Beha, 2011, pp. 51–57). Enrollment numbers of for-profits like the University of Phoenix indicate very successful marketing and recruitment; they may also index broad and swelling demand. Votaries of this model tout it as the answer to a failing system of higher education, and point out that for-profit education serves mainly minority and low-income groups. President Obama himself signed an executive order on April 27, 2012, to protect veterans from for-profit educational institutions trying to 'swindle' and

'hoodwink' them. It is a scandal that such for-profit institutions can essentially get the government to pay more simply by charging more. Phoenix, among the largest for-profit institutions, earned $4.5 billion and boasted 500,000 students in 2010. Institutions extract most of their money from the federal government, not something that most people seem to register when they are told that Phoenix or DeVry University are exemplars of the for-profit model. More oversight is needed (Beha, 2011, p. 52).

Though enrollment rates among these 'diploma mills' are among the highest in the world, according to a recent PBS program, there are embarrassing contradictions. Phoenix's admitted overall graduation rate is 31 percent and its first-time-student graduation rate is only 12 percent, lower than among comparable not-for-profit institutions. Founded by John Sperling, who proudly admits never having earned a degree himself, Phoenix attracts many first-time-enrollees. It offers courses designed by a corporate development team, not professors (Beha, 2011, p. 54). Indeed there are no professors, and no tenure, only contracted 'course facilitators,' and it favors online over physical classrooms. There are much broader issues too. About 50 percent of American high school graduates taking the ACT Examination do not qualify as college-ready. Two-year colleges students often perform worse than peers at four-year for-profits, even Phoenix. Whereas four-year U.S. schools have a college completion rate of 56 percent, the rate for two-year colleges is 29 percent (College Board, 2011, p. 9).

What is to be done? The Obama administration has set ambitious educational goals. The College Board projects a less optimistic goal for young American adults (25- to 34-year-olds), of 55 percent attainment of an associate degree or higher by 2025, submitting this as a reliable indicator of America's progress toward the goal of being a world leader in educational attainment (College Board, figure 6). Beha doubts that even this will be enough, given that 45 percent of Americans will lack a degree.

But does educational renewal require getting everybody through college? Not according to a recent Harvard School of Education study (Harvard Graduate School of Education, 2011). It suggests that although by the middle of the nineteenth century the U.S. 'already had the most educated youth in the world,' and by 2000, per capita inflation-adjusted income was 'five to six times as large as it had been in 1900,' America seems to have lost its lead. It recommends a more pragmatic educational system. Renouncing universal education, it advocates occupational certifications and other vocationally oriented curricula that, like comparable

European apprenticeship programs in Germany, Switzerland, and Scandinavia, prepare students for 'middle-skill' jobs – electricians, police officers, construction managers, health care workers. These jobs are difficult to outsource and demand something less than a college degree; they do not seek to satisfy the traditional shibboleth of 'college readiness.' Such training has been a casualty of the Obama Administration's degree obsession: the President's proposed 2012 budget. His 'Race to the Top' initiative will increase overall education spending but cut funding for vocational and technical schools by 20 percent (Ferguson, 2011, p. 88). Then Presidential hopeful Romney countered Obama's campaign with his own proposal to allow recipient of federal monies to take that money with them if they choose to go to a different school, effectively increasing parents' choice of schools, but also motivatedly jeopardizing the financial security of public schools where teachers unions have some power. Meanwhile, many are pursuing graduate degrees to distinguish themselves from typical college graduates, in a 'credentials race' with an uncertain finish (Ferguson, 2011, p. 57).

The Harvard study is not without merit. Yet it betrays something crucial in education: the exploratory, critical, and aesthetic dimensions of an education. Most of all, it pays scant deference to the most signal feature of any educational endeavor, namely enjoyment in learning. This enjoyment is the foundation of what I call the aesthetic dimension. Could a re-emphasis on enjoyment as core value renew American education?

In some ways it could certainly make a person's pursuit of an education more purposive – in the Kantian sense of *Zweckmassigkeit*, or goal-directed, as opposed to merely purposeful (willed or willful) – given that many students endure education as a necessary rite of passage and see no *intrinsic* value in it. A purposive pursuit of education would emend that. It is well to remember here Max Weber's distinction between the professional and the intellectual type of student. Weber's distinction between profiting from ideas (the professional attitude) and being committed to them (the intellectual attitude) is often lost in contemporary debates. The Harvard study doesn't foreground *intrinsic* aesthetic and intellectual *rewards* of education; its measure is the practical and commercial *benefits* of an education.

By contrast, Beha seems a votary of such enjoyment. Enrolling at Phoenix, Beha unsparingly criticizes the delivery of class materials: '[e]ntirely absent from those classes was any sense that learning could be exciting, or even valuable for its own sake' (p. 56). This critique endorses Matthew Arnold's and Cardinal Henry Newman's own championing of education for its own sake, an aesthetic of pedagogical pleasure (Newman, 1852). Here I argue that our critique of for-profit institutions should be founded on a hybrid value system, attentive to pragmatic and business needs, but simultaneously committed to the liberal humanistic values of the intrinsic pleasure of learning.

The time seems ripe for such a recalibration towards intellectual and aesthetic renewal and the 're-creation' of the human through education. This will entail a dual or hybrid vision: an eye to what global business needs and another on truly 'disinterested' learning motivated by aesthetic pleasure, a readiness to be surprised by joy. As Louis Menand suggests, to strip joy and pleasure from life or work is worse than death, a vivid example being clinical depression. Even when not driven by financial profit, knowledge adds to the general human fund of fundamental capital that drives all entrepreneurship: knowledge, Menand quips, 'is our most important business' (Menand, 2010, p. 13). Business students make better citizens if inculcated with a meaningful liberal perspective on human life; humanities students need business savviness, perhaps more urgently, to participate in productive civic life.

Reacting against nineteenth-century anti-intellectualism, a small, powerful coterie of educators including Princeton's Woodrow Wilson and Harvard's new President Abbott Lawrence Lowell began around 1900 to champion a renewed commitment to the classical model of liberal education as envisioned by Arnold and Newman. At Johns Hopkins (founded in 1876), a parallel rejection of utilitarianism emerged, patterned after German universities' Fichtean paradigm of *Wissenschaft*, the pursuit of scientifically oriented pure research untrammelled by practical concerns. But paradoxically this reform also insisted education be 'worldly.' Today, I argue, we need a similarly enlightened and updated hybrid approach.

Contemporary students often complain of the distractions of information technology's shiny appurtenances. Kate Crawford reports that Australian and Indian users of cell phones and social media frequently confess a desire to escape the 'noise' of technology and recreate themselves in 'technology sabbaticals' (Crawford, 2009, pp. 64–69). Enslaved to the siren call of a lucrative career, many yet thirst for a more intellectually and aesthetically rewarding 'disinterested' educational experience.

Structural renewal

The renewal I propose is not 'aesthetic' just in the weak sense. Rather, I propose that aesthetic renewal must be supported by structural renewal.

Yale's Anthony T. Kronman, Sterling Professor of Law, confirms that contemporary students crave education that addresses questions of life's 'ultimate meaning' (Kronman, 2007, p. 75). Kronman's secular culturalism finds corroboration from Bill Readings, who writes that liberal education 'has lost its organizing center'; the idea of culture as 'both origin and goal' of the human sciences has faded (Readings, 1996, p. 10). More unstinting liberals include Frank Lentricchia, Fredric Jameson, and Henry Giroux; they are committed to a progressive approach in education (Lentricchia, 1983, p. 2; Jameson, 1979/1980, pp. 31–32; Giroux, 2001, pp. 40). Skeptics contesting this vision include Stanley Fish, who question the spirit of Jacques Barzun's pedagogical cultural Platonism, in which 'Education…is synonymous with civilization' (p. 12). There are also right-wing ideologues defending Western (high) culture. Allan Bloom, Roger Kimball, and Dinesh D'Souza all castigate progressive defenders of liberal education (Bloom, 1987, p. 337; Kimball, 1990; D'Souza, 1991).

What defenders and critics share is the recognition that good citizenship is founded on sound education. For example, the recent report on the Massachusetts Common Core points up a universal desire to reverse the trend toward soundbite culture ('Why Text Complexity Matters,' p. 2) The report emphasizes the need to teach *how to read complex texts* – in business, arts and sciences. My argument therefore is that a fusion or hybrid renewal is what we need. This should not be visualized as indifferentiation (a conception that motivates the argument of a book entitled by Thomas Donaldson and Edward Freeman *Business as a Humanity*).

Universities have traditionally been constructed as credentializing institutions. As a recent piece in the *Washington Post* put it, '[f]or thousands of years now, the university has been the middleman of the higher education system.' But this image has undergone significant change, in response to the 'immense pressure to do something about the prohibitive cost of higher education,' immense enough to be the first key topic of the President's post-State of the Union tour at the University of Michigan. In the twenty-first century, he said, 'higher education is not a luxury – it's an economic imperative.' Some professors, such as Sebastian Thrun, formerly tenured professor of computer sciences at Stanford, are leaving academe in frustration. He left to found Udacity, an education start-up offering cheaper online courses to what de Vise terms 'buyers of education' (students). The revolution in education, what de Vise calls an 'Arab Spring,' is also due to the ongoing transformations in IT. De Vise argues that it is part of the mission of an institution higher education to 'curate' this information, to provide technical skills to students, to build necessary infrastructure, to cater to a broader and more diverse student profile in terms of age, work background, life experience, ethnicity, country of origin.

Philosophical renewal

The final element of the hybrid renewal I am proposing is a philosophical renewal, informing the structural changes we make and the reorientation towards an aesthetic reimagining of the purposes of education. There remains a need, indeed a hunger, for an education for its own sake – for enjoyment, as exemplified in Martha Nussbaum's classicist and cosmopolitanist defense of the university and a liberal education based on the Socratic 'examined life' in which the mind is not a slave to 'habit' or 'custom' but produces 'people who can function with sensitivity and alertness as citizens of the whole world' (Nussbaum, 1997, p. 8). A vigorous defense of learning as pure enjoyment or 'flow' (even play and recreation) is articulated by Mihaly Cziksentmihalyi (p. 4). Such flow, which can also emerge from an engagement in practical learning, e.g., in an apprenticeship in carpentry or mechanical engineering, is what would be enabled by the kind of hybrid educational vision I am promoting.

Hofstadter points out, however, that 'in the United States the play of the mind is perhaps the only form of play that is not looked upon with the most tender indulgence...' (Hofstadter, 1963 [1962], p. 33). To advocate a simple return to the old ideal of liberal education is to invite skepticism. The intellectual heroes of America, as Washburn remarks, have tended to be Thomas Edison and Benjamin Franklin rather than 'pure' academics, scientists and intellectuals such as Josiah Willard Gibbs, a father of modern physical chemistry and obscure Yale professor (Hofstader, 1963 [1962], pp. 25–26). Yet 'it is precisely because [American universities] have stubbornly resisted forsaking their independence and refused to adopt narrow market values (even as their responsibilities have grown) that universities have played a unique and vital role in American life' (Washburn, 2005, pp. 26–27).

There is then hope for a kind of *Aufhebung* or sublation of the ideal of autotelic education through a hybrid of pragmatism and idealism. Rather than presenting an idealistic case for a return to liberal education for its own sake, we can take seriously the demands of a defining American pragmatism. A hybrid approach is not oblivious to the painful bifurcation Van Wyck Brooks in 1915 identified in American writing and thought between 'the world of the practical [and] sensibility, refinement, theory, and discipline' – the world of the aesthetic (Hofstadter, 1963 [1962], pp. 403–404). We *can* be active proponents of an *aesthetic* as well as critical interdisciplinarity: a pragmatic, pluralist education. In a book tellingly titled *The Academic Revolution*, Christopher Jencks and David Riesman suggest that 'the question has always been *how* an institution mixed the academic with the vocational, not *whether* it did so' (Jencks and Riesman, 1968, p. 199).

Allow me to highlight some modest efforts at my home institution, a small business university. It promotes the liberal arts as an indispensable supplement to a business education. We administer a liberal studies major (LSM), a double major expressly for business majors. I am a coordinator for the LSM, and I emphasize to students that this is a good way to combine the practical and the creative. The LSM has been a small part of a renewal of the institution, as it has transformed itself from a 'college' to a 'university.' The university is also striving to encourage interdisciplinary collaboration. My own small participation in such efforts include attending a seminar at Harvard Business School as a member of a Humanities department, as well as co-facilitating a seminar on globalization with a business school professor. I have taught a course on Postcolonial Literature and Culture emphasizing a cultural studies approach that engages seriously with commercial and cultural dimensions of colonialism and globalization.

These I offer only as first-hand accounts of efforts to blend a business and a humanities orientation. Far more significant examples can be adduced. Steve Jobs dropped out of Reed College, but took classes and learned calligraphy for 'recreational' reasons. As he stressed in his famous Stanford Commencement speech, this may have been a secret to his success as the business leader he became, because the aesthetic sense he refined there informed Apple's distinctive style. Washburn also provides the example of Nobel Prize-winning Stanford biologist Paul Berg. He has made key contributions to the biotech transformation of genetics, including basic research on DNA splicing, foundation for the $1 billion biotech industry. Significantly, his research was not produced for commercial ends. As Berg himself wrote, 'The biotech revolution itself would not have happened had the whole thing been left up to industry. Venture capital people steered clear of anything that didn't have obvious commercial value or short-term impact. They didn't fund the basic research that made biotechnology possible' (Washburn, p. 27). Instead, nearly all the research was paid for by the taxpayer as 'pure' research.

It was precisely this kind of research that the Bayh–Dole Act would have made legal for a private biotechnology firm *subsequently* to win a patent for and profit from, not having supported in the first instance. The taxpayer would ultimately have to pay a second time for any benefits that the private firm then sold back to the taxpayer. This, Berg said, was only one of the many risks of corporate control of research in the academy. Far better to foster a climate of open, 'disinterested' inquiry. This is true not only in the sciences but in the arts. Van Gogh was famously neither successful nor famous in his lifetime. If only practically useful education were underwritten by state, federal, or private interests, it would be seriously distorted. Yet we just cannot ignore the demands of a defining American pragmatism with regard to the mission of education. To repeat, we *can* be active proponents of an *aesthetic* as well as critical interdisciplinary and pragmatic, pluralist model of education.

Let me conclude by suggesting two general recommendations: at the policy level, we should vote for better and more thorough governmental oversight and *regulation* of the educational system, notwithstanding the inevitable objections this recommendation will draw; and at the institutional level, we should honor pragmatic as well as disinterestedly intellectual motivations for seeking a university education by offering students not only more interdisciplinary approaches but also a greater integration of practical, critical, and aesthetic perspectives in a mutually informing and mutually reinforcing way.

References

Beha, Christopher R. (2011) 'Leveling the Field: What I Learned from For-Profit Education,' *Harper's Magazine* (October), pp. 51–57.

Bloom, Allan (1987) *The Closing of the American Mind: How Higher Education Has Failed Democracy and Impoverished the Souls of Today's Students* (New York: Simon & Schuster).

Bok, Derek (2006) *Our Underachieving Colleges: A Candid Look at How Much Students Learn and Why They Should Be Learning More* (Princeton: Princeton University Press).

The College Board's Completion Agenda, Available: http://completionagenda.collegeboard.org/about-agenda, p. 9. Accessed September 1, 2011.

Crawford, Kate (2009) 'Noise, Now, Listening to Networks,' *Meanjin*, 69(2), pp. 64–69.

Czikszentmihalyi, Mihaly (1991 [1990]) *Flow: The Psychology of Optimal Experience* (New York: Harper & Row).

Donaldson, Thomas J. and R. Edward Freeman (1994) *Business as a Humanity* (New York: Oxford University Press).

D'Souza, Dinesh (1991) *Illiberal Education: The Politics of Race and Sex on Campus.*

Ferguson, Andrew (2011) *Crazy U: One Dad's Crash Course in Getting His Kid into College* (New York: Simon & Shuster).

Giroux, Henry A. (2001) 'Introduction,' in Henry A. Giroux and Kostas Myrsiades (eds), *Beyond the Corporate University: Culture and Pedagogy in the New Millennium* (Oxford: Rowman & Littlefield).

Harvard Graduate School of Education (2011), 'Pathways to Prosperity: Meeting the Challenge of Preparing Young Americans for the 21st Century,' February. Available: http://tinyurl.com/46jq9nh. Accessed July 22, 2011.

Hofstadter, Richard (1963 [1962]) *Anti-Intellectualism in American Life* (New York: Alfred A. Knopf).

Jameson, Fredric (1979/1980) 'Marxism and Teaching,' *New Political Science*, 2/3, pp. 31–32.

Jencks, Christopher and David Riesman (1968) *The Academic Revolution* (New York: The Doubleday Company).

Kimball, Roger (1990) *Tenured Radicals: How Politics Has Corrupted Higher Education* (Chicago: Rowman & Littlefield).

Klein, Julie Thompson (2005) *Humanities, Culture, and Interdisciplinarity: The Changing American Academy* (Albany, NY: State University of New York Press).

Kronman, Anthony T. (2007) *Education's End: Why Our Colleges and Universities Have Given Up on the Meaning of Life* (New Haven, CT: Yale University Press).

Lentricchia, Frank (1983) *Criticism and Social Change* (Chicago: University of Chicago Press).

Menand, Louis (2010) *The Marketplace of Ideas* (New York: W.W. Norton).

The New York State Commission on Higher Education Report, esp. 12, 55. https://docs.google.com/viewer?a=v&q=cache:VlH2leC21MIJ:www.ppinys.org/innovation/CHEPreliminary-Report. Accessed September 1, 2011. Online.

Newman, John Henry Cardinal (1999 [1852]) *The Idea of a University* (Washington, DC: Regnery Press).

Nussbaum, Martha C. (1997) *Cultivating Humanity* (Boston: Harvard University Press).

Readings, Bill (1996) *The University in Ruins* (Boston: Harvard University Press).

Robinson, James Harvey (1923) *The Humanizing of Knowledge* (New York: George H. Doran Company).

Vesey, Laurence (1973) 'Stability and Experience in the American Undergraduate Curriculum,' in Carl Kaysen, ed., *Content and Context: Essays on College Education*, 1, pp. 58–59.

Washburn, Jennifer (2005). *University Inc.: The Corporate Corruption of Higher Education* (Cambridge: Basic Books).

'Why Text Complexity Matters,' Appendix A of the *Common Core Standards for English Language Arts & Literacy in History/ Social Studies, Science and Technical Subjects*, Research Supporting Key Elements of the Standards, esp. p. 2; Available: http://tinyurl.com/7pbapbj, accessed December 10, 2011.

19
Service-Learning, Business Education, and the Civically Engaged Professional

Edward Zlotkowski

In *Rethinking Undergraduate Business Education: Liberal Learning for the Profession* (Colby et al., 2011), researchers at the Carnegie Foundation for the Advancement of Teaching point out that business is now the largest undergraduate major in the United States. This fact, they maintain, suggests that what happens in undergraduate business programs is of more than parochial interest. Because business has become such a powerful force in the contemporary world, how students are prepared for it is, or should be, of concern to all of us. If, as Colby et al. maintain, undergraduate business programs are delivered in a way that does not lead students to ask how market-based thinking relates to other important social perspectives and cultural values, we run the risk of entrusting a powerful social sector to individuals not qualified to run it wisely.

The primary strategy Colby et al. (2011, p. 60) recommend to ensure that this does not happen is the deliberate cultivation of what they call 'liberal learning.' Liberal learning, they tell us in chapter 4, represents a *way* of learning, not a particular set of disciplines. It is learning that prioritizes (1) analytical thinking, (2) multiple framing, and (3) the reflective exploration of meaning. Ideally it is complemented and enriched by forms by practical reasoning, which allows it to be embodied in real-world practice.

But if liberal learning does not actually belong to any particular set of disciplines, Colby et al. make it clear that in their view it naturally resides in the arts and sciences, at least in comparison with the business disciplines. Thus, the best way to ensure that the latter do not operate in an overly narrow, exclusively market-focused context is to take steps to bring them into closer proximity with the arts and sciences. Central to the book's argument is the proposition that if the business disciplines and the arts and sciences were positioned less as the weights at the ends of a barbell and more as the intertwined strands of a double helix (Colby et al., pp. 6–7), much of what ails undergraduate business education could be effectively addressed.

This is an attractive strategy, in part because it seems to draw upon resources already at hand. Since most business programs have arts and sciences counterparts, linking these already established curricular areas should be less daunting than creating something entirely new. Furthermore, the linkage can take many forms: paired disciplinary courses, cross-disciplinary readings, interdisciplinary team-taught courses, integrated capstones, assignments requiring integrative thinking and writing. But the strategy also raises questions. Indeed, it makes a number of claims and assumptions that deserve further examination.

For example, the authors pay relatively little attention to strategies for broadening the business disciplines from within. Towards the end of the chapter in which they articulate their understanding of liberal learning they assert that if students 'gain experience with…liberal learning exclusively within a business context, their college experience will be impoverished and they are unlikely to graduate with a deep understanding of the world and their place in it' (Colby et al., p. 69). This certainly has been the assumption behind the widespread requirement of general education courses not just for business students but for all undergraduates at most colleges and universities. However, as many critics have pointed out, this requirement often results in little serious engagement, either academic (Erickson et al., 2006) or civic (Schneider, 2000). On its face, a broad-based education would seem to be desirable, but curricular breadth may be less important than the way in which a given disciplinary area is itself intellectually, culturally, and civically positioned. Many business faculty members have undergraduate degrees in the humanities and the social sciences. Surely this is a circumstance to be valued and explored. Relatedly, the past decade has seen the rise of many initiatives from within business education that have challenged the prevailing market-dominated paradigm on social and ethical as well as economic grounds. Why are the intellectual resources generated by, to take but one example, conscious capitalism (www.consciouscapitalism.org) less important in opening up the undergraduate business curriculum than a link to, for example, literary studies?

Indeed, from a purely practical standpoint, can we realistically expect business educators to be open to significant influences from without?

Are they likely to accept the idea that they 'need' their non-business colleagues to get business education 'right'? How open, in turn, are those non-business colleagues to weaving business cases and texts into their own teaching – even when the majority of their students are business majors?

Finally, and perhaps most importantly, it is not at all clear that the liberal arts as taught today are as suitable as Colby et al. (2011) assume for promoting the liberal learning they recommend. Clearly, what is driving their conviction that undergraduate business education needs to be reformed is a belief that the perspectives and values that dominate market-based thinking must be put in a context that includes not just other academic disciplines but, far more importantly, perspectives and values that lead to civic engagement. As they explain in their first chapter, '[college education] means, in the American tradition of liberal education, that students need to be prepared for their futures as citizens...' (p. 3). But over the past few decades, we have seen the humanities in particular slide into a miasma of impenetrable critical jargon and self-reference that is no less destructive of 'liberal learning' than the most narrowly vocational business program. As the intellectual historian Thomas Bender (1993) has observed, 'Academe is threatened by the twin dangers of fossilization and scholasticism (of three types: tedium, high tech, and radical chic). The agenda of the next decade, at least as I see it, ought to be the opening up of the disciplines, the ventilating of professional communities that have come to share too much and that have become too self-referential' (p. 143).

Bender's critique is pointedly *not* a critique of business education alone. As Eugene Lang (2000), chairman of the Board of Managers Emeritus of Swarthmore College, has written about the commitment of America's most prestigious liberal arts institutions to civic engagement,

> Today, unlike their forebears, liberal arts colleges do not as a general rule feel impelled to exercise a proactive role in preparing students for service in their communities. Contemporary liberal arts curricula are seldom designed to implement that civic dimension of their missions by reaching beyond the campus environment. Rather, conscious of their established prestige and historic role in higher education, they are substantially consumed by internal academic agendas.... Qualities of responsible citizenship as demonstrated by student engagements with social issues are applauded; but rarely do colleges engage these issues in ways that meaningfully prepare

students for active roles as citizens in recognizing, understanding, and responding to them. (p. 135)

It was for this reason that in 2001 Lang founded Project Pericles, a 'not-for-profit organization that encourages and facilitates commitments by colleges and universities to include social responsibility and participatory citizenship as essential elements of their educational programs' (http://www.projectpericles.org/projectpericles/).

Thus, even the 'double helix' model Colby et al. recommend may well lead to a string of juxtaposed courses *all* of which fail to develop liberal learning in any meaningful civic sense. As Matthew Fisher, associate professor of Chemistry at St. Vincent's College in Pennsylvania, notes in a chapter he wrote for *Citizenship Across the Curriculum* (2010), 'Undergraduate science education assumes that majors who have a basic understanding of the scientific concepts will automatically make the connections between those concepts and global challenges... this, however, is unlikely unless the connections be made explicit' (p. 113). Or, as Carol Schneider (2000), president of the American Association of Colleges and Universities (AAC&U), has observed of the academy's poor record of civic preparedness:

> ... there emerged across the academy two fundamental disconnections between the undergraduate curriculum and concepts of citizen engagement and responsibility. The first disconnect was between the departmental programs... and the marginalized 'civic' content of the general education curriculum.... The second disconnect was that between the actual content of Western Civilization courses and the students' self-identification as American citizens responsible for the policies and practices of a particular set of communities... in these courses most directly tied to issues of civic values and participation... instructors left it to the students' own determination how the study of Western Civilization related to either the immediate problems or the constitutive practices of American democracy. (pp. 104–105)

In short, it is difficult to be optimistic that even *academically* rigorous liberal arts programs have themselves the kind of commitment to *civic* engagement that would allow them to play the pivotal role the authors of *Rethinking Undergraduate Business Education: Liberal Learning for the Profession* would like to see them play. What would seem to be needed are strategies that allow the full range of academic disciplines to rediscover their social utility and public purposes.

Experiential resources

Considerations and reservations such as these call into question neither the value of *Rethinking Undergraduate Business Education* nor the potential benefit of linking the business disciplines with the liberal arts. Rather, they suggest that this linkage will not be by itself sufficient to bring about a rethinking of undergraduate business education. For that to happen, other factors will have to be brought into play, especially the natural inclination of business faculty to value educational experiences outside the classroom. As Colby et al. point out on several occasions, one significant lesson the liberal arts can learn from the business disciplines is the importance of including real-world practice in a discipline's pedagogical strategy:

> ...we set out to examine programs that explicitly announced the intent to provide their undergraduate business majors with the benefits of liberal learning... [these efforts] also provide an opportunity for liberal arts disciplines to learn from business education, especially about strategies that help students practice and refine their knowledge in real-world circumstances. (p. 3)

Indeed, Schneider (2009), speaking from her perspective as president of the country's most important liberal arts association, would seem to endorse this view when she suggests that the future of the liberal arts depends, to no small extent, on our ability to not only 'erase the distinction' 'between "practical" or career studies and the "true liberal arts"'. She also states that a 'good liberal arts education should take pride in preparing students for "effective practice"' but also link liberal learning with "real-world practice"' (www.aacu.org/liberaleducation/le-fa09/le-fa09_president.cfm).

Such a stress on moving beyond the classroom as the only important locus of learning, regardless of the disciplinary area in question, should not be surprising given the volume of educational research that supports this position (see, for example, Abbott 1996 and Ewell 1997 for summary statements). Still, many faculty members – including some business faculty members – continue to resist course-based real-world experience for a variety of personal and cultural reasons, and real-world experience plays a surprisingly small role in *Rethinking Undergraduate Business*

Education (2011). To be sure, one of the staples of experiential education in business programs, the corporate internship, has little to contribute to the book's emphasis on broadening, not reinforcing, an already narrow focus on market values. Still, corporate internships represent only one kind of experiential education and not the one that has most recently received the most public attention. That would be service-learning, the deliberate linking of course objectives and academic rigor to projects that strengthen community-based organizations and/or further the common good. Ironically, at least five of the ten schools Colby and her colleagues feature have major service-learning programs. Perhaps some of these programs contribute little to undergraduate *business* education at their institutions? Theoretically, this should not be so.

Even a quick review of key features of service-learning will make clear why it should be seen as central, not peripheral, to efforts to broaden business students' perspectives and to help create an educational context in which all students – business and liberal arts alike – are able to appreciate the civic relevance of their disciplines. Let us imagine service-learning as the product of two intersecting axes, each of which embodies a productive tension. A horizontal axis spans the need to connect discipline-specific skills and concepts to an awareness of their civic utility and social implications. A vertical axis links traditional campus-based activities and assignments to field-based work designed to respond to community needs and interests. In any given service-learning initiative the emphasis can fall more on academic skills development or social and civic awareness, can stress the campus or community as worksite. However, in every instance all four factors will be present. Neither academic gain nor social/civic awareness can be left out of consideration, nor can faculty guidance or community voice.

Such a pedagogical design ensures that academic learning – regardless of the discipline – is always a vehicle of social and civic awareness, and vice versa. It also ensures that academic courses, in the words of Ernest Boyer (1996), are viewed 'not as isolated islands, but as staging grounds for action' (p. 20). The campus functions as a site for citizenship even as the community functions as a site for learning. In this way 'contact' complements 'concepts' (Kolvenbach, 2000), and the educational process becomes far more naturally holistic. Indeed, it is not just the educational process itself that becomes more naturally holistic; so does student understanding of how problems must be framed and addressed. Business-focused projects take place in a context of organizations dealing with significant social issues. Projects based in the liberal arts expose students to questions of implementation and organizational capacity.

Thus, the inherent multi-disciplinarity of real-world problem-solving works to break down, or at least to render more porous, academic silos. Bender's (1993) agenda of 'the opening up of the disciplines, the ventilating of professional communities that have come to share too much and that have become too self-referential' (p. 143) receives a tangible assist.

Colby et al.'s suggestion of the intertwined strands of a double helix (pp. 6–7) as a useful way to conceptualize the relationship that should prevail between the business disciplines and the arts and sciences also receives an assist. Community-based projects that raise questions related to social purpose as well as resource utilization and organizational efficiencies are the sugar and phosphate molecules that naturally bind the two stands of the double helix. To address a social issue adequately one simply cannot ignore questions of implementation; to design and implement a resource well one simply cannot ignore questions of social purpose. There is here no need to create artificial structures to link the two stands. As a matter of fact, it would be artificial to separate them.

The Bentley Service-Learning Center (BSLC)

As we have stressed, service-learning is not the only effective way to strengthen liberal learning in business education and/or to link that education to the kinds of benefits associated with the liberal arts. Institutions need a variety of strategies to accomplish this goal, and many of them are described elsewhere in this volume. Furthermore, service-learning can contribute to a business-liberal arts dialogue only if its design possesses genuine integrity. Such integrity demands that one carefully attend to all four of the key factors identified above. If, for example, projects arising in the business disciplines fail to make room for an examination of relevant social issues and content themselves with some kind of technical 'fix,' the power of service-learning to generate multiple perspectives will have been squandered. If projects arising in the liberal arts do not ask students to take seriously the real-world circumstances in which social and cultural issues play themselves out, students will not learn to use practice to test theory and generate new knowledge. Lack of sufficient faculty investment will result in academically questionable work; lack of a strong community voice will result in disrespect for the importance of 'lived' expertise.

For this reason it is highly desirable that colleges and universities develop effective service-learning centers that can assist all constituencies – faculty members, students, community partners, and the administration – in maximizing both the academic and the social benefits of such work. The Bentley Service-Learning Center has been playing such a role for over two decades, and annually facilitates connections between approximately 50 community partners, over 1,000 students, and 100 faculty members. Central to the center's success has been its organizational structure, which not only allows staff members to develop and sustain relationships with each of the four key constituencies but also to create and constantly renew academic, social, and civic resources. Thus, the center's faculty director focuses on the role of service-learning in the institution as a whole and the ways in which community-based work can contribute to the university's core objectives as well as its national reputation. The director reports to the dean of arts and sciences but also has ready access to the entire deans' council, the provost, the president, and the directors of other campus-wide initiatives such as the Center for Business Ethics, the Center for the Arts and Sciences, and the Center for Women and Business. Whenever possible, the director seeks not only to facilitate collaboration on a programmatic level but also to articulate areas of shared concern.

Working with the faculty director are three professional staff members: a senior associate director, an associate director, and an administrative assistant. While the first of these focuses primarily on the recruitment, training, and monitoring of the BSLC student leaders as well as the health of key community relationships, the second focuses on the faculty: their recruitment, development, and support. The third not only runs the center office but also oversees a service-learning certificate program and some non-academic service opportunities.

However, as important as the professional staff is to achieving the program's objectives, it would be difficult to underestimate the student role in everything the center does. From the very beginning, the BSLC has deliberately fostered a culture of strong student leadership and ownership. Students, trained to function as project managers, provide a reliable and sustainable link between courses and most community partners. They identify project opportunities for faculty and fellow students, monitor the quality of face-to-face community work, and provide faculty with both feedback on their students and suggestions for strengthening the academic as well as the social value of ongoing initiatives. In some cases they may even work with individual instructors as 'teaching assistants,' leading in-class reflection sessions and critiquing some assignments. Especially during the 2011–2012 academic year, their responsibility for ensuring that faculty fully appreciate the importance of academic rigor in community-based work and that their student peers process their experiences from a civic as well as an academic perspective has significantly increased. Naturally, this heightened responsibility has entailed still more training, including a set of professional development opportunities designed to make project managers more comfortable functioning as faculty colleagues.

In short, the prominent role played by student leaders in making community-based work a powerful and inclusive learning opportunity for the entire undergraduate student body points to still another way in which service-learning, at least at Bentley, functions as a vehicle of liberal learning. Drawing upon both business-related organizational skills and a set of broad social commitments, the BSLC's project managers – comprising approximately 2.3 percent of the undergraduate population – represent precisely the kind of 'creative, ethical and socially responsible organizational leaders' (http://www.bentley.edu/about/mission-and-vision) the university seeks to graduate.

Conclusion

American higher education has entered a period of major change. Everywhere inherited certainties are losing their power to convince. At one time we assumed that the liberal arts prepared one not just for life-long personal development but also for civic engagement. Documents such as 'A Crucible Moment: College Learning and Democracy's Future' (AAC&U 2012), a national report on the failure of colleges and universities in all academic sectors to prepare students for citizenship, calls at least the second part of that assumption into question. At one time we believed that exemplary business education meant teaching students to worship shareholder value. *Rethinking Undergraduate Business Education* (2011) and the Aspen Institute's Center for Business Education have forcefully challenged that claim. At one time we thought the 'true' liberal arts and career studies had nothing in common. No less than the president of the country's leading liberal arts association has challenged that certainty (Schneider, 2009). When Richard Light, professor of Education and Public Policy at Harvard, set out to discover 'what choices...students themselves [can] make to get the most out of college' and 'what are effective ways for faculty members and campus leaders to translate good intentions into practice' (2001, pp. 2–3), some of his research results surprised him. His very first 'finding' included the following:

> ...I assumed that most important and memorable academic learning goes on inside the classroom, while outside activities provide a useful

but modest supplement. The evidence shows that the opposite is true.... When we asked students to think of a specific, critical incident or moment that had changed them profoundly, four-fifths of them chose a situation or event outside of the classroom. (2001, p. 8)

Hence, it is not surprising that 'Those students who make connections between what goes on outside and inside the classroom report a more satisfying college experience' (Light, 2001, 14).

Whether or not Einstein actually said that 'We can't solve problems by using the same kind of thinking we used when we created them,' it is clear that the academy cannot hope to address the challenges of this new educational era by limiting itself to the pedagogical strategies of the past. How many of the 'high-impact practices' identified by George Kuh (2008), founding director of the National Survey of Student Engagement, would have been so designated even 30 years ago: first-year seminars, learning communities, global learning, internships, service-learning (http://www.aacu.org/leap/hip.cfm)? As more and more students make business their major of choice, we cannot help but choose to use every resource we have to make that choice a wise one for all of us.

References

AAC&U (2012) 'A Crucible Moment: College Learning & Democracy's Future.' Accessed May 31. http://www.aacu.org/civic_learning/crucible

Abbott, John (1996) 'The Search for Next-Century Learning,' *AAHE Bulletin*, 48(7), pp. 3–6.

Bender, Thomas (1993) *Intellect and Public Life: Essays on the Social History of Academic Intellectuals in the United States* (Baltimore, MD: Johns Hopkins Press).

Bentley University (2012) 'Mission and Vision.' http://www.bentley.edu/about/mission-and-vision, accessed May 31.

Boyer, Ernest L. (1996) 'The Scholarship of Engagement,' *Journal of Public Service and Outreach*, 1(1), pp. 11–20.

Colby, Anne, Ehrlich, Thomas, Sullivan, William M., Dolle, and Jonathan R. (2011) *Rethinking Undergraduate Business Education: Liberal Learning for the Profession* (San Francisco: Jossey-Bass).

Conscious Capitalism (2012) http://consciouscapitalism.org, accessed May 31.

Erickson, Bette LaSere, Calvin B. Peters, and Dian Weltner Strommer (2006) *Teaching First-Year College Students* (San Francisco, CA: Jossey-Bass).

Ewell, Peter T. (1997) 'Organizing for Learning: A New Imperative,' *AAHE Bulletin* 50(4), pp. 3–6.

Fisher, Matthew A. (2010) 'Educating for Scientific Knowledge, Awakening to a Citizen's Responsibility,' in *Citizenship Across the Curriculum*, Michael B. Smith,

Rebecca S. Nowacek and Jeffrey L. Bernstein (eds), pp. 110–131 (Bloomington, IN: Indiana University Press).

Kolvenbach, Rev. Peter-Hans., S. J. (2000) 'The Service of Faith and the Promotion of Justice in American Jesuit Higher Education.' http://www.scu.edu/ ignatiancenter/events/conferences/archives/justice/upload/f07_kolvenbach_keynote. pdf, accessed May 31.

Kuh, George D. (2008) 'High Impact Educational Practices,' http://www.aacu. org/leap/hip.cfm, accessed May 31.

Lang, Eugene M. (2000) 'Distinctively American: The Liberal Arts College,' in *Distinctively American: The Residential Liberal Arts College*, Steven Koblik and Stephan R. Graubard (eds), pp. 133–150 (Somerset, NJ: Transaction Publishers).

Light, Richard J. (2001) *Making the Most of College: Students Speak Their Minds* (Cambridge, MA: Harvard University Press).

Project Pericles (2012) http://www.projectpericles.org/projectpericles/, accessed May 31.

Schneider, Carol Geary (2000) 'Educational Missions and Civic Responsibility: Toward an Engaged Academy,' in *Civic Responsibility and Higher Education*, Thomas Ehrlich (ed.), pp. 98–123 (Phoenix, AZ: Oryx Press).

Schneider, Carol Geary (2009) 'The Clark/AAC&U Challenge: Connecting Liberal Education with Real-World Practice,' *Liberal Education*, 95, pp. 2–3.

20
The Multi-Disciplinary Nature of Experiential Learning

Diane M. Kellogg

Introduction

The depth and breadth of what one can learn from the experience of living and working in the world is – and always has been – radically different from the learning potential of the classroom.

The need for students to learn from the experience of living and working in the world, and not just the business world, has become an increasing imperative for a variety of reasons. Most would agree that classroom curriculums lag behind the real world, as new knowledge is constantly being generated and the conditions of the world are, as a consequence, also constantly changing. New textbooks take time to get published and new curriculums take time to develop and implement. Though these knowledge-dissemination processes have been shortened by technology, instant access to information has meant that the world is changing at an even faster pace. New knowledge affects people and programs and policies and products globally. Today, more than ever, we cannot count on classroom education alone to prepare students for the business world in a changing global environment.

Though the service-learning movement offers an exception, it is most common that students are asked to read, listen to lectures, and articulate their learning, and sometimes their own ideas, through discussion or in writing. Traditional business education also encourages internships. Internships do give students some experience in the business world, but there is a rarely an imperative that a faculty supervisor make a site visit or meet with the intern's corporate supervisor. It is more common that students submit a final paper to report on or analyze their internship experience. Students often perform their internship for the sake of the 'line on the resume' and are not challenged to maximize the learning potential of the experience.

If the traditional role of the classroom educator continues to be knowledge-focused, staying a chapter ahead of their students will become increasingly impossible. Motivated students already have easy access to knowledge. Alternatives such as distance and online learning, with automated quiz answers and natural-language analysis of student writing, challenge the notion that traditional educators are critical to the learning process.

The changing world is demanding changes to traditional approaches. Experiential learning is one such approach. By placing the student in an unfamiliar environment, often accompanied by an experienced educator, the student learns about the world in a way vastly different from the familiar, and somewhat safe, classroom setting with traditional testing methods.

Students will be graduating to live and work in a world they haven't been prepared to encounter. While this has always been the case, and always will be, the gap between education and experience is getting wider given the pace of change in the world, and the slow pace of curriculum change in academic institutions.

The need for all of us – faculty and students alike – to view experience as a critical catalyst for ongoing education becomes increasingly important in a fast-changing world where knowledge is expanding at an exponential rate. This emerging reality mandates multi-disciplinary education in the context of experiential learning.

This chapter will explore how educators can capitalize on global travel experiences as a source of multi-disciplinary learning. The challenges and benefits are framed through the use of examples from Bentley's multiyear engagement with partner organizations in Ghana that address social and economic challenges the country faces. Twelve professors from six different academic departments have collaborated to offer students a choice of (1) a three-credit, semester-long course that includes about two weeks of travel in Ghana; or (2) an eight-week, six-credit summer course that immerses students in Ghanaian life and gives them an opportunity to use their business skills while working alongside Ghanaians in partner organizations.

The world as classroom

Students who find themselves in Ghana recognize very little in the world around them. The unpredictably paved, potholed, and sign-free roads are lined with vendors selling all manner of goods. Unexpectedly to the western business student, each seller sells only one product. And they don't stick with their 'store,' such as it is: they walk from car to car when the traffic is stopped. You find yourself window-shopping through the window of a car as products come to you, one at a time.

It's not a classroom, but students are taking a class and are expected to be in learning mode in this new world. The newness of the environment is part of the key to its learning potential: people pay more attention to the unfamiliar than they do to the familiar. In our everyday familiar environments we go on 'auto-pilot' and fail to notice nuances or details that might in fact be quite different from one day to the next.

For example, the routine trip from class to campus might mean that students don't notice whether there are or aren't any squirrels in the woods that day. However, turkeys on the quad might get their attention. The very newness of the experience might lead them to ask questions: why are the birds here? Do they like to eat something on campus? Did that new housing development nearby push them out of their habitat? For the most part, experiences not new to us don't raise our curiosity nearly as much as out-of-the-ordinary experiences.

For American students, Ghana is out of the ordinary. Global travel, especially to the developing world, leads to curiosity and openness to learning. Students become curious about economic development and a myriad of different, yet interdependent topics, fostering that elusive and hard-to-promote process of learning. And it leads to learning about oneself, too. Why am I reacting as I am to these street vendors? Should I buy from them? Why shouldn't I buy from them? Can I relate to them? Can they relate to me? Whether positive or negative, with self-reflection one's reactions can be instructive about one's own attitudes, beliefs and values. People question themselves while experiencing economic development to an extent they most certainly would not if they were reading or writing or talking about economic development in a classroom setting. Self-knowledge, still an important by-product of college life, can become an extremely important aspect of experiential learning, if educators value, encourage, and facilitate the development of insights and self-knowledge.

We have found that offering students experiences in Ghana leads to opportunities to broaden and deepen students' understanding of any number of academic topics: economic development, geography, global health, sustainability, leadership, diversity, marketing, financial management, and political science, among others.

For example, students enrolled in the Global Health course on campus learned about malaria, and most could answer the exam questions related to malaria. Students who take the same course when Ghana travel is included also set mosquito traps in thatched-roof homes, and return to the village the next day to count and classify the population of mosquitoes captured overnight. They put captured mosquitoes under a microscope to determine how many are of the *anopheles* strain, and therefore potential carriers of the malaria parasite. While this same exercise could have been conducted (with some trouble) in a laboratory setting on campus, students wouldn't have seen the living conditions of the people in the village and met the families who slept in the rooms where the mosquitoes were trapped. While doing lab assignments in the villages, students learn the ages of family members and therefore know the very people who are more and less susceptible to being bitten, to being infected, and to dying as a result of sleeping in that room that night. They know how far it is to the clinic, and what treatment would cost as a percentage of that total family income for that month. The experience stays with them emotionally, as book learning seldom does.

In Ghana, students experience the broader economic conditions that keep villagers working so hard to maintain their families at a subsistence level, often unable to send their children to school or provide them with medical care. Students come to shed their judgments of families who don't send their children to school. Empathy emerges and the motivation to address root causes of problems, instead of just the symptoms, becomes a valuable perspective that impacts students' future thinking and analysis of societal problems.

Benefits to experiential learning

In the context of experiential, off-campus learning, we find that students are:

- more motivated to learn;
- ask better questions;
- care more about problem-solving – the practical application of knowledge;
- are better able to think analytically about the problems they witness or experience.

Here are some examples of each.

Motivation. On one Ghana journey the students met a man named Isaac Adjaottor. Isaac had a full-time job as a medical lab technician, but he worked in his community as a volunteer between 5 am and 10 am, and then again between 5 pm and 10 pm. Students felt his passion for educating his people about malaria prevention, and were in awe of his commitment to his people. It made them curious. They may have never felt so passionate about anything in their lives, yet they were meeting a very likeable person who was not much older than they, who lived his life with deep purpose. They wanted to know more; they *really* wanted to know more. How did he become so passionate? Doesn't he feel a need for more personal time? Has he seen any progress given all the hours, weeks, months and years of his life he's invested?

Questions. Their genuine motivation to learn about global health, too, was evidenced by the number and excellence of the questions they asked. They learned about the complexity of diagnosing and treating schistosomiasis, giardi, and wuchereria bancrofti, and about efforts being made to remove those organisms from the water supply and from the insect population.

A student named Malini who met Isaac as part of a Sustainability course had previously received top grades in the on-campus Global Health course. She could name, and even pronounce well, the complicated names of the parasites and worms that infect children and adults who live on the banks of the Volta river. Her knowledge was quite impressive. The first day she arrived for her eight-week internship experience, we toured the clinic and were brought right to the front of the long, winding cue of patients waiting to be seen by a doctor. We spent a good deal of time learning about how, given no funding, public health education nevertheless took place, in a sustainable and personal way, through the interactions of doctor and patient. We also learned about the process for detecting parasites and worms in the blood and urine and feces of children and adults. Malini asked many questions, and the doctor gave us his time freely, and encouraged us to ask until we could think of no more questions.

Care more and better analytical skills. As we left, Malini was visibly disturbed. She stumbled to find the words to express her horror that our presence in the clinic that day extended the waiting time for patients by almost an hour. Why were we more important than the people who had come to be treated? How wrong. Why are Western visitors given priority over local patients? Should we have gotten in line and waited our turn? Could we have met the doctor for dinner instead, and asked our questions then?

This led to learning on a whole new set of topics: sociology, psychology, global aid, philanthropy, and colonialism were all part of the multi-disciplinary conversation.

The quality of questions and the depth of self-reflection are just the starting point when higher education moves from the classroom to the world. Giving students experiences opens them to deeper understanding of the problems, including emotional investment in the solution. Students become more intimately engaged in problem-solving discussions, and come to see the interdependence of issues related to health, education, employment, political stability, and even climate change that would influence how practical any given solution would be.

Topics that once had only academic value become matters of urgency. Students not only come up with better questions in 'real time' than they do in the abstract setting of classrooms, but they also care more about the answers because they know the people who will be affected. Meeting Isaac put a name and a face to the problems of people living in the Volta river estuary. He introduced us to his father, his neighbors, his cousins, and many women selling goods in the local market. Students know people in Ghana, and care about the quality of their lives.

What are the challenges?

Inevitably, faculty members in experiential settings will face questions that are outside of their own discipline when they take students into the real world. 'I don't know' proves to be an excellent answer, modeling to students that experts don't have to know everything. 'I don't know' sets up the question, 'How should we find out?', giving students the opportunity to develop their own learning strategies on the basis of their own experiences, using the resources and people available to them at the time. The challenge to faculty members is to stretch beyond their own discipline and broaden their own focus of study and preparation.

Single-discipline faculty members become less and less valuable as educators in experiential settings, being replaced by a new generation of multi-disciplinary scholars. The definition of the term 'interdisciplinary' is still being debated but tends to mean that one professor teaches from the merged perspective of several disciplines. It's not necessarily team teaching, but requires a melded understanding of several disciplines. The assertion here is that interdisciplinary experts aren't the only ones who can guide multi-disciplinary exploration. Instead, what faculty members need is to increase their skills and value as *facilitators* of experiential learning, using a multi-disciplinary approach. Simply helping students recognize the relevance of several different disciplines is the starting point. Questions without immediate answers are not only acceptable, but desirable.

Without guided facilitation of discussion and learning, new experiences don't necessarily result in learning. Human beings develop their understanding of a situation through the use of their existing beliefs, values, and assumptions. Rarely do we even realize that we are limited by our existing frameworks. For example, when seeing a group of children playing unsupervised and noticing that fairly young children are carrying babies on their backs, American students might conclude that parents are shirking their duty to supervise children at play. If, when walking further through the village, mothers are seen in small groups chatting and laughing among themselves, American students might find their original conclusion confirmed: mothers are being irresponsible. Why aren't they caring for their own babies?

How can faculty members help students develop completely new frameworks for understanding new experiences (or past experiences, even)? In African tradition, children learn how to be caretakers and parents while they are still young by learning how to care for younger siblings. Older children take on responsibility for newborns, leaving mothers without babies on their backs. But assumptions and existing attitudes preclude 'seeing' the village situation more accurately.

Experiences analyzed from several perspectives means that existing values and beliefs must be challenged, to enable people to develop more sophisticated understanding of the world. Learning evolves only when the mind can shed frameworks and beliefs that limit what we 'see.'

Multi-disciplinary experiential learning, with pre-defined curricular requirements, is certainly a challenge. However, the global nature of business makes success imperative. As commerce brings disparate cultures closer together, travel and cultural understanding become even more valuable for developing a close-up, personal feel for others.

Multi-layered, experiential learning in Ghana: a final example

At a seaside fishing village in West Africa, newly arriving students for our eight-week Global Social Responsibility Practicum were greeted by happy children who giggled as we extended our 'abruni' (white) hands to them as if to say 'come walk with me.' They did, and we walked together through an idyllic setting of coconut trees, enjoying the sounds of the surf and the low pitched tones of men singing as they dragged in heavy fishing nets while the women collected the mackerel into large pans. Carrying the catch from seaside, the women spread the tiny wriggling fish over drying racks above charcoal-burning fires.

We walked to the small homes in the same village, where the previous Bentley class on Global Health had set mosquito traps one night, and returned the next morning to count mosquitoes. The earlier travelers told the summer students that there were *anopheles* mosquitoes (carriers of malaria) among the catch, so my students started to wonder whether any of the family members were infected the night before. Why no mosquito nets in this home?

Charity, a mother who opened her home to our Global Health students in January, welcomed us back. The summer students already knew that 15 percent of the mosquitoes caught were *anopheles*. From Charity we learned about this village's effort to use solar power for cooking rice. Charity is the leader of eight women who have named themselves the Sun for Life group. They use a solar oven to cook rice on sunny days. When they use solar power instead of charcoal to cook, they put the money saved (one cedi, or $.70) into a Sun for Life kitty. Forty solar-powered cooking days yields enough cedis to buy one solar-powered lamp, which can also recharge a cell phone using solar power. This bonus of a power source for recharging results in more money saved: instead of spending money on the trip to town (two cedis) to recharge their cell phone (four cedis), the first woman to get a solar-powered lamp can now put six cedis into the community kitty each time she recharges her cell phone.

The kitty grows faster now. Once the kitty has 40 cedis again, the second woman gets a solar-powered lamp. On and on, as the Sun for Life program promises to eventually give each of the eight women a solar-powered lamp at no cost. In essence, the sun is buying lamps for them. The solar-powered lamp let children read past 6 p.m., which is sunset on the equator all year round. Enough sun-cooked pots of rice and enough solar-powered cell phone recharging hours, and the kitty will eventually have enough cedis to send another child to school. And that child will also be able to study well into the evening.

So what do Bentley students learn from this experience?

They learn a lot. Experiential learning stimulates questions. The class included students majoring in accounting, marketing, finance, management, and managerial economics; but the questions they asked centered on their experience:

- How many of these children we laughed with and played with will die of malaria?
- Why don't the women just get a micro-loan and buy a solar-powered lamp and then sell the recharging ability as their way of repaying the loan?

- What would be their incentive for kicking in money if they are the eighth person on the list to get the lamp?
- Isn't capitalism more motivating than communal living? Are you sure these women really understand the finances behind charcoal versus solar power?
- What happens if someone doesn't pay into the kitty?
- Why start with solar power for cooking rice, when they're buying a lot more charcoal for drying the mackerel they catch every day?
- What about the woman who sells charcoal for a living?
- Can the women feel good about putting one of their sisters out of business? What about the business in town that makes four cedis for each hour of cell phone recharging?
- What good does it do to educate a child who received so little protein in its infancy that its brain is under developed?
- Shouldn't mothers be taught to feed their children eggs along with the rice, so their brains develop normally?
- Why don't they eat eggs, but they will eat chickens?
- Why do they catch such small fish?
- Don't they have any guidelines on length of fish, to assure a stable population?
- Why do they keep bathing and swimming in the river water, even when public health officials have warned them of the parasites and worms that infest the water?
- Did you notice that the paved road got washed away by the ocean and we were driving on a dirt road through a field of onions instead?
- Doesn't the government keep up the roads around here?

Bentley's business majors are interested in careers that will assure them an income, yet their success in the business world is contingent on their ability to live and work in the real world of people and problems and social issues. Experiential learning offers that, sometimes (as we see in Africa) in dramatic and unexpected ways.

21
Prospects for Fusing Liberal Learning and Business Education in the Changing Environment of Higher Education

Daniel R. LeClair

Previous chapters in this book leave little doubt about the powerful learning created by integrating liberal arts, sciences, and business education. The central question for this chapter is whether such an approach is likely to take hold and thrive in the rapidly changing environment of higher education. It is a challenging question, for it would be naïve to believe the future of business education will be shaped solely by professors from liberal arts, science, and business disciplines working harmoniously together. In reality, the future of business education depends on a wide range of institutions and constituents interacting in a complex, dynamic industry.

The changing higher education sector

Business education is a large part of a higher education sector that is changing dramatically. At the heart of these changes are three powerful trends: first, public (government, taxpayer) support for higher education has been shrinking as a proportion of the total. For example, U.S. government appropriations for four-year public institutions shrunk from 32.1 percent to 24.6 percent between 2001 and 2009 (*Chronicle* August 27, 2004, p. 30; August 26, 2004, p. 8). Conversely, an increasing portion of total expenditures on higher education has come from private sources, mostly students and parents who make up for this shortfall by paying higher tuitions and fees. There is evidence that this 'privatization' of funding is happening around the globe. For example, the share of public funding for higher education institutions fell on average from 74 percent in 1995 to 67 percent in 2008 among 19 comparable OECD countries (*Chemistry World*, August 26, 2011).

The second powerful trend is the 'massification' of higher education. Although there are more formal definitions, massification is applied here to describe the rapid expansion in higher education enrollments. For example, since 1990 U.S. higher education enrollment has grown from 15 million to more than 22 million. One hundred years ago, only three percent of the population attended college; today more than 50 percent do so. (Knowledge @ Wharton, February 29, 2012) This trend has had a particularly important impact on business education because much of the increase has come from older students who are more interested in business and management degrees. Like privatization, massification has occurred around the world, especially in emerging economies.

The third trend, globalization, has been characterized by increasing numbers of internationally mobile students and faculty, cross-border partnerships, and multinational campuses. It has been motivated by a massive shift to knowledge and service economies and facilitated by efforts to harmonize degree structures. Globalization has expanded access to higher education while intensifying competition in many dimensions. By most accounts, higher education globalization is in the early stages of development; international borders still matter tremendously and many of the positive outcomes from globalization have yet to be realized. For a fuller treatment of globalization, especially as it relates to business education, see *The Globalization of Management Education* (2011).

Together, these trends have had profound implications for higher education. Two implications are most relevant to this chapter. First, privatization, massification, and globalization have all contributed to a rapid increase in the number and diversity of higher education providers. For example, although it has long been considered a mature market, in the United States 439 new four-year institutions were added between 2001 and 2011, including 60 public, eight private nonprofit, and 371 private for-profit institutions. (*Chronicle*, August 31, 2001, p. 7; August 26, 2011, p. 4) Even larger expansions have occurred in many countries and regions around the globe.

Second, the trends have been a catalyst for innovation in higher education. The industry has spawned new degree programs to satisfy unmet demand; new faculty structures to leverage content experts and increase efficiency; new financial models to diversify funding sources and align incentives; new collaborative agreements between institutions to take advantage of relative strengths, enhance reputations, and improve educational experiences; and new technological applications to scale education, reduce marginal cost, and improve outcomes. As we shall explore in this chapter, these two developments impact the motivation and ability of universities and business schools to move in the direction of fusing liberal learning with business education.

Prospects for fusing liberal learning with business education

What are the implications of the changing higher education sector on the likelihood that the fusion of liberal learning and business education will take hold and prosper, and have a significant impact on how we educate managers and leaders? Let us investigate the impact on motivation and ability.

Mission, vision, and strategy – rediscovering the social purpose of business education

The relevance and value of the fusion model depends on an institution's mission, vision, and strategy – why it exists, what it wants to achieve, and how it intends to get there. The changing higher education environment has made it much more important for universities and business schools to articulate and carry out a clear and distinctive mission. It is important for schools to position themselves and their programs effectively within an increasingly crowded field of providers. Yet, while having a distinctive mission has become more important, many factors have conspired to make it easy for schools to imitate others. Stringent regulations and established customs limit choices while powerful media rankings tend to create 'arms races' and foster homogeneity. One increasingly important strategic choice for any institution is about which constituents and communities it intends to serve. Unfortunately, shifting alignments caused by the changing economics of higher education signal that there may be little room for liberal learning in the future of business education.

Privatization has tilted universities and business schools toward serving the needs of students and parents, who are increasingly focused on jobs as they graduate than on the value of a broad-based education that might benefit them in the long term. They question the value of courses they perceive as irrelevant to practice or landing their first or next job and ask for more hands-on applications and practice problems, and less reading and abstraction. They want step-by-step instructions about how to minimize the time to degree and make themselves more employable. Students and parents are more likely to compare schools on the basis of job placement rates and initial salaries than on research achievements and community impact. Meanwhile, companies are sending mixed signals. Executives often speak eloquently about wanting graduates with broader competencies and critical thinking, not just specialized knowledge and analytical thinking. Meanwhile, onsite recruiters hire students based primarily on their technical skills and hunt for graduates with majors or concentrations in a particular subject, such as finance or marketing.

Despite the market pressures, there are signs that universities are taking on broader social problems, putting the needs of the society at the center of their mission. In the wake of the Great Recession many business schools, in particular, are rediscovering their underlying social purpose. Many of these business schools are tired of being type-cast as career factories, places where people go to maximize the chances of getting their first job or next promotion. Business schools have been good at generating high salaries and placement rates, but many critics believe they lost their way as a consequence. As INSEAD dean, Dipak Jain, said, 'business schools have been better at performance than purpose' (Jain, 2010).

A stronger sense of social purpose provides a 'center of gravity' or context for higher management education. By defining their purpose in terms of society rather than individuals, institutions are more likely to find relevance and value in the fusion model. They are more likely to see overlap rather than conflict in the interests of students, employers, and society. And they are more likely to collaborate with other academic units on campus. For example, Stanford University and its Graduate School of Business have long been associated with innovation and now, with support from a major gift, are building a multidisciplinary platform to help alleviate poverty worldwide (Stanford, 2011).

Social purpose comes in many forms. Of course, Bentley University serves a leading example; its mission is to create new knowledge within and across business and the arts and sciences and to educate creative, ethical and socially responsible organizational leaders. Following Hurricane Katrina, Tulane University and its Freeman School of Business committed strongly to active civic engagement and 'became the first national research institution to integrate public service into its core curriculum for undergraduates' (Solomon, 2012). Then there are institutions like Morehouse College (for young black males), Simmons

College (for women), Yeshiva University (for Jewish people), and U.S. Coast Guard Academy (for officers) where students and faculty alike find inspiration and purpose from shared experiences and expectations. They each have 'something more' that provides context and purpose to the curriculum, as well as guides behavior, connects alumni, and shapes the strategy of the school.

The lens of social purpose is also useful to distinguish the for-profit sector from the public and non-profit sectors in higher education. Deming et al. (2012) wrote that 'the for-profits almost always offer training for a vocation or trade. In that sense, they are 'career colleges'' and they offer 'almost no general education and liberal arts programs' (Deming et al., 2011, p. 144). Continuing, they state:

> For-profit higher education is more likely to flourish in providing vocational programs that lead to certification and early job placement – programs that have clear short-run outcomes that can serve to build institutional reputation in the labor market. But the for-profits are likely to be in a far less advantageous position where external benefits (and subsidies from donors and government) are important and where the qualities of inputs and outputs are difficult to verify. (Deming et al., 2011, p. 85)

This distinction also raises the question of how a larger social purpose can be supported by institutions in an environment of rising costs, shrinking public funding, and increasing competition. Even if schools are motivated to integrate liberal learning with business education, it seems extraordinarily difficult to actually do it. The question is whether trends in higher education are making the 'crucial fusion' more or less difficult to implement.

Structure and organization – autonomy, collaboration, and innovation

The structure of an organization, including the way its people are connected to each other and policies and traditions regulating their interaction, can enable an organization to achieve its mission and vision. Unfortunately, higher education is far from ideal. Universities are replete with structural limitations that more often stall than enable strategic action. For example, many people argue that faculty governance distorts university strategic decision making and that tenure inhibits action. Because they are not changing any time soon, let us set aside these structural limitations for the time being. Instead, consider aspects of the structure that are evolving, changing in ways that will make liberal learning either more or less feasible in universities and business schools.

A critical assumption is that effectively fusing liberal education and business education requires extensive integration and coordination. The authors of the recent Carnegie Foundation report, *Rethinking Undergraduate Business Education*, explain it this way:

> If students gain the full array of Analytical Reasoning, Multiple Framing, Reflective Exploration of Meaning, and Practical Reasoning entirely within arts and sciences disciplines, they will almost certainly have difficulty translating that understanding to their preparation for business. If they gain experience with these dimensions of liberal learning exclusively within a business context, their college experience will be impoverished and they are unlikely to graduate with a deep understanding of the world and their place in it.
>
> For that, a good deal of what is traditionally understood to be liberal arts and sciences content is needed as well. The two content areas are therefore interdependent and must be coordinated. In the best examples we encountered, they are. (Colby et al., 2011, p. 85)

Thus, organizational structures that facilitate integration and coordination are viewed as more conducive to the fusion of liberal learning and business education.

Independence and autonomy

Privatization has usually been accompanied by more independence and autonomy for universities and the business schools that operate within them. More and more institutions are gaining control over the assets, strategies, and policies that impact their competitiveness and sustainability. As a consequence they are able to create new programs more quickly in response to market opportunities and invest in their own brands, prompting some critics to say there is now more 'business' than 'school' in today's business schools.

On the surface, this trend seems to oppose the fusion model. Wouldn't more autonomous, financially independent schools be more aligned with a career focus than a social purpose? Wouldn't greater independence across academic units, including business schools, arts, and sciences, be inconsistent with the types of integration and coordination required to fuse liberal education with business education? Not necessarily.

It is quite possible that more autonomy could enable business schools to create stronger foundations in liberal learning. First, autonomy does not mean isolation. Business schools can strengthen their emphasis on liberal education by collaborating with other academic units, both inside and outside university boundaries. An independent business school can seek partners that most fully complement its strengths and support its strategic objectives.

Second, more autonomous business schools could be free to hire their own arts and sciences faculty. They might teach their own courses or assist to infuse liberal learning into business courses. Bentley University has the benefit of one faculty organized across business, arts, and sciences. The absence of internal barriers has made it easier for their faculty to communicate and coordinate and, by virtue of being a business-focused institution, there is a guiding 'center of gravity' for arts and sciences that usually doesn't exist in the liberal arts divisions of general universities. This approach can be particularly important in countries where the undergraduate educational systems have a highly specialized focus or lack 'general education' components.

Third, more autonomy could increase financial support to fuse liberal learning with business education. Other things being equal, the fusion model is more costly to implement than other models. But with proper financial models that make cross-subsidies transparent, entrepreneurial ventures can be seen as a way to generate margins to subsidize and invest in important, but less profitable, educational models.

Globalization

Globalization in higher education has contributed intensifying competition – for students and parents, for example – and pressures to align with rankings criteria and the interests of students, parents, and employers. However, globalization has also brought new opportunities to universities and business schools. International study experiences are increasingly viewed as essential and occurring at the intersection of liberal learning and business education. And globalization has caused structural changes that may further enable business schools to develop deeper liberal learning as a critical component of business education.

First, international collaborations are growing in numbers and in depth. In its 2011 report the AACSB (Association to Advance Collegiate Schools of Business) Globalization of Management Education Task Force (2011) argued that, unlike the past, the future of business education will depend less on the number of institutions than on the connections between them (AACSB, 2011). Currently, most international collaborations are bilateral and one-dimensional, often focused exclusively on accommodating student exchanges between two schools. But from the seeds of these initial agreements are springing new multilateral opportunities to deepen cross-border collaborations, especially to create educational projects involving students from different countries and stimulate more cross-border research, leading to new curricula perspectives.

Second, harmonization initiatives, such as the Bologna Process, which is restructuring degree programs across Europe, are making it easier for degree programs to fit more readily together, inspiring and enabling curriculum reform. In countries such as Australia, where undergraduates specialize from the beginning of tertiary education, innovative curricula models aim to build on the general education tradition of North America (University of Melbourne, 2006). However, doing so in Australia is possible only if the content is integrated within business education. That is, by necessity Australia must integrate liberal learning with more specialized business education rather than stack them like most U.S. institutions have done.

Third, from initial experiences in globalization has emerged a deeper understanding about how curricula and extra-curricular strategies must complement each other. The Globalization of Management Education Task Force argued that too few business schools have paid enough attention to how the vast array of global activities fit together. Similarly, the authors of the Carnegie Foundation report also make the point that 'students need intentional, institutional support in actively connecting liberal learning with learning that is directed specifically toward preparation for business careers' (Colby et al., 2011, p. 85).

Applications of technology

Online education is the most visible aspect of technology's impact on higher education. However, to many people in the higher education community, online courses are not conducive to the kind of education that fuses liberal learning with business education. They believe online learning allows for too little of the deep synchronous interaction and reflection needed to develop critical thinking and framing skills. But there is emerging confidence that new and future applications can increase student engagement and facilitate the kinds of education implied by both liberal learning and experiential learning. Technology has brought more plentiful and diverse information to the learner. Information technology has also created opportunities to engage students more intensely in education through interactive simulations.

New technologies are helping schools to track student progress more effectively and coordinate across programs and schools. In general, information technology holds the potential to expand liberal learning opportunities beyond its current comfortable domain of residential undergraduate education into, for example, part-time education.

Trends in faculty and research

As research has become more specialized and narrowly defined, it has become more difficult for faculty to integrate and coordinate curricula content. Meanwhile, in some countries shortages of doctoral faculty have dramatically increased salaries while decreasing teaching loads. In some environments, teaching loads are so high and research expectations so low that faculty spend most of their time consulting. In some schools, the vast majority of faculty teach part-time and are not engaged in curriculum and course development. From almost every perspective, no matter where you are, it appears that the faculty are not especially likely to provide the leadership necessary for liberal learning in business.

On the other hand, there are a couple of faculty developments that suggest a more optimistic view. First, more schools are introducing models to 'leverage' faculty content experts by engaging other teaching professionals. Many business schools have begun to complement research faculty (content experts) with experienced coaches in communications and leadership, for example, so that courses can provide deep business knowledge and help students to master important skills at the same time. Adopting such models, even on a limited basis, can be expensive, but signals a strong commitment to fusing liberal learning with business education. Similarly, as business professors are increasingly specialized in either teaching or research, schools have had to design new faculty structures in which the teachers are informed by the researchers, perhaps encouraging teachers to incorporate and integrate content from a variety of disciplines.

Second, there is a revolution brewing in academic research that, if realized, holds the potential to increase multidisciplinary research. One factor changing the research model is privatization of higher education finance. The shift in funding from public to private funding sources has raised questions about the value of research to parents and students (who care more about instruction than research), causing schools to focus more on creating practical insights at the intersection of disciplines. Another driver is information technology, which could 'disintermediate' academic publishers and shift peer-review from pre- to post-publication. As more and more faculty communicate about their research with colleagues through open scientific blogs rather than through the traditional closed pre-publication review process, we should expect more cross-fertilization and integration.

Summary and recommendations for business schools

What is the likelihood that the fusion of liberal learning and business education will take hold and have a significant impact on the future of higher education? For proponents of integrating liberal learning with business the answer is not immediately encouraging. The changing environment compels universities and business schools to focus more on satisfying short-term demands and organize for independence and competitiveness rather than integration and coordination.

However, deeper exploration reveals a different, more positive future. Under the surface, higher education is changing in ways that could both encourage and enable the fusion of liberal learning and business education. Universities and business schools have found that their stakeholders have more expectations in common than in conflict when considered in the context of social purpose. Through the lens of social purpose, the integration of liberal learning and business education is seen not only as desirable, but it is also viewed as necessary in the emerging environment. Changes in higher education have also fostered new, innovative approaches (e.g., new platforms for deeper interaction, opportunities to engage a wider range of experts in education, more transparent financial models, and interdisciplinary partnerships) and opportunities that enable schools to achieve the deep kinds of integration and coordination necessary to fuse liberal learning and business education.

The lessons for management educators, including organizations such as AACSB International, are straightforward. First and foremost, to foster deep, broad-based education in business, it is most important for business schools to articulate clear, distinctive missions defining their purposes in society. Schools should stick to their mission even in the face of market pressures to conform. Second, schools should be encouraged and supported to adopt innovative approaches to achieve the integration and coordination necessary to fuse liberal learning with business education. Major changes in higher education – increasing independence and autonomy, globalization, technological advances, new faculty models, and changing research environment – all provide opportunities to combine the content and pedagogies of liberal learning and business education in deep ways for the benefit of society.

References

AACSB International Globalization of Management Education Task Force (2011) *Globalization of Management Education: Changing International Structures, Adaptive Strategies, and the Impact on Institutions* (Tampa, FL: AACSB International).

Burke, Maria (2011) 'Higher Education Spending Rises Around the World,' *Chemistry World*, September 19, electronic document, http://www.rsc.org/chemistryworld/News/2011/September/19091103.asp, accessed December 1, 2011.

The Chronicle of Higher Education Almanac Issue 2001–2002, August 31, 2001, and *The Chronicle of Higher Education* Almanac Issue 2011–2012, August 26, 2001.

The Chronicle of Higher Education Almanac Issue 2004–2005, August 27, 2004, and *The Chronicle of Higher Education* Almanac Issue 2011–2012, August 26, 2011.

Colby, Anne, Ehrlich, Thomas, Sullivan, William M., Dolle, Jonathan R. (2011) *Rethinking Undergraduate Business Education* (San Francisco: Jossey-Bass).

Deming, David J., Goldin, Claudia, and Katz, Lawrence F. (2012) 'The For-Profit Postsecondary School Sector: Nimble Critters or Agile Predators,' *Journal of Economic Perspectives*, Winter, 26(1), pp. 139–164.

Jain, Dipak (2010), keynote speech, Annual Conference of CLADEA, Cartagena, Colombia, November 4.

Solomon, Ira (2012) 'Doing Well by Doing Good: Public Service in Business Education,' AACSB eNEWSLINE Dean's Corner, February 2012, electronic document,   http://www.aacsb.edu/enewsline/deanscorner/solomon.asp, retrieved March 6, 2012.

'Stanford Graduate School of Business Launches Institute to Alleviate Poverty with $150 Million Gift.' Stanford Graduate School of Business Press Release, November 4, 2011, electronic document, http://www.gsb.stanford.edu/seed/press-release.html, retrieved March 6, 2012.

University of Melbourne (2006) 'The Melbourne Model: Report of the Curricular Commission.'

Index